W9-DAS-660

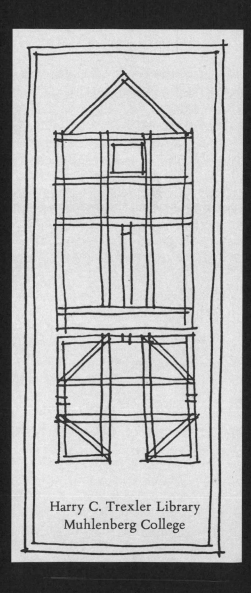

Harry C. Trexler Library
Muhlenberg College

International Production

WITHDRAWN

ASPECTS OF POLITICAL ECONOMY
Series Editor: Geoffrey Harcourt

Published

A Asimakopulos, *Investment, Employment and Income Distribution*
Pat Devine, *Democracy and Economic Planning*
Paul Dunne (ed.), *Quantitative Marxism*
Richard M. Goodwin
& Lionello F. Punzo, *The Dynamics of a Capitalist Economy*
Heinz Kurz, *Capital, Distribution and Effective Demand*
Marc Jarsulic, *Effective Demand and Income Distribution*
Peter Nolan, *The Political Economy of Collective Farms*
Bob Rowthorn
& Naomi Wayne, *Northern Ireland: The Political Economy of Conflict*
Ian Steedman, *From Exploitation to Altruism*
Christopher Torr, *Equilibrium, Expectations and Information*
Warren Young, *Interpreting Mr Keynes*
Grazia Ietto-Gillies, *International Production: Trends, Theories, Effects*

Forthcoming

Ravi Kanbur, *Risk Taking, Income Distribution and Poverty*
Jose Salazar, *Pricing Policy and Economic Development*

International Production

Trends, Theories, Effects

Grazia Ietto-Gillies

Polity Press

Copyright © Grazia Ietto-Gillies 1992

The right of Grazia Ietto-Gillies to be identified as author of this work
has been asserted in accordance with the Copyright, Designs and Patents
Act 1988.

First published in 1992 by Polity Press
in association with Blackwell Publishers

Editorial office:
Polity Press
65 Bridge Street
Cambridge CB2 1UR, UK

Marketing and production:
Blackwell Publishers
108 Cowley Road
Oxford OX4 1JF, UK

3 Cambridge Center
Cambridge, Massachusetts
02142, USA

All rights reserved. Except for the quotation of short passages for the
purposes of criticism and review, no part of this publication may be
reproduced, stored in a retrieval system, or transmitted, in any form or
by any means, electronic, mechanical, photocopying, recording or
otherwise, without the prior permission of the publisher.

Except in the United States of America, this book is sold subject to the
condition that it shall not, by way of trade or otherwise, be lent, resold,
hired out, or otherwise circulated without the publisher's prior consent in
any form of binding or cover other than that in which it is published and
without a similar condition including this condition being imposed on the
subsequent purchaser.

ISBN 0 7456 0576 1

A CIP catalogue record for this book is available from the British
Library and the Library of Congress.

Typeset in 10 on 11½ pt Times
by Photo·graphics, Honiton, Devon
Printed in Great Britain by Billing and Sons, Worcester

This book is printed on acid-free paper.

Contents

List of Tables

Preface

In the past three decades the study of international business has increased at a rate almost comparable to the spread of international business itself. This growth is, largely, the result of work that has taken place in business schools and business studies departments or in economics departments with a strong business studies orientation. The number of such schools and departments, and of students within them, has been increasing, and this has helped to increase the production and dissemination of research work in international business. Unhappily, economics departments have, on the whole, shied away from this area of work, in terms of both teaching and research. It is a pity that this should be so for a variety of reasons, in particular because economics and economic modelling cannot seriously claim to deal with the 'real world' until this most important area of development in the economic environment is fully incorporated into the body of analysis. We should not worry too much if such an incorporation leads to less tidy, less formalized, less manageable models and conclusions: the advantages gained in terms of realism and new paths of discovery will more than compensate for any such shortcomings.

One area of 'international business' largely dealt with in the economics literature is international trade. However, it is increasingly clear – and this book will emphasize it – that the study of international trade in modern economic systems must proceed in conjunction with the study of international production, as trade and production have now become indissolubly linked. Thus the analysis of international production, its determinants and its effects should help economists to deal with international trade issues.

Given their multi- and interdisciplinary focus, business schools have tended to take a particular route in terms of research and pedagogy into international business and international production. The route is one that takes account of the body of knowledge in disciplines other than economics, thus giving the benefits of a realistic, multi-faceted, real world approach. However, it is also a route that has, often, tended to shy away from rigorous analysis; more seriously still, it has tended to shy away from theoretical analysis and to be – at times – too preoccupied with 'business' in a narrow sense. This has led to the following problems. First of all, the teaching of international production is often presented in a rather dogmatic way with the most common theories presented as generally accepted truths rather than hypotheses to be tested, criticized, compared and improved. Secondly, the excessive preoccupation with the micro and managerial spheres has led to a neglect of macro elements of international production, particularly in terms of explanations and theories. This is a serious problem since, given the size, spread and impact of transnational corporations, micro and macro issues are interlinked to a higher degree than in any other area of economics.

It is, partly, with these issues in mind that the present book has been written. I wanted to try to give an analysis of international production which, while firmly rooted in facts and trends at both the micro and macro level, would also give the reader a full excursion into theories, their historical development, their degree of corroboration and their contribution to our knowledge of international business.

The analysis of effects will, similarly, take account of methodological issues, of micro–macro elements, of conflicts between various groups, of new developments and patterns of international business activity. The picture that emerges is likely to be less tidy, less dogmatic, less certain than the one often presented on the assessment of effects. I make no apologies for it: uncertainty, contradictions, conflicts, knowledge via hypotheses and their testing, these are what the real world is about.

The wealth of theories and approaches presented will, I hope, convince the reader of the degree of 'maturity' of this area of economics. I hope that the twin approach considered here (theoretical/empirical) and the issues raised, in terms of theories, effects and strategies, will make this book appealing to lecturers, students and researchers in both business studies and economics departments.

If this book stimulates the reader and researcher to read other works on international production and to further research in this area, and, mainly, if it stimulates teachers to introduce this body of knowledge of a most relevant aspect of modern economic systems into their classrooms, the present writer will have achieved her aim.

Grazia Ietto-Gillies
London

Acknowledgements

I would like to thank the following people: Owen Adikibi, Donald Gillies, David Green, Geoff Harcourt and an anonymous reader from Polity Press for reading a first draft of the book and offering useful comments. My gratitude also to: John Taylor for his excellent work on the script, which has extended far beyond copy-editing; Yukta Dixit for some empirical work related to chapter 18; Christopher Clarke for his help with the empirical work for chapters 2 and 18; Oonie Gordon for considerable help in the work leading to table 18.4; Konstantinos Hatzivalasis for some editorial help; Doreen Barker, Kate Lloyd and Jennifer Simmons for help with processing my words.

I am grateful to South Bank Polytechnic for granting me study leave, which has made it possible for me to finish this book.

The author and publisher would like to thank the following: the President and Fellows of Harvard College and John Wiley and Sons, Inc. for permission to reproduce fig. 8.1; the International Review of Applied Economics for permission to reproduce chapter 18; the British Review of Economic Issues for permission to reproduce chapter 14; GATT for permission to reproduce table 2.7; The Macmillan Press Ltd. for permission to use data from tables 5.1 and 5.2 from *The Growth of International Business* edited by Mark Casson and table 13 from *Multinationals Company Performance*; Paul Chapman Publishing Ltd. for permission to reproduce table 3.2, p. 57 of Dicken, *Global Shift*; Acocella for permission to reproduce fig. 6.1; the Oxford Bulletin of Economics and Statistics for permission to reproduce table 2.4.

Abbreviations

AICs	advanced industrialized countries
DMEs	developed market economies
EPZ	export processing zone
FDI	foreign direct investment
GDFCF	gross domestic fixed capital formation
GDP	gross domestic product
GNP	gross national product
IFT	intra-firm trade
IIT	intra-industry trade
LDCs	less developed countries
JVs	joint ventures
MNC	multinational corporation
MNE	multinational enterprise
NICs	newly industrialized countries
NIDL	new international division of labour
R&D	research and development
SIC	Standard Industrial Classification
TNC	transnational corporation
TNE	transnational enterprise

Note: The *italics* in passages quoted from other authors should be understood to be in the original text, unless otherwise specified.

To my parents, and to Donald and Mark

Introduction: Plan of the Book

This book is about international production and thus about the activities of transnational companies.

The book starts by considering the conditions which have led to the tremendous growth of transnational activities in the past few decades and the agents responsible for such activities. Thus chapter 1 deals with issues related to the organizational structure and control of companies as well as with developments in transportation and communications. The second chapter is devoted to the main trends in the internationalization process resulting from transnational activities. The trends presented relate to both international production and trade. With regard to international production, consideration is given to trends in the geographical and sectoral structure of foreign direct investment, in equity and non-equity involvement, in the size of transnational companies and in the geographical spread of the network of activities. International trade will be dealt with mainly in relation to the activities of transnational companies; overall trends in world trade and production will be considered as well as developments in patterns of trade, with particular reference to intra-industry and intra-firm trade.

Most of the data presented come from official sources, which will be used whenever possible in preference to other sources. Many of the data presented are macro and refer to nations. I follow the official convention and ascribe to country X as a whole the foreign direct investment originating with companies based in X. This does not mean that the interests and motivations of companies are identified with those of nations: they are separate and indeed the nation as a whole has different interest groups. The need to keep the separation in mind is particularly relevant when dealing with economic agents that are transnational. Account will be taken of this when considering the effects of transnational activities (part III) and, whenever applicable, in analysing theories (part II).

In chapter 1 I deal with some necessary conditions for the growth of internationalization; these conditions tell us why such growth was possible. However, it is still necessary to explain why companies wanted to take the transnational route on such a scale. In trying to explain 'why international production' we are faced with a wealth of theories, to which part II is devoted.

Attempts at explaining international production have produced a very considerable number of interesting theories; we are thus faced with the problem of assessing competing theories – a common problem in the methodology of science. The 'facts' presented in chapter 2 will, therefore, assist the reader in two ways. First, by providing a general description of the various aspects of internationalization and their relative importance; secondly, as evidence in the corroboration or refutation of the theories presented in part II. No overall general conclusion is given as to the 'best' theory for two reasons: first because, in this writer's view, the state of the art at present is such that no simple theory can be considered to be the most plausible and best corroborated for all countries and sectors; secondly because it is felt that the readers should be left to draw their own conclusions and their own overall assessments according to the particular circumstances analysed.

The chapters on theories are organized according to the following general principles. First, the exposition of each theory is kept separate from my own criticism; this is done in order to facilitate the didactic function of the book and to allow readers to form their assessments of each theory. Secondly, the presentation will be made on the basis of historical principles; this allows the reader to see how theories have evolved from each other and how they have changed in response to changes in the internationalization process. Thus, part II starts with a section on Marxist writers mainly because it was in this tradition that the first attempts at explaining the causes and effects of foreign investment began.

The organization of the theories into four main sections is done with the aim of grouping together theories with common elements; inevitably some theories have elements belonging to more than one group, but this is a problem common to any system of classification. A subsidiary aim in the grouping is to facilitate the readers, and the teachers, in finding the types of theory they want to read or recommend to their students. For example, business schools have, traditionally, been interested in the theories presented in section III more than the ones in sections I and II.

Part III is devoted to effects. The conventional distinction between effects on home and host countries is rejected in favour of a more global approach; the motivations and consequences of this course of action are set up in the chapter on methodological issues (chapter 16). The last chapter presents some empirical comparative analyses of multinational domination of national economies; the concept, indicators and estimates are arrived at using the methodological approach of chapter 16.

Part I

Agents and Trends

PUCK: How now, spirit; whither wander you?
FAIRY: Over hill, over dale,
        Thorough bush, thorough briar,
        Over park, over pale,
        Thorough flood, thorough fire –
        I do wander everywhere
                Shakespeare, *A Midsummer Night's Dream* II.1

1
The Internationalization Process: Agents and Conditions

Whence are we, and why are we? Of what scene
The actors or spectators?

P. B. Shelley, *Adonais* XXI

1.1 Terminology

The term 'international production' is here used with reference to production organized and controlled by transnational companies. The actual organization and management of business activities across frontiers can take different forms. Similarly, the type of business involvement leading to the control, organization and management of production can take various forms ranging from foreign direct investment (FDI) to licensing to sub-contracting to joint ventures. While most international production takes place via foreign direct investment, there are various other ways – through both equity and non-equity involvement – by which large companies can organize, manage and control production in various countries. For this reason the terms 'international production' and 'internationalization' are here used in a way that includes other forms of involvement besides production directly related to FDI. This more comprehensive use leads to less precision than a definition based on FDI only; however, it offers advantages in terms of analysis, on which there is more in section 1.4 and the next chapter.

The terms 'multinational', 'international' and 'transnational' are usually used interchangeably. The last is becoming more widespread, partly because it is the one more recently used by the United Nations and partly because it seems more comprehensive than multinational since it does not involve decisions on how many nations should be involved in the concept of 'multi'. Similarly in the literature on international production the terms 'firms', 'enterprises', 'companies' and 'corporations' are used more or less interchangeably, although the last seems more common as, again, it is the one used by the United Nations.

The *definition* of a transnational company (TNC) is not straightforward. Probably no definition ever is, but in the case of TNCs there seem to be many problems, some of which are considered in the appendix to this chapter. The definition that emerges from the analysis in this and later chapters is one that sees a *transnational as a corporation that organizes and controls production and/or related activities in more than one country*.

The modern transnational corporation is no passive spectator of the changing scene in the internationalization process: rather it is the main actor. What are the origins of international firms?

1.2 Historical antecedents

The modern TNC has evolved and grown mainly in the decades following the Second World War. However, its *antecedents* go much further back in history. Transborder institutional control and transborder business operations go a long way back. The Catholic Church is a prime and most powerful example of an institution with transborder multistate control in which the elements of religion and temporal assets strengthen each other in terms of control. However, the Catholic Church, powerful and effective in its control though it is and has been, cannot, strictly, be considered as a business institution. Transborder business operations as such have existed for many centuries, indeed before the existence of nations: the Medici bank – based in fifteenth-century Florence – could be considered a company involved in such transborder business operations.

More recent companies, such as the East India Company, the Royal African Company and the Hudson Bay Company, and similar ones dating back to the seventeenth and eighteenth centuries, are often considered the real forerunners of modern TNCs. While their business operations truly spanned many nations, their type of business as trading companies had only some of the characteristics of modern TNCs. These companies were the forerunners of modern general trading companies such as the Japanese *sogo shosha*. However, they can be considered forerunners of the modern transnational corporations only in a very limited sense: only with regard to the multinationality of business activities.[1] In other relevant aspects of most modern TNCs the transformation is so substantial that many authors (including the present one) are inclined to play down the similarities. The differences lie in the type of operations – manufacturing rather than just trading – and related different internal organization of production. Thus Hymer (1971) writes on the issue of old trading companies:

But neither these firms, nor the large mining and plantation enterprises in the production sector, were the forerunners of the multinational corporations. They were like dinosaurs, large in bulk, but small in brain, feeding on the lush vegetation of the new worlds (the planters and miners in America were literally *Tyrannosaurus rex*). The activities of these international merchants, planters and miners laid the groundwork for the Industrial Revolution by concentrating capital in the metropolitan centre, but the driving force came from the small-scale capitalist enterprises in manufacturing. . . . It is in the small workshops, organized by the newly emerging capitalist class, that the forerunners of the modern corporation are to be found. The strength of this new form of business enterprise lay in its power and ability to reap the benefits of cooperation and division of labor. (pp. 115–16)

1.3 Internal organization

Modern international production is not just doing business in many countries and with many countries. It involves the ability to plan, coordinate and control production in many countries from a centre and under common, centrally determined objectives and strategies; it also involves the ability of the central headquarters to assess the performance of individual units. The ability to perform all these functions is closely linked to having an appropriate organizational structure and to facilities in communications, transportation and data gathering, transmission and processing. In effect the existence of appropriate organizational structures and the existence of facilities in transportation and telecommunication can be considered *two necessary conditions* for the full take-off of internationalization of production on a large scale, as witnessed in the past few decades. The issue of *internal organization* is dealt with in this section and the related wider issue of control in the next. Section 1.5 considers developments in communication and transportation.

The causes of changes in the internal organization of companies, and its historical development, have been analysed under two different 'paradigms': the 'efficiency' and the 'strategic' one. Williamson (1981, 1984) sees internal organizations changing mainly in response to efficiency criteria and to the needs to cut costs – including transactions costs – and to minimize the pursuit of individual goals within the organization. Chandler (1962) sees the internal organization of corporations evolving mainly in response to strategies, in particular growth strategies. I follow this second strategic strand mainly through Hymer's analysis of the development of the international firm.

Hymer (1970) analyses the relationship between evolution in the internal structure of firms and multinationality. Following Chandler, he distinguishes 'three major stages in the development of corporate capital. First, the Marshallian firm, organized at the factory level, confined to a single function and a single industry, and tightly controlled by one or a few men, who, as it were, see everything and decide everything' (p. 42). The second stage sees large corporations, vertically integrated and increasingly moving towards mass production, develop a new business organization. The new organization was developed through the experience of managing railways, with their widely dispersed operations and their need for coordination and commitment of vast resources. It developed through administrative functions: finance, personnel, purchasing, engineering and sales. It is sometimes referred to as the 'central office functionally departmentalized' (COFD) or 'unitary' (U-form) structure.

The twentieth century saw further economic developments. Industry became more concentrated, large corporations followed diversification strategies which created the need to plan, coordinate, control and manage different products; these corporations were also operating over large geographical areas, particularly in the case of the US ones. The new corporation needed a different, more flexible structure, which emerged as the multidivisional structure. The 'multidivisional form' (M-form) of organization was first introduced by General Motors and Du Pont after the First World War; it soon spread to other US corporations and, after the Second World War, to European ones.

In this structure, corporations are divided and decentralized into divisions, each dealing with a product and each run fairly autonomously. Thus the new organization differed from the U-form in three main respects:

1   it centred on products rather than functions;
2   it focused on the establishment of a central office;
3   it relied on 'information' for its centralization/decentralization scheme to work.[2]

The new structure provided flexibility because new divisions could be added or closed down as business evolved without too much disturbance to the rest of the organization. Channon (1973, pp. 3–4) writes on this point: 'In theory . . . the quasi-independent divisions could be likened to a series of portfolio investments which could be bought or sold without serious impact on the overall corporation.' The new organization also provided the opportunity to extend the divisional structure to the international set up; thus the spread of activities into many countries could occur by the addition of new divisions as necessary. Further developments in the M-form have seen TNCs organized into divisions on a geographical or product basis. In some cases the conflicting demands of products and geographical areas have led to 'grid' organizations which exhibit mixed product/geography features (see Channon, 1973). In the divisional structure each division is a profit centre and its performance is thus assessed separately from the others. The central office receives profits from the various divisions and allocates capital to them, thus having an overall planning and strategic role.

Parallel to the evolution in internal organization, there has been an evolution in the division of managerial labour. Hymer (1971), following Chandler and Redlich, distinguishes three levels of business administration, which also identify the levels of managers. Level three (the lowest) managers deal with day-to-day operations at factory level; level two managers coordinate the work of level three managers, while level one managers are responsible for setting objectives and for strategic planning. In the Marshallian firm the three levels are managed by the same person or group of persons; in the medium-size vertically integrated corporation, level three is separated from levels two and one; the functions of these last two levels are likely to be performed by the same people. The M-form sees a full division of managerial labour with the three levels completely split among different people or groups of people.

Thus changes in growth strategies (mass production, diversification, internationalization) led to changes in internal organization and this brought a sharper internal division of managerial labour. At the same time the evolution of the organizational structure paved the way for the full take-off of internationalization of production: with the M-form it was possible to expand into new countries by creating entirely new divisions without much disturbance to the rest of the organization. Thus the constraints of organization and control on geographical expansion were removed.

The M-form is not without its problems, however: it has recently come under attack by economists on the grounds that it is no longer suited to institutions and macroeconomies operating in the 1980s and 1990s. Michael Best (1986) writes mainly, but not exclusively, with UK problems in mind; he sees the structural problems of the UK economy as due to a new type of worldwide competition. The old competition was price-led, the new one is product-led, and thus led by elements such as quality, novelty and design. This type of overall product improvement is best achieved by linking operations from various products lines and also linking planning to production. Best sees the M-form as badly suited to helping companies to move towards a product-led competition as this structure is characterized by the following:

1 Planning is divorced from production: the division of managerial labour may have gone too far.
2 Various divisions do not cooperate and exchange experiences at the level of production; they therefore miss opportunities for cross-fertilization of ideas and improvements in products and processes.

3 The planning horizon tends to be short- or medium-term while the new competition, with its emphasis on technology and innovation, needs a long-term horizon.

The new competition needs an organization and structure that enables companies to plan long term, integrate production and planning, and explore the interconnections between various products and processes. At the industry and macro level, Best sees a need for an agency that fosters links between products, processes and sectors.

Marginson (1985) claims, however, that the M-form is needed by large companies, particularly in the UK, as it 'provides an organizational framework within which management can retain control over the work process on the shopfloor' (p. 55), following the growth of shopfloor trade union organization of earlier decades.

The debate about the advantages and problems of the M-form will, no doubt, continue; at the same time, changes in organizational forms will occur. We are already witnessing developments from the M-form and it is to be expected that, as globalization proceeds and further advances are made in technology and communications, new organizational forms will emerge.

1.4   Control

The issue of *control* is central to the process of internationalization. There are various aspects of control, all important to the process. First, we have the aspect related to internal control by headquarters of its divisions and periphery in general: control directed towards achievement of set goals, general quality control and assessment of performance. There is the old controversy over the possible separation of control from ownership in companies whose share ownership is widely spread.[3]

There is an issue of control over acquired units, whether foreign subsidiaries or not: what percentage of holding will guarantee control to the parent company? All the literature on this point assumes that ownership of assets of the subsidiary by the parent is the main or only prerequisite for control and hence for inclusion of the subsidiary in the domain of the corporation. The disagreement, whenever it exists, is over the percentage of holding necessary for control and hence over the cut-off point for inclusion or exclusion. However, in a recent work Cowling and Sugden (1987a) take a wider view on the issue of control. These authors criticize the legalistic view of the firm, which, going back to Coase (1937), focuses on market versus non-market transactions in defining the existence and limits of the firm.

Cowling and Sugden focus on *control* rather than legal ownership of assets in order to arrive at definitions of firms and TNCs. They write:

. . . control implies the ability to determine broad corporate objectives despite resistance from others. In other words, to make decisions over such strategic issues as a firm's relationship with nation states and workers, its rate and direction of capital accumulation, its sources of raw materials, and its geographical orientation. (Cowling and Sugden, 1987a, p. 59)

Starting from the standpoint that 'strategic decisions play a prime role because, by definition, they determine the direction of the firm' (pp. 59–60), they arrive at the following definitions of firms and TNCs:

A firm is the means of coordinating production from one centre of strategic decision making. A transnational is the means of coordinating production from one centre of strategic decision making when this coordination takes a firm across national boundaries. (p. 60)

Such coordination can take place within the boundary of a firm *legally* defined or outside this legal domain; in this second case a 'legal' firm is in a position to exercise control over the production activities of another 'legal' firm. For example, through sub-contracting the principal can exercise a considerable amount of control over the sub-contractor. Sub-contracting is one of the various ways in which a large corporation can become involved in the coordination of production and can exercise some control over another 'firm' without the existence of equity participation. Such forms of participation are increasing in type (sub-contracting, licensing, etc.) and in quantity (number of firms involved and value of activities). Hence the issue of control without ownership involvement may become more and more relevant.

Cowling and Sugden, in bringing the issue of control to the forefront of debate, follow one of the many seeds sown by Hymer in his dissertation (1960). Their approach is full of theoretical and practical problems, and they mention in particular the following: how to get data on firms defined on the basis of control and how to identify who makes strategic decisions. In spite of these problems, Cowling and Sugden (1987a) consider it better to work with a concept that is sound and realistic, from an economic standpoint, than to make 'apparently sound conclusions based upon inadequate concepts' (p. 64).

I tend to agree with these authors and for this reason the definition presented in section 1.1 is a wide one; it is a definition of international production that includes not only production stemming from foreign direct investment but also that related to other more indirect forms of involvement in which there is 'control' by TNCs. As the network of joint ventures, alliances, licensing agreements and sub-contracting arrangements widens, the need to consider the corporation in terms of control over assets and production rather than in terms of ownership also grows.

1.5   Technological change and the growth of TNCs

In section 1.2 the necessary conditions for the growth and spread of international production were mentioned. These were considered as conditions without which the big post-Second World War take-off in internationalization could not have occurred. The first is the development of appropriate internal organizational structures to enable corporations to deal with large, diversified, geographically spread and complex institutions: we have touched on such developments in section 1.2. The second necessary condition has to do with developments in the areas of *transportation and communications*. Considerable advances in the technology of transportation and communication have led to a decrease in the costs of such services and to more reliable services as well as to completely new possibilities. Dicken (1986, p. 107) writes:

> Transport and communication technologies perform two distinct, though closely related and complementary roles. *Transport systems* are the means by which materials, products and other tangible entities (including people) are transferred from place to place. *Communication systems* are the means by which information is transmitted from place to place in the form of ideas, instructions, images and so on. For most of human history, transport and communications were effectively one and the same. Prior to the invention of electric technology in the nineteenth century, information could only move at the same speed, and over the same distance, as the prevailing transport system would allow. Electric technology broke that link, making it increasingly necessary to treat transport and communication as separate, though intimately related, technologies.

If the size of the world is measured in terms of the time necessary for moving people and commodities from country to country, there is no doubt that the world has 'shrunk' considerably throughout the centuries and that a large part of the 'shrinkage' has occurred during this century. The main developments in transport technology during the twentieth century have been 'the introduction of commercial jet aircraft, the development of much larger ocean-going vessels (superfreighters) and the introduction of containerization which greatly simplifies transhipment from one mode of transport to another and increases the security of shipments' (Dicken, 1986, pp. 107–9). The technology of communication has made even more striking advances via innovations in telephone, telex, radio, cable and satellite. Satellite communication not only provides virtually simultaneous transmission and reception but it does so at relatively low and decreasing cost and at more or less the same cost for any distance.

Considerable evidence on the technological developments, growth in markets and reduction in costs of the telecommunication services is given by the United Nations Economic Commission for Europe (1987). Two striking examples in their volume relate to the cost of satellite communication and the real cost of telephone calls. Their table II.7 shows that the total cost for satellite communication has steadily decreased and is expected to show further reductions. The cost in real terms per half circuit per year is expected to decrease from US$13 500 in 1983 to $6730 in 1990 and to $2460 in the year 2000. The real cost of a three-minute telephone call between the United Kingdom and the United States has decreased from £173 in 1927 to £1.63 in 1983 (UNECE, 1987, figure II.18). The UN Commission's overall assessment of the price of telecommunication equipment is:

> Owing to continuous rapid technological advances and to economies of scale in production as a result of constantly increasing demand, prices of telecommunication equipment have increased less rapidly than those in manufacturing as a whole. In the United States, for instance, prices of telephone and telegraph apparatus increased by an average of 6.9 per cent per year during the period 1972–1982. . . . This can be compared with a yearly average of 8.9 per cent for capital equipment as a whole for the same period. . . . the price increases became successively smaller during the late 1970s and during the 1980s. Between 1982 and 1985, prices increased by a yearly average of only 1.5 per cent. (p. 30)

In 1937 Coase (p. 343) wrote: 'Changes like the telephone and the telegraph which tend to reduce the cost of organizing spatially will tend to increase the size of the firm. All changes which improve managerial technique will tend to increase the size of the firm.' We could add that these changes will also tend to increase internationalization and the geographical spread of activities.

Besides these two necessary conditions for growth in internationalization there have been other developments related to advances in computer technology that have further *facilitated* the internationalization process. Technological advances have helped internationalization through their effects on markets and on production processes.

Technological developments in the mass media and the widespread diffusion of radio and television, even in relatively poor countries and areas, have led to increasing uniformity of consumer demand for products supplied by TNCs. Demonstration effects carry with them considerable social and political effects. Mass media and new communication technologies render complete censorship difficult; awareness of high consumption levels in other societies or countries adds to discontent and to political destabilization.

In some services, such as banking, the advances in data transmission and communications are leading more and more towards the development of international banking without the creation of bank branches. As we shall see in the next chapter the volume of international banking and insurance services has increased at a very fast rate, while the number of foreign branches and subsidiaries has remained stagnant and shown little increase.

In terms of manufacturing production, advances in computerization and its application to the technology of product design have helped the internationalization process. Products and productive processes can be and are divided into various components and stages. The way the division is done is dictated by technological constraints and by cost-minimization strategies, in particular for labour costs. Various components may require different skills and thus involve different labour costs. In a multi-country set up different skills can be purchased in different countries, thus minimizing labour costs worldwide.[4]

The relationship between the division of products into components and the location of production is likely to be one in which causation goes both ways. This means that technology and design have an effect on the division of products into various components and of processes into various stages; such division will, therefore, have effects on how components are located in different countries. But conversely the availability of labour and labour skills, and the relative costs of labour in various countries, may have an effect on the way the products are divided into components and, therefore, on the design of products.

It is clear that the actual and potential capability of dividing the productive process into elementary units has facilitated internationalization because it has made possible the location of different stages of production in different countries; from this point of view, the technology of decomposition into elementary units has acted as a cause of internationalization. At the same time the drive towards internationalization is likely to have encouraged a type of technological development that has led to the decomposition of the productive process; this decomposition allows TNCs to make the best use of the worldwide supply of skilled and unskilled labour force in various locations. These developments would not have been possible without the widespread use of computing technology in the design of products and processes.

Computerization is helping in the more efficient use of transport equipment (e.g. full use of vessels and airfreight space) and infrastructure (e.g. ports, traffic controls etc.). It is also helping in the planning of supply according to demand via full control of stocks in time and space. This is allowing organizations to move increasingly from a 'just in case' system of production to the 'just in time' system, with consequent decreases in stocks and thus decreases in costs and risks.

It should be noted that the two necessary conditions for the growth of internationalization (developments in technology of transport and communication plus developments in internal organization), as well as advances in the facilitating technologies, do not just add to each other in contributing to the final result of growth in internationalization. Their combined effect is more likely to be multiplicative or exponential than additive. The technology of data transmission combined with the technology of data elaboration and analysis and an appropriate organizational structure can dramatically improve the efficiency of widespread operations and thus lead to more and more globalization.

Technological and organizational changes have created the basic necessary conditions for the growth of internationalization, and at the same time their developments have been enhanced by the requirements of transnationalism. Other post-Second World War conditions have also helped the internationalization process. The climate of international political stability and cooperation in the industrial Western countries has helped transnational activities; at the same time the requirements of TNCs worldwide have helped in the achievement of this international political situation. Thus changes in the political environment in Eastern Europe will, no doubt, increase transnational activities directed towards those areas.

Appendix: On Definitions

There are almost as many definitions of TNCs as there are writers on the subject. The United Nations Department of Economic and Social Affairs (1973) devotes a whole annex (II) to definitions.

Dunning (1981, p. 3) adopts a deliberately simple definition when he defines multinational enterprises (MNEs) as 'firms that engage in foreign direct investment'. He considers this to be a 'broad definition'; however, in practice, this definition rules out international involvement other than via direct investment. Hood and Young (1979) define an MNE as a corporation which 'owns (in whole or in part), controls and manages income-generating assets in more than one country. In so doing it engages in international production, namely production across national boundaries' (p. 3). Caves (1982) sees the MNE 'as an enterprize that controls and manages production establishments – plants – located in at least two countries' (p. 1).

Aharoni (1971) devotes a whole article to the issue of definitions. If his paper does not help to give us a clear, simple, agreed definition, at least it helps us to see the problems and pitfalls. He traces the term 'multinational firm' to D. E. Lilienthal, who 'suggested the definition of "multinational corporations" as "corporations which have their home in one country but operate and live under the laws and customs of other countries as well" ' p. 27). Aharoni sees many possible definitions according to whether one wants to stress the structure, performance or behaviour of companies.

In a *structure* related definition one may want to emphasize various elements, such as:

1   the geographical criterion (number of countries in which operations take place);
2   the ownership criterion (spread in the nationality of shareholders);
3   the national composition of top managers as decision-makers;
4   the organizational structure of the company: to what extent is the organization of the company structured 'on the basis of a worldwide concept of operations' (Aharoni, 1971, p. 30).

One general problem with (2) and (3) is the fact that 'control' may not coincide with ownership or management.

Definitions based on the *performance* criterion are again very problematic as they involve various parameters. In particular, we would have to decide whether to consider *absolute* or *relative* measures of resources committed. Whether the absolute or relative measures are considered, decisions will have to be taken on their cut-off point for inclusion in the multinational league. Aharoni identifies four possible elements as performance indicators, all of which have a valid claim to be considered in defining a multinational company: assets, number of employees, sales and earnings. They all present difficulties.

The *behavioural* criterion sees the multinational firm as one whose top management 'thinks internationally' (Aharoni, 1971, p. 33). This is probably the most problematic definitional criterion; the problems (highlighted by Aharoni) range from tautology to difficulties in differentiating *ex ante* from *ex post* measures.

The overall difficulties in arriving at agreed definitions are compounded by the fact that the various indicators of structure, performance and behaviour are not connected. Thus companies that would be considered TNCs under a particular structural indicator may not meet the multinationality criterion under a different structural indicator or under the performance indicators.

With regard to *foreign direct investment* there are differences between the theoretical concept used by most writers in the field and the definition used in the official statistics. Although the definition is rarely stated with full precision, most writers work with a concept of direct investment based on control and on ownership of assets.

Regarding official statistics, the IMF (1977, p. 136) gives the following definition: 'Direct investment refers to investment that is made to acquire a lasting interest in an enterprise operating in an economy other than that of the investor, the investor's purpose being to have an effective voice in the management of the enterprise.' The same IMF Manual includes in the category of *portfolio investment*, 'long-term bonds and corporate equities other than those included in the categories for direct investment and reserves' (p. 142).

The United Nations Department of Economic and Social Affairs (1973, pp. 4–5) draws the following distinction between subsidiaries, affiliates, branches and associates:

> A foreign branch is a part of an enterprise that operates abroad. An affiliate is an enterprise under effective control by a parent company and may be either a subsidiary (with majority or sometimes as little as 25 per cent control of the voting stock by the parent company) or an associate (in which case as little as 10 per cent control of voting stock may be judged adequate to satisfy the criterion).

It should be noted that the definition of direct investment used by the IMF and implicit in all the countries' statistics on FDI is a rather problematic one for the following reasons.

1   First, the cut-off point between direct and portfolio investment is based on the criterion of 'control'. There is, however, no properly defined concept of 'control'. As the IMF manual states: 'many countries rely for evidence of direct investment on the proportion of foreign ownership of the voting stock in an enterprise' (IMF, 1977, p. 137). However, the proportion considered relevant for inclusion can vary from country to country. A relevant element in establishing what proportion of ownership gives 'control' – thus leading to inclusion in the FDI category – is whether foreign ownership is dispersed into many foreign investors or is concentrated into one investor or a group of associates. In the latter case 'the percentage chosen as providing evidence of direct investment is typically quite low – frequently ranging from 25 per cent down to 10 per cent' (IMF, 1977, p. 137).
2   Secondly, there are again some variations between countries in the forms of investment that are included in FDI. 'The equity capital supplied by the direct investor and the reinvested earnings attributed to him . . . are two types where the direct investment relationship is undoubtedly a primary factor' (IMF, 1977, p. 139). The UK Central Statistical Office (CSO. 1988) writes thus on the forms of investments included in the FDI category:

> Direct investment consists of the parent company's share of the unremitted profits less losses of subsidiary and associated companies, the cash acquisition, net of sales, of share and loan capital of subsidiaries and associated companies, changes in indebtedness on inter-company accounts and changes in branch–head office indebtedness. (p. 8)

3   Thirdly, the concept used by the IMF definition and statistics is essentially a financial concept based on balance of payments criteria. Therefore, it 'is not the same as capital expenditure on fixed assets or the growth in a company's net assets' (CSO, 1988, p. 8).

4   Fourthly, there is no attempt at separating foreign direct investments that result in the creation of new productive capacity from those that are the result of acquisition of existing capacity. From a micro point of view increased real assets via mergers or via greenfield operations may result in increased capacity for the individual firm. However, from a macro point of view the acquisition of existing production facilities (e.g. via mergers) does not result in increased productive capacity for the economy as a whole. This problem is further complicated by the fact that FDI results in legal ownership claims across countries. The ownership of real assets and productive capacity by companies based in one country will increase. In the case of greenfield operation this increase is accompanied by an overall increase in productive capacity; in the case of acquisitions, the operation results in a transfer of legal claim from one company and country to another. As estimates of international production are normally based on FDI statistics, we must be careful to distinguish the micro from the macro interpretations of such estimates.

2

Trends in Internationalization

It is a capital mistake to theorize before one has data.
A. Conan Doyle, *Scandal in Bohemia*

2.1 Trends in international production

The post-Second World War period has seen very considerable qualitative and quantitative changes in the internationalization process. Both international production and international trade have been affected, often in an interactive way. With regard to international production the following main trends have occurred.

(1) There has been a tremendous increase in foreign direct investment by companies based in the developed market economies (DMEs) (table 2.1).[1] The USA is by far the largest foreign investor; other countries with a long tradition of large outward investment are the UK and the Netherlands. However, the past 30 years have seen the emergence and growth of outward involvement by newcomers into the field, such as the Federal Republic of Germany (FRG) and Japan. The FRG increased its share of outward stock from 1.2 to 8.7 per cent between 1960 and 1985; the corresponding percentages for Japan are 0.8 and 12.1. The shares of the USA and UK have progressively declined: the USA share was 47.6 per cent in 1960 and 36.2 in 1985; the corresponding figures for the UK are 18.5 and 15.1.

(2) Many DMEs are heavily involved in both outward and inward FDI. The UK and the Netherlands are the main examples in this category although other countries are moving in the same direction (e.g. the USA and the FRG), as indicated by the trends in tables 2.1 and 2.2, which give the position of each country in relation to other developed Western countries through time. The FDI position of each country in relation to

Table 2.1 Outward stock of foreign direct investment, selected years 1960–1985, major developed market economies

Country	1960			1967			1973			1975			1978			1980			1985		
	Value	%	Rank	Value	%	Rank	Value	%	Rank	Value	%	Rank	Value	%	Rank	Value	%	Rank	Value	%	Rank
United States	31.9	47.6	1	56.6	50.3	1	101.3	49.0	1	124.2	45.1	1	168.1	45.2	1	220.3	41.1	1	250.7	36.2	1
Canada	2.5	3.7	5	3.7	3.3	5	7.8	3.8	8	10.4	3.8	8	13.6	3.7	8	21.6	4.0	7	36.5	5.3	7
France	4.1	6.1	4	6.0	5.3	4	8.8	4.2	7	10.6	3.9	7	14.9	4.0	7	20.8	3.9	8	21.6	3.1	8
Federal Republic of Germany	0.8	1.2	8	3.0	2.7	7	11.9	5.8	4	18.4	6.7	5	31.8	8.5	3	43.1	8.1	3	60.0	8.7	4
Italy	1.1	1.6	7	2.1	1.9	8	3.2	1.6	9	3.3	1.2	10	3.3	0.9	10	7.0	1.3	10	12.4	1.8	9
Netherlands	7.0	10.5	3	11.0	9.8	3	15.4	7.4	3	19.9	7.2	4	23.7	6.4	6	41.9	7.8	4	43.8	6.3	6
Sweden	0.4	0.6	10	1.7	1.5	9	3.0	1.4	10	4.7	1.7	9	6.0	1.6	9	7.2	1.3	9	9.0	1.3	10
Switzerland	2.3	3.4	6	3.7	3.3	5	10.2	4.9	6	22.4	8.1	3	27.8	7.5	4	38.5	7.2	5	45.3	6.6	5
United Kingdom	12.4	18.5	2	17.5	15.6	2	26.9	13.0	2	37.0	13.4	2	41.1	11.1	2	81.4	15.2	2	104.7	15.1	2
Japan	0.5	0.8	9	1.5	1.3	10	10.3	5.0	5	15.9	5.8	6	26.8	7.2	5	36.5	6.8	6	83.6	12.1	3
Other	4.0	6.0		5.6	5.0		8.2	3.9		8.5	3.1		14.7	3.9		17.4	3.3		25.6	3.7	
Total developed market economies	67.0	100.0		112.4	100.0		207.0	100.0		275.4	100.0		371.8	100.0		535.7	100.0		693.3	100.0	

Values in billion US dollars.

Source: UN Centre on Transnational Corporations, 1983a, p. 34; 1988, p. 24

the size of the country itself will be considered in chapter 18. Various indicators of the impact of FDI on national economies are presented in that chapter and estimates are given in various tables.

(3) Not only is there considerable cross-border investment among DMEs but a large amount of such investments is intra-industry. Intra-industry investment means that investment across countries takes place in the same industries. This is a concept similar to intra-industry trade, on which there is more later (section 2.2, point 2). Estimates of intra-industry FDI in Dunning (1982) and Norman and Dunning (1984) point to high values for the main industrialized western economies.[2]

(4) The DMEs are by far the main recipients of FDI and over the long term their share has been increasing (table 2.3). The developing countries receive by far the smallest share of world FDI; this share declined from about 30 per cent in the 1960s and early 1970s to around 25 per cent in the 1970s and 1980s. The decline is even more dramatic if one considers the period before the Second World War, which shows shares well above 60 per cent for the developing countries. This high share going to less developed countries was a reflection of the different structural composition of FDI in the pre- and post-war periods. Before the Second World War the majority of FDI was made with the aim of securing supplies of natural resources to developed countries and hence was more likely to be directed towards LDCs. It is with the increased scope for foreign investment in manufacturing that the considerable changes in FDI have occurred. These changes have taken the form of both large increases worldwide and changes in the geographical structure, with more FDI directed towards DMEs. The present situation is therefore one in which most FDI originates with DMEs and by far the largest share (approximately 75 per cent) is directed towards the same group of countries.[3]

(5) Recently we have witnessed the emergence and relative growth of TNCs from developing countries, mainly newly industrializing countries. The UNCTC (1988, p. 38) writes on this issue: 'While FDI undertaken by corporations parented in developing countries amounted in 1985 to less than 3 per cent of the world's outward stocks of FDI, the number of TNCs belonging to these countries is not unsubstantial.' A very considerable share (almost half) of the FDI from developing countries is directed towards extractive and mineral-processing industries; most TNCs from LDCs tend to invest in other LDCs. Only a handful of LDCs are involved in outward investment: 'Some 10 of the 17 large corporations have their home bases in only three countries: the Republic of Korea alone accounts for six of those corporations, while Brazil and Mexico are home to two each' (UNCTC, 1988, p. 38).

Table 2.2 Outward and inward foreign direct investment: world total, main areas and selected market economies, averages 1975–1985

Countries and areas	Average annual flow							
	Inward				Outward			
	1975–1980		1981–1985		1975–1980		1981–1985	
	Value	%	Value	%	Value	%	Value	%
United States	7 894.6	24.5	19 155.8	39.3	17 091.5	42.4	8 639.7	19.1
Western Europe	13 873.5	43.1	14 859.5	30.5	17 912.8	44.5	25 247.7	55.7
France	2 127.3	6.6	2 144.5	4.4	1 825.1	4.5	2 692.5	5.9
Federal Republic of Germany	1 052.6	3.3	869.2	1.8	3 153.4	7.8	3 870.2	8.5
Italy	553.7	1.7	1 048.4	2.2	419.0	1.0	1.669.9	3.7
Netherlands	1 276.7	4.0	1 434.8	2.9	3.841.3	9.5	4 019.9	8.9
Sweden	100.2	0.3	167.1	0.3	571.2	1.4	1 032.7	2.3
United Kingdom	5 195.4	16.1	4 331.5	8.9	7 024.5	17.4	9 408.8	20.8
Japan	152.3	0.5	331.1	0.7	2 172.5	5.4	5 083.6	11.2
Total developed market economies	24 642.0	76.6	36 593.4	75.1	39 774.3	98.8	44 453.5	98.1
Developing countries	7 539.1	23.4	12 141.7	24.9	500.7	1.2	858.6	1.9
All countries	32 183.4[a]	100.0	48 735.5[a]	100.0	40 277.5[a]	100.0	45 312.1[a]	100.0

Values in million US dollars.
[a] There are many reasons for the discrepancies between inward and outward flows, including missing data and different methods of data collection in the various countries.

Source: Calculated from UN Centre on Transnational Corporations, 1988, pp. 504–10

Table 2.3 Percentage stock of inward foreign direct investment, selected years 1914–1985, developed market economies and developing countries

Host area	1914	1938	1960	1971	1975	1978	1980	1983	1985
Developed market economies	37.2	34.3	67.3	65.2	75.1	69.6	71.1	75.6	75.0
Developing countries	62.8	65.7	32.3	30.9	24.9	27.8	26.6	24.4	25.0
Unallocated	n.a.	n.a.	0.4	3.9	n.a.	2.6	2.3	n.a.	n.a.

For some years the percentages do not add up to 100 because of some unallocated amounts. The figures for the various years are not fully comparable as they relate to different samples. n.a. = not applicable.

Sources: For 1914 and 1938, Dunning, 1983, tables 5.1 and 5.2; for 1960, 1971, 1978 and 1980, Stopford and Dunning, 1983, p. 12; for 1975, 1983 and 1985, UNCTC, 1988, table 13.

Similarly, there has been an increase in FDI from centrally planned countries, which has grown in the 1970s and 1980s. State enterprises in socialist countries had established some 590 branches, subsidiaries and affiliates abroad by the mid-1980s; over 70 per cent of these were established in developed market economies.

However, TNCs from developing countries and from socialist (or former socialist) countries are, of course, still very small in number, in spite of their recent growth.

(6)   There has been a big shift in the sectoral composition of FDI worldwide. As already mentioned, the bulk of FDI before the Second World War was in primary products and particularly raw materials; from the late 1950s there was a shift towards manufacturing, which has become the dominant sector for FDI since the 1960s. However, the 1980s saw a considerable increase in FDI in services. The UNCTC (1988), in a comprehensive survey of TNCs and services, writes:

> By the mid-1980s, about 40 per cent of the world's total FDI stock . . . was in services, compared to approximately one quarter at the beginning of the 1970s and less than 20 per cent in the early 1950s. Moreover, FDI in services has increasingly become the most dynamic part of the growth of FDI in general. (p. 370)

The process indicates not a displacement of manufacturing FDI with services FDI but rather an increased transnationalization of services, which has led to increased FDI in both manufacturing and services. The bulk of services FDI originates in and is directed towards DMEs. Very fast growth in the share of total outward FDI attributable to services has occurred in Japan and the Federal Republic of Germany. Japan's share of services in total FDI changed from 25 per cent in the mid-1960s to 57 per cent in the mid-1980s; the corresponding figures for the FRG in the same period are 10 per cent and 48 per cent. The largest recipient of FDI in services is the USA but other DMEs have also experienced rapid increases in the inflow of services FDI.

Regarding the composition of services FDI, the UNCTC (1988) writes:

> . . . in most home and host countries for which data are available, the dominant positions are occupied by FDI in finance-related services (banking, insurance and other financial services) and in trade-related services (wholesale and retail trade and marketing). . . . As a percentage of the outward FDI stock in services of 11 home countries, the share of finance-related services ranged from 27 to 84 per cent in the first half of the 1980s. That of trade related services for the same countries was, with three exceptions, between 22 and 42 per cent. Similarly, as a proportion of inward FDI stock in services, and both for developed and developing countries, finance-related services and trade-related services together typically account for 50 to 90 per cent. (p. 382)

Transnational banking has increased to a very considerable degree. The UNCTC (1988, p. 102) reports that international financial activities, as measured by funds raised in international financial markets, increased at an annual rate of 23 per cent between 1972 and 1985; the increase in subsidiaries abroad of banks has, however, been much lower as financing can be done internationally through other channels than subsidiaries.[4] This internationalization process of financial markets was speeded up by the use of financial surpluses from oil and by 'the advances in computer and telecommunications technology, the trend towards abandonment of many financial regulations and the introduction of a range of new financial instruments on the securities markets' (UNCTC, 1988, p. 103). The breakdown of the Bretton Woods agreements and the progressive movement towards lower levels of government regulation in currency markets have also contributed towards the internationalization of financial markets.

The UNCTC (1988, pp. 390–1) reports also a very large expansion in transnational activities in the health-care industry due, in particular, to the establishment of private hospitals abroad by US TNCs. In absolute terms, the industry is still very small but it is increasing at a very fast rate.

The relevance of trading companies has also increased recently because of increasing export potential from some developing countries. Some of these countries have developed good export platforms but not equally good distribution and marketing networks and this has created an increasing role for the general trading companies, such as the Japanese *sogo shosha* (see UNCTC, 1988, pp. 164–6).

The rapid increase in services FDI results from the increased transnationality of services companies, coupled with increased work in services on the part of industrial TNCs as part of their diversification and integration strategies. The process has been helped by the growth of non-equity arrangements, the abolition of exchange controls in some countries, the deregulation of financial markets, by improved data transmission and communications technology (which has led to increased use of transborder data-flows) and, last but not least, the increased demand for services as a by-product of increased incomes in DMEs.

(7)   There is evidence that large TNCs have increasingly been widening the geographical network of their operations. Vernon (1979) has used data from the Harvard Multinational Enterprise Project relating to the 316 largest TNCs to derive data on the geographical spread of operations through time. The data in table 2.4 show that the percentage of large corporations operating in less than six countries decreased from 80 to 12.7 per cent between 1950 and the 1970s.

By contrast, Dicken (1986, p. 57) points out how the increase in the geographical spread of operations has occurred mainly in very large TNCs; the majority of TNCs are not so widely spread. When a wider, more representative sample than that in the Harvard Project is considered, we see that almost 80 per cent of companies had affiliates in no more than five countries in 1973 (table 2.5). However, table 2.5 does not allow us to see what has happened through time. We know from table 2.4 that the network of operations of the largest companies has grown wider; we are not sure whether the same conclusion applies to the larger sample considered in table 2.5.

Table 2.4 Network of foreign manufacturing subsidiaries of 316 USA and Europe based MNCs, 1950 and 1970s; percentage distribution

Networks in	1950	1970/75
Fewer than six countries	80.4	12.7
Six to 20 countries	18.7	64.2
More than 20 countries	0.9	23.1

Source: Adapted from Vernon, 1979, p. 258, table 1

(8) The popular image sees TNCs as very large, very powerful organizations; this view is broadly correct, although some qualifications are
necessary. According to UNCTC (1988, p. 34), in the 1980s, 'As in the
past, a small number of transnational corporations were responsible for
a large share of economic activity: six hundred corporations generated
one fifth of the total value added in manufacturing and agriculture, with
only 69 corporations accounting for half of total sales.'
Small and medium-sized corporations represent half the total universe
of TNCs, however. The technological developments in transport and
communication may have helped small and medium-sized firms to become
TNCs. As such developments continue, leading to further 'shrinkage' of
the world, the possibility of small and medium-sized firms becoming
TNCs, once they have reached a minimum size, will increase. Many small
and medium-sized TNCs originate in LDCs and socialist countries, while
the bulk of very large TNCs are located in DMEs. Table 2.6 gives the
breakdown by country of origin of the 600 largest TNCs in the 1980s.
Almost half of the largest TNCs originated in the USA. The UK was
parent to over 10 per cent of these companies while Japan generated
almost 16 per cent.

(9) New forms of international involvement in business activities have
developed in the past 20 years. They include, in particular, non-equity
forms of involvement, joint ventures (JVs) and export processing zones
(EPZs).
Non-equity forms of involvement can take different forms, including
management contracts, international sub-contracting, licensing agreements and turnkey operations.[5] These various forms involve contractual
arrangements over the supply of goods and materials for further pro-

Table 2.5 Geographical distribution of the foreign affiliates of 9481
transnational corporations, 1973

	Percentage of TNCs with links in the following number of countries					
	1	2–5	6–10	11–15	16–20	> 20
Percentage	44.9	34.8	10.2	4.4	2.3	3.4
Cumulative percentage	44.9	79.7	89.9	94.3	96.6	100.0

Source: Dicken, 1986, p. 57, table 3.2. Original source: Commission of the European
Communities, 1976, Survey of Multi-national Enterprises, Volume 1, table B. Brussels:
Commission of the European Communities

Table 2.6 Geographical origin of the world's largest 600 transnational corporations in mining and manufacturing by home country, 1985

Country	Total number	Percentage
USA	275	45.8
UK	62	10.3
France	26	4.3
Federal Republic of Germany	37	6.2
Italy	5	0.8
Netherlands	8	1.3
Sweden	17	2.8
Switzerland	9	1.5
Japan	95	15.8
Australia	4	0.7
Canada	22	3.7
Other	40	6.7

Source: Calculated from UNCTC, 1988, annex B.1, pp. 533–45

cessing, know-how, management skills and access to technology; one or more of these transfers may be involved in any specific arrangement. In return, the TNC receives royalties, fees and revenue from sales of materials and components. Although it is largely non-equity, the agreement may, at times, entail some equity involvement between the TNC and the local firms; these firms are usually, but not exclusively, located in LDCs. While of undoubted benefit to TNCs, the new forms of involvement can also be of benefit to the domestic firm and host country as employment is generated, know-how may be transferred and export opportunities are increased. The UNCTC (1988, p. 157) writes: 'TNCs and domestic manufacturing firms have through non-equity forms of relationships particularly sub-contracting, played an important role in expanding the exports of manufactures from many developing countries and territories.'

Evidence on non-equity forms of involvement is not readily available, so indirect indicators often have to be used. For licensing agreements a good proxy is given by data on receipts of royalties and fees; these data show a considerable increase for the main DMEs in the past two decades (see, for example, Stopford and Dunning, 1983; UNCTC, 1988, table XI.1).

There has been a considerable increase in sub-contracting arrangements between big corporations and smaller production units. There are various definitions of sub-contracting. Michalet (1980), following a UNIDO group of experts, states:

> . . . a sub-contracting relationship exists when a firm (the principal) places an order with another firm (the sub-contractor) for the manufacture of parts, components, sub-assemblies or assemblies to be incorporated into a product which the principal will sell. Such orders may include the treatment, processing or finishing of materials or parts by the sub-contractor at the principal's request. (p. 40)

Sub-contracting has both a domestic and an international basis. International sub-contracting refers to a sub-contracting arrangement between firms located in different countries. Whether it is done in developed or less developed countries, sub-contracting is usually likely to originate with a TNC as 'the principal'.

There is, unfortunately, no overall comprehensive empirical evidence on sub-contracting. Friedman (1977) gives some international comparisons on the motor industry:

> British Leyland maintains sub-contracting relations with about 4,000 firms and about 65 per cent of the value of an average Leyland car represents 'bought out' parts and components. Ford, on the other hand, buys out about 50 per cent of the value of its cars on average. . . . In Japan around 45 per cent of car value is bought out by car manufacturers and in Italy, Germany, France and the United States the proportions are from 25 per cent to 40 per cent. (pp. 118–19)

It is worth remembering, however, that in the motor industry the 'buying out' of parts and components often involves large firms on both sides.

Murray (1985) gives some interesting facts on a different sector:

> A good example of the 'new production' is that of the Italian clothing firm, Benetton. Their clothes are made by 11,500 workers in Northern Italy, only 1,500 of whom work directly for Benetton. The rest are employed by sub-contractors in factories of 30–50 workers each. The clothes are sold through 2,000 tied retail outlets, all of them franchised. Benetton provide the designs, control material stocks, and orchestrate what is produced according to the computerised daily sales returns which flow back to their Italian head-quarters from all parts of Europe. (p. 30)

Sharpston (1975) uses the value of imports under USA Tariff Items 806.30 and 807.00 as a proxy for observations on international sub-contracting by US multinationals.[6] His evidence shows (p. 97) that the total value of imports from LDCs under these two items increased by approximately 25 times between 1966 and 1973. Enderwick (1984, p. 354) writes on the same issue: 'Estimates suggest that between 1965 and 1970 almost half of the increase in clothing imports into western Europe was accounted for by goods supplied by sub-contractors.'

A particular type of sub-contracting arrangement common in transbor-der agreements is the original equipment manufacturing arrangement (OEM): a 'type of long-term contractual relationship between a manufacturing firm and its main supplier of components and sub-assemblies' (UNCTC, 1988, p. 166). Its origins may be traced back to the United States automobile industry in the 1920s.[7]

(10) The term joint venture refers to a partnership between two or more enterprises in a specific business 'venture'. The partnership may involve both equity and management participation and can be on the basis of equal or different shares for the partners. It can involve the setting up of new production facilities or the buying of existing ones. Increasingly, international business involvement has taken the form of joint ventures. The advantages for individual companies over other forms of involvement are many and include the following:

1 Lower risk, as the risk of a particular investment is spread among the participants.
2 The possibility of using complementary resources, skills and know-how on the part of the participating enterprises.
3 The avoidance of competition in a particular market.
4 Ease of penetration into a particular market or country. In some countries joint ventures with a domestic enterprise may be the only acceptable entrance route for a foreign TNC.
5 Easier repatriation of profits for the TNC involved.
6 The opening up of further possibilities for production and marketing in a new country.
7 Flexibility with respect to the equity share, which can vary from case to case and can vary for the same venture through time according to the agreement between the participants. Flexibility is also achieved in the overall organization of the participating companies: the new venture can be set up or closed down without excessive disturbance to the main corporate structure and organization.

Joint ventures are often related to involvement in LDCs; the local firm (usually a medium-sized one) will have the advantages of access to technology and managerial and marketing skills as well as to equity capital.

Transnational joint ventures can take the form of an arrangement between a foreign owned firm and a local privately owned or state enterprise. They can, however, also be a venture undertaken by various foreign-owned companies in a particular country without any local partici-pation (see Grimwade, 1989, pp. 242–50).

Transnational joint ventures have been increasing, particularly in LDCs and Eastern Europe. The UNCTC (1988) reports a considerable increase in joint ventures between TNCs from DMEs and Eastern European state enterprises: 'By the end of 1987, their total number, although still relatively small, had reached nearly 850' (p. 300). The participating enterprises in Eastern Europe are mainly small and medium-sized enterprises; the main sector of operations is manufacturing; the main host countries Poland and Hungary. Western TNCs see joint ventures as a way of penetrating into Eastern Europe and its high skilled, low-cost labour force; Eastern governments see it as a method for penetration of new markets, as part of their export expansion and/or import substitution strategies and as a source of access to new technology, managerial skills and external financial resources.

The general increase in JVs throughout the world, their pattern, determinants and effects are well documented in the volume edited by Contractor and Lorange (1988).[8] Hergert and Morris (1988) give evidence of a very considerable increase in JVs between partners from major developed countries between 1975 and 1986; the largest share of total JVs is within the European Community (30.8 per cent) followed by agreements between EC and US partners (25.8 per cent). Motor vehicles, aerospace and telecommunications are the industries where most JVs have taken place (respectively 23.7, 19.0 and 17.2 per cent); the purpose of the collaboration is given mainly as 'joint product development' (37.7 per cent) and 'production' (23.3 per cent). The further increase in JVs in the late 1980s and in 1990 has sparked off serious worries about the formation of international cartels (see Leadbeater, 1990; Marsh, 1990). These worries seem very justified particularly since the Hergert and Morris (1988) research found that 71.3 per cent of JVs are between rival partners. It is significant that the FIAT president Agnelli (1990) puts the case for more international JVs and dismisses the cartelization issue on the ground that these cooperative agreements are only limited and hence lead to overall 'competitive cooperation'.

(11)　An export processing zone (EPZ) 'is an adaptation, for the purpose of modern export oriented industrialization programmes, of the 18th century concept of a commercial free trade zone. Its original purpose was to speed re-exports and the victualling of ships, and a major later aim was to stimulate entrepôt trade' (Currie, 1985, p. 1). The main change from the original free trade zone is that the type of business has moved from commercial to manufacturing, thus leading to the modern EPZs. 'The central features of EPZs are that imports and exports are free of tariffs or other trade restraints, that infrastructural facilities for manufacturing production are provided, and that regulatory and administrative procedures entailed in the establishment and operation of enterprises are simplified. Fiscal or financial incentives may also be provided' (UNCTC, 1988, pp. 169–70).

The EIU report by Currie (1985) mentions the existence of nine zones by the end of the 1960s; this increased to 35 zones by the end of 1974 and 57 zones by the end of 1979; the UNCTC reports 260 zones in 1988. Concomitantly with the growth in number of zones, there has been a very considerable growth in employment which by 1988 had risen to about 1.3 million from 500 000 in 1975. The countries where EPZs are located are mainly LDCs and newly industrialized countries (NICs); 95 per cent of world employment in EPZs is accounted for by 14 countries with Singapore, Mexico and the Republic of Korea as leaders. The labour employed is mainly young and female: some 80 per cent of the workforce is composed of women between 20 and 24 years of age. The labour force employed has a high turnover and is, on the whole, non-unionized; wages are much lower than in DMEs, though often higher than the average wages in the host country. Location in EPZs is mainly by foreign TNCs, generally not the very large ones but 'smaller firms, often only just beginning to expand their international operations' (UNCTC, 1988, p. 170). Sometimes domestic firms are also allowed to use EPZs. Various forms of involvement may be used in EPZs, from sub-contracting arrangements to joint ventures to direct foreign investment.

The industries that thrive most in EPZs are electronics and textiles. These are industries characterized by labour-intensive techniques and low weight and bulk in relation to value. This last feature renders it efficient to ship around the commodities processed.

2.2   Trends in international trade

(1)   Trade volume and patterns have also undergone considerable changes in the past few decades. The value of world trade has increased not only in absolute terms but also, significantly, as a proportion of world production. Table 2.7 shows that the growth rates of world volume of exports have been considerably and significantly higher than the growth rates of output for both manufacturing and total merchandise.

TNCs account for a large and increasing percentage of world trade. In the United Kingdom TNCs account for some 80 per cent of total exports; of this about 30 per cent is the responsibility of non-UK corporations with subsidiaries in the UK. In the USA, home country TNCs account for about half of total imports and over three-quarters of exports (UNCTC, 1988, chapter VI).

(2)   A considerable proportion of world trade is intra-industry. Intra-industry trade consists of a simultaneous export and import, by the same country, of products belonging to the same industrial group. The growth of intra-industry trade poses theoretical and practical problems. Theoretically, this growth seems to refute explanations of trade based

Table 2.7 World merchandise trade and production, average annual percentage growth rates in volume, 1960–1985

	1960–9	1970–9	1980–3	1984	1985
All merchandise					
Exports	8.5	5.5	0.5	9.0	3.0
Production	6.0	4.0	0.0	5.5	2.0
Manufacturing					
Exports	10.5	7.5	2.0	12.0	6.0
Production	7.5	4.5	1.0	7.0	4.0

Source: GATT, 1986

on inter-industry specialization, comparative advantages and factor endowment, thus adding to the wealth of problems in this branch of economic theory.[9]

At the practical level, the measurement of intra-industry trade depends mainly on the definition of 'industry' and therefore on the industrial classification used for the estimates. The definition of industry could be so wide that most or all trade would be intra-industry. Conversely, if no grouping is accepted and products are considered different whenever they exhibit even very small differences, then no trade is intra-industry. Thus estimates crucially depend on definitions, classifications and groupings. Within any accepted classification, such as the Standard Industrial Classification (SIC), estimates at higher aggregation level give different results from estimates at a lower level of aggregation, with the more comprehensive 'industry' giving higher values for intra-industry trade.

Grubel and Lloyd (1975) have developed an index of intra-industry trade that has formed the basis for most work in this area. However, they recognize that their index has an aggregation bias such that 'the measure of intra-industry trade at a more aggregate level is greater than, or at least no less than, the measured intra-industry trade with a given commodity breakdown. Aggregation increases the measure of intra-industry trade' (p. 23).

The Grubel–Lloyd indicator of intra-industry trade (IIT) is based on the following formula:

$$\text{IIT} = \frac{[(X_i + M_i) - |X_i - M_i|]}{(X_i + M_i)} \times 100$$
$$= \left[1 - \frac{|X_i - M_i|}{(X_i + M_i)} \right] \times 100$$

where X_i and M_i are exports and imports of a given country for industry i. If imports and exports for industry i are exactly balanced, the IIT index is equal to 100, the maximum level of intra-industry trade. If there is an imbalance, then IIT will be less than 100. If all trade is one-way (i.e. either M_i or X_i is equal to zero) then IIT will be equal to zero and there is no intra-industry trade in industry i.

The average level of IIT in a given country is calculated by Grubel and Lloyd using a weighted mean in which the weights for each industry are determined by the relative sizes of imports and exports of the industry concerned. Alternative formulae and measurements are introduced by Aquino (1978), Belassa (1974) and Bergstrand (1983).

Many explanations have been put forward for the high and increasing levels of IIT. They include: product differentiation and consumer demand for more variety in products, particularly in countries with high per capita income; economies of scale; degree of product innovation; increase in FDI and in the general level of TNCs' activities worldwide.

A comprehensive, clear survey of approaches to, explanations of and estimates on intra-industry trade is given by Grimwade (1989, chapter 3). His summary of findings reports high and increasing levels of intra-industry trade, with Western European countries (France, the United Kingdom, Belgium–Luxembourg and the Netherlands) sharing higher ratios than the USA, Canada, Japan and Australia.

> The level of intra-industry trade increased as a share of total trade in all ten countries except the Netherlands. The biggest increases were recorded for Belgium–Luxembourg and the United Kingdom . . . the highest levels of intra-industry trade were to be found in chemicals and machinery products. . . . Intra-industry trade as a proportion of total trade increased most quickly in manufacturing goods. (p. 107)

There is, essentially, no agreement on the measurement or explanation of intra-industry trade; it is clearly an area in which more theoretical work needs to be done. However, all the authors who have dealt with this area of work seem to agree that the levels and growth of intra-industry trade in the past few decades have been considerable; thus this aspect of trade cannot be ignored in either its causes or effects.

(3)   Intra-firm trade is a concept directly related to the activities of TNCs. Intra-firm (or intra-group or intra-enterprise or intra-company or in-house) trade refers to imports and exports involving firms related by ownership and operating in different countries. Measurement is usually made by considering exports (or imports) that are intra-firm as a percentage of total exports (or imports) in a country. The main conceptual problem is related to the definition of ownership: what percentage holding should one firm have of another for the trade to be classed as intra-firm?

The main practical problem, however, arises from the fact that, worldwide, there are very few statistics on intra-firm trade, particularly on the imports side. The only countries that collect systematic data on both imports and exports that are intra-firm are the USA and Japan. Table 2.8 gives data for three countries; for the UK, data on intra-firm imports are not available. All three countries show high and growing ratios of intra-firm trade in general with intra-firm imports significantly higher than intra-firm exports for the USA.[10] Intra-firm trade is particularly significant in manufacturing, with chemicals and transport equipment sharing very high levels in both the UK and the USA (UNCTC, 1988, table VI.2).

The growth of intra-firm trade raises a variety of issues linked to the effects of TNCs activities; these are discussed in chapter 17. The problems are reinforced by the fact that intra-firm trade gives scope for manipulation of transfer prices; that is, prices charged for commodities and services that are transferred across borders although internally to the company. The scope for manipulation of transfer prices is quite wide, affecting not only the transfer of goods, but also the transfer of services, and therefore of fees for managerial services, payment of royalties and payment of interest on loans. The manipulation can consist of charging higher or lower prices than the arm's length prices and/or exercising leads and lags in payments.[11]

There are various motives that induce TNCs to charge internal prices different from arm's length ones. In particular, differences in corporate taxation between countries will make it profitable to shift recorded profits to the low tax-rate country. Similarly, expected changes in currency values may prompt shifts of funds towards the country where the currency is expected to appreciate. In general, risks connected with currencies may be diminished by appropriate use of transfer prices plus leads and lags in the payments; similarly, underpricing a commodity may lead to payment of a lower *ad valorem* tariff. Obstacles to the repatriation of profits may be removed by appropriate internal pricing. A company may also have political reasons for wanting to have low declared profits in a particular country; for example, such a strategy might allow the company to avoid pressure for wage increases or pressure for more competition in the market and hence for tighter competition policies.

The manipulation of transfer prices can sometimes be detected but in general this is quite difficult as, for most commodities transferred, comparable market products with which to compare prices do not exist.

The manipulation of transfer prices is not without its problems for the company. There may be pressure from local shareholders and unions for a more open and accountable system of transfers. There may also be strong pressures from local managers not to see local profits syphoned off. The need for proper accountability and assessment of the performance

Table 2.8 Share of intra-firm transactions in the international trade
of the United States, Japan and the United Kingdom; percentages

Country	Trade associated with home country TNCs	Trade associated with TNCs of other home countries	Trade associated with all TNCs
United States			
Exports			
1977	26.7	2.6	9.3
1982	21.9	1.1	23.0
1985	29.0	2.0	31.0
Imports			
1977	21.7	20.5	42.2
1982	17.1	21.3	38.4
1985	16.1	24.0	40.1
Japan			
Exports			
1980	24.1	1.7	25.8
1983	30.6	1.2	31.8
Imports			
1980	31.5	10.6	42.1
1983	18.4	11.9	30.3
United Kingdom			
Exports			
1981	16.0	14.0	30.0

Source: UNCTC, 1988, p. 92, table VI.1.

of divisions may clash with the desire for higher overall profits which
the manipulation of transfer prices allows. This situation can create not
only difficulties in accountability and the assessment of performance but
also a high level of managerial conflict, which is detrimental and time-
consuming.[12]

This is one instance of conflicts generated within (and to a large
extent caused by) the centralized/decentralized structure typical of the
M-form of organization considered in chapter 1. Conflicts over internal
pricing arise between managers of 'buying' and 'selling' divisions as
well as between headquarters and local divisional managers. Conflicts

arise between the wish for high profits in the organization as a whole, and the use of profitability as a performance indicator for single divisions or units.

Part II
Theories

Felix qui potuit rerum cognoscere causas
(Lucky is the one who has been able to understand the causes of things)
Virgil, *Georgics*

Introduction to Part II

In this part I shall deal with various theories and approaches to foreign investment.

The theories are presented in four sections: section I deals with Marxist approaches; section II deals with explanations of foreign investment within the neo-classical paradigm; section III deals with the prevalent, most widely accepted theories of TNCs and FDI; section IV considers some approaches that stress strategic elements.

In the presentation of the theories a historical approach is adopted and thus most theories are presented chronologically. This historical approach has two main aims: it allows us to see how theories evolve and how authors develop concepts which may have been touched on by previous theorists; it also allows us to see the relationship between the real economic situation and the theories developed during particular periods of time. Thus the Marxist theories are considered first, partly because they were the first ones put forward, and partly because they relate to an early phase of foreign investment when colonialism and the securing of raw materials were still of paramount relevance.

No doubt some readers will disagree with the groupings here presented; however, any classification and grouping is bound to be problematic. Readers may also feel that the inclusion of theories and writers is arbitrary, and of course to some extent it is. The aim here is to try to include the most popular and representative theories or those that have some special feature. Inevitably, some theories have been omitted. This is partly to avoid some repetition of arguments, partly to keep the volume of material under control. In the final choice of what to include, no doubt a role has been played by this author's preferences and degree of knowledge or ignorance of the various theories.

In relation to the classification and grouping of theories, it might be worth making a few points and highlighting some problems. The first problematic area is related to Marxist theories: Marxist literature is often filled with fierce polemics as to which theory, development or approach is 'really' Marxist. The usual benchmarks of a Marxist approach are elements such as class analysis, analysis of conflicts and contradictions etc. However, there are elements on which there is more disagreement, such as the extent to which a Marxist analysis should contain elements of production rather than mainly elements of demand and exchange. This last point leads on to the issue of theories based on under-consumption: to what extent can they be considered part of the Marxist analysis? Very often it is a matter of the sort of prescriptions and predictions they lead to, including predictions about the inevitability of imperialism and/or the inevitability of the downfall of capitalism.

Within the more 'prevalent' group of theories Hymer's forms a case in itself. Hymer's theory is quite radical in terms of departure from the neo-classical paradigm; it is also susceptible to very radical interpretations and developments. However, as first presented by Hymer himself, and as later developed and interpreted by other authors, it does not seem to be a Marxist theory. Later work by Hymer has a more Marxist flavour. Hymer's approach contains many strategic elements and thus it could have been included in section IV; one reason for its inclusion in section III, at the start of the main prevalent modern theories, is to allow the reader to see how the modern theory of FDI began and the extent to which Hymer's approach served as stimulus for further developments.

The theories are not always fully comparable as some of them deal with explanations of TNCs' activities in general, some with FDI only, some with overall foreign investment. In summarizing a particular theory, attention will be given to explanations of foreign direct investment and international production in general.

Most Marxist literature on foreign investment is concerned with imperialism, whether colonial (as in the early theories) or not. The focus of this book is not imperialism and development, but international production; this means that the Marxist theories included are those concerned with foreign investment, whether they touch on it in the course of exploring imperialism or not. Development theories *as such* have been excluded, even though some of the authors presented deal with development.

The assumptions behind the neo-classical paradigm are very much at variance with the reality of TNCs and their operations; there never was a greater example of economists 'assuming away' their problems! Given this situation readers may well wonder why the neo-classical theory was included at all. The answer is: partly because it was felt that such a considerable part of the literature should not be ignored, and partly for historical reasons.

Each theory is commented on and criticized. I try, as much as possible, to keep exposition and critique separate, thus allowing readers a better chance to form their own critical assessment. The main assessment criteria used in my criticism are the explanatory and predictive power of theories; other elements, such as internal consistency or clarity of exposition, may also be commented on.

A critique of theories presented is useful, as an intellectual exercise in itself but also, and mainly, because it is through critical appraisal of existing theories that science progresses. Popper (1972) writes on this issue:

> Thus we can say that science begins with problems, and proceeds from there to competing theories which it evaluates *critically*. . . . The evaluation is always *critical*, and its aim is the discovery and *elimination of error*. The growth of knowledge – or the learning process – is not a repetitive or a cumulative process but one of error-elimination. (p. 144)

Criticism is an important element (the most important?) in the advancement of science in general; in the social sciences – so ridden with value judgements – a positive critical approach becomes essential. We must also remember that no single theory is likely to be perfect and fully satisfactory; all those chosen for inclusion in this book will contain some interesting elements and that is why they have been chosen. Often a theory may be relevant to a special historical, geographical or industry situation if not to all, or many, situations.

Throughout many years of teaching I have always been keen to present my students with alternative approaches and to criticize each approach as much as possible. Students often find this method disturbing because it does not give them ready-made answers to problems, does not give them *the* 'acceptable' view of the world and leaves them at a loss in finding out which answers the teacher might like to see in the exam papers!

I am convinced that this critical approach to teaching is the correct one and that part of the reason why students find it difficult at first is that most of them are used to years of uncritical presentation of concepts in the school classroom. It is rewarding to see that as time goes by in their course my students sharpen their critical sense and learn that the best answer to give to an exam paper is a critical one!

Section I
Marxist Approaches

---

per che una gente impera ed altra langue
so that one people rules and another languishes
                    Dante, *La Divina Commedia, Inferno*. VII.82

3

Classical Writers on Imperialism

3.1   Hobson's analysis of imperialism

Hobson's book *Imperialism*, first published in 1902, contains a very clear analysis of the economic and political implications of the growing imperialist tendency of developed countries in the nineteenth century, and particularly of Britain.

He starts his analysis by giving an assessment of the magnitude and growth of imperialism in terms of size of colonized territories and populations; these measures are set against comparative data for the related developed imperialist country. The main focus of the study is Britain: its very considerable expansion in the last 30 years of the nineteenth century is emphasized.

Does the nation as a whole need imperialism and does it benefit from it? Hobson asks and analyses this question in relation to: (a) the need to generate exports to sustain domestic activity and employment; and (b) the need to expand the territorial areas in which the growing population of Britain can find settlement.

He considers both of these 'needs'. In particular the 'need' for colonial trade is discussed from various points of view: first, because a possible cut in colonial exports could be counterbalanced by increased domestic demand for consumption provided the 'appropriate' distribution policy on income and wealth were followed; secondly, because trade with the colonies was becoming a decreasing proportion of total trade at the time; thirdly – and connected with the second point – because political annexation and subjugation are not necessary to the generation of trade. Indeed he points out the inconsistency between the free trade doctrine of British economists and politicians and the imposition of 'protected' trade via colonialism when he writes: 'In total contravention of our theory that trade rests upon a basis of mutual gain to the nations that engage in it, we undertook enormous expenses with the object of "forcing" new markets, and the markets we forced were small, precarious and unprofitable' (pp. 65–6).

His conclusion is, therefore, that 'imperialism' is not needed by the nation as a whole. Indeed when the economic and human costs of imperialist and related distortions in the structure of public expenditure are considered, one is led to conclude that the nation as a whole does not benefit from imperialist expansion.

Why, then, is it done? The answer is that although the nation as a whole may lose out from imperialism, a section of the population benefits from it. Hobson spells this out clearly when, in answer to his own question, 'How is the British nation induced to embark upon such unsound business?', he writes: 'The only possible answer is that the business interests of the nation as a whole are subordinated to those of certain sectional interests that usurp control of the national resources and use them for their private gain' (p. 46). The sections of the population that benefit are a variety of people drawn from the educated middle and upper classes: engineers, people working in armaments, planters, missionaries etc. However, the prime movers and instigators are the financial investors.

One of Hobson's best insights is to realize that imperialism has little or nothing to do with trade and more to do with investments as prime motivators. 'By far the most important economic factor in Imperialism is the influence relating to investments' (p. 51). This is made clear, among other things, by looking at data on incomes from foreign investment and profits from exports; the first set of incomes has grown much faster than the second. Hobson's own words on the relevance of investment and the interests of investors are very clear:

> It is not too much to say that the modern foreign policy of Great Britain has been primarily a struggle for profitable markets of investment. . . . If, contemplating the enormous expenditure on armaments, the ruinous wars, the diplomatic audacity or knavery by which modern Governments seek to extend their territorial power, we put the plain, practical question, *Cui bono*? the first and most obvious answer is, the investor. (pp. 53, 55)

The financiers manage to impose their line by control of the press and by their manipulation of political power. Why are financiers seeking investments abroad, why not in their own country? Is the country generating more savings than it can absorb? The answer is affirmative and this is connected with the tendency of the economic system towards overproduction, glut and under-consumption, and generally towards a lack of 'effective' demand.

'Everywhere appear excessive powers of production, excessive capital in search of investment, . . . the growth of the powers of production . . .

exceeds the growth in consumption, . . . more goods can be produced than can be sold at a profit, and . . . more capital exists than can find remunerative investment' (p. 81). This tendency to under-consumption or over-saving increases with improvements in methods of production and concentration of ownership and control as these lead to higher profits and concentration of incomes. The question now is: to what extent is this over-saving and over-production the inevitable outcome of progress and improvements in the economic system? Hobson vehemently rejects this line and explains over-saving and under-consumption through the distributional structure, which favours the wealthy classes against those classes that have a greater need and ability for consumption, but are denied 'consuming power' by the unfair distribution of income.

> The over-saving which is the economic root of Imperialism is found by analysis to consist of rents, monopoly profits, and other unearned or excessive elements of income, which, not being earned by labour of head or hand, have no legitimate *raison d'être*. (p. 85)

So the 'taproot' of imperialism is under-consumption and this is generated by a mal-distribution of income: the remedy is to move towards substantial reforms which distribute more income to the working classes and shift public expenditure from armaments towards public and community projects.

The economic system is condemned for the political and economic distortions it generates and for generating 'an economic waste which is chronic and general throughout the advanced industrial nations, a waste contained in the divorcement of the desire to consume and the power to consume' (p. 87).

3.2 Some comments

Hobson's analysis contains many interesting points, some specific to his historical period, some of more general value and interest. His view of imperialism is closely linked to colonialism. In his treatment, investment is almost exclusively portfolio investment and the flow of funds considered goes mainly from developed countries to the underdeveloped ones. The era of foreign direct investment was clearly still far away. It is, however, interesting that the issue of investment in natural resources is given relatively little weight, with the big role being played by financial investment. There is a clear analysis of public versus private benefits and costs of imperialism. Very interesting, of course, is the link between under-consumption and distribution, and their link with the tendency towards concentration and monopolistic structures.

Clearly, Hobson's analysis cannot be fully extended to the conditions of present day internationalization for many reasons, including: modern TNCs operate via FDI and via a range of new patterns of foreign involvement; the investments made by private companies (what he referred to as 'free market investments') are clearly no longer linked to colonial expansion; investment is no longer directed exclusively from advanced industrial countries to underdeveloped ones – on the contrary the bulk of FDI is directed towards other developed countries. However, in Hobson's work there are many points that can still be considered of interest to the analysis of modern economic systems. For example: the role he ascribes to financial investment; the role of pressure groups and classes in the distortion of public expenditure in their favour; the growing relevance of incomes from foreign investments; the link between under-consumption, distribution and a monopolistic structure.

3.3   Lenin's theory of imperialism

In 1916, while in exile in Switzerland, V. I. Lenin wrote his 'pamphlet' on *Imperialism, the Highest Stage of Capitalism*, which was first published in 1917. The work takes account of two related relevant works to which Lenin had access: the books by Hobson (1902) and Hilferding (1912).

Lenin sees the stage that capitalism had reached at the turn of the century as new. This new stage is characterized thus:

1 There is a very considerable and increasing concentration in production: an increase in 'combination'[1] of production or in what we would now call degree of integration, both horizontal and vertical. 'Combination' or integration gives firms various advantages, among which are: elimination of costs of market transactions; evening out of the trade cycle; scope for further technical advances; and a stronger monopolistic position *vis-à-vis* competitors or rivals. All these lead to an increased monopolization of production.
2 Monopolies are spreading in the sphere of banking and finance as well as in other sectors.
3 Finance capital and banks are increasingly exercising power and hold over production and industry.
4 A vast increase in colonization, and 'partition' of the world among the great powers.
5 Large exports of surplus finance capital from developed countries.

This state of affairs led to capitalism reaching its highest stage: that of imperialism. Lenin's definition of imperialism includes five basic features (p. 86):

1 The concentration of production.

2   'The merging of bank capital with industrial capital, and the creation, on the basis of this "finance capital", of a financial oligarchy'.
3   'The export of capital as distinguished from the export of commodities'.
4   'The formation of international monopolist capitalist associations which share the world among themselves'.
5   The complete 'territorial division of the whole world among the biggest capitalist powers'.

Imperialism is the *inevitable* consequence of the development of capitalism. Competition inevitably leads to monopolies in banking; this furthers the tendency towards monopolistic production and creates a subjection of production and industry to finance. Monopoly leads to a decrease in profitable investment opportunities at home, and to the search for more profitable opportunities abroad; this leads to colonization, which in itself creates further monopolies in terms of markets and investment opportunities. Throughout his 'pamphlet' Lenin stresses the role of 'finance' capital in imperialism, both in terms of its role in the developed countries and the need to search for outlets for the surplus finance capital, and in terms of the colonies' abilities to offer investment opportunities to surplus capital.[2] Any issue of land settlements or sources of raw materials becomes therefore of secondary importance in relation to the role of finance capital. In this, Lenin's analysis is very close to that of Hobson, who also sees the push towards imperialism as coming from surplus finance (over-saving in Hobson's terminology) and monopolistic finance capital (in Lenin's scheme) rather than from any need to secure raw materials: the raw materials could, after all, be bought on the open market.

The new stage of capitalism produces various effects and consequences, in particular:

1   Capitalism spreads its net. Capitalist relations are introduced into larger and larger parts of the world. Development in these countries spreads while growth in industrial countries is retarded. Lenin sees investment in the host countries (colonies) as adding to their total investment while detracting from the investment in the home country (motherland).
2   Capitalism in industrial countries becomes parasitic as the *rentier* capitalists live by 'clipping coupons' and thus become more and more divorced from production (Lenin, 1917, p. 96).
3   The profits from foreign investments are only part of the total profits flowing from the colonies to the advanced countries. Investments in railways, general infrastructures, etc. are likely to require imports of products from the motherland into the colonies, thus creating extra profits for the manufacturer and exporter. Lenin therefore sees investments and exports as complementary.
4   Imperialism allows the bourgeoisie to give the upper strata of the

working class in industrialized countries special concessions and a share of the profits, thus 'bribing' them into acquiescence and opportunism.

5 The monopolization of production leads to its increasing socialization. 'When a big enterprise assumes gigantic proportions, and, on the basis of an exact computation of mass data, organises according to plan the supply of primary raw materials . . .; when the raw materials are transported in a systematic and organised manner to the most suitable places of production . . .; when a single centre directs all the consecutive stages of processing the material right up to the manufacture of numerous varieties of finished articles; when these products are distributed according to a single plan among tens and hundreds of millions of consumers . . . then it becomes evident that we have socialisation of production' (pp. 121–2).

6 This socialization of production combined with the private appropportion of its fruits, will, increasingly, create further and further conflicts and will lead to the ultimate demise of capitalism.

3.4 Some comments

Any comments on Lenin's theory must inevitably start with a comparison with Hobson's imperialism. Lenin's treatment has benefited from Hobson's work in content; however, in presentation, it is not as clear and polished as Hobson's.

Both authors stress the role of 'finance'. In both the issue of 'raw materials supply' plays a subservient role: it forms an outlet for investment opportunities, not the primary reason for an imperialist policy. Hobson's link between under-consumption and surplus finance capital (over-saving) constitutes a strong economic link in the theory; whether we accept his under-consumptionist stance or not, we must accept that the reasons for the existence of surplus finance capital and declining investment opportunities in industrial countries are less clear in Lenin than in Hobson. One by-product of Hobson's under-consumptionist stance is his emphasis on 'mal-distribution' as cause of a lack of effective demand and hence of imperialism. Under-consumption does not appear – in any form – in Lenin's theory.

Lenin stresses, much more than Hobson, the role of concentration and monopolization in both industry and finance. He also stresses the inevitability of monopolization and the inevitability of its consequences: imperialism and the ultimate end of capitalism. Hobson's approach in terms of remedies is a reformist one and this is clearly linked to the inner logic of his theory: he sees the problems stemming from mal-distribution of income and wealth. However, as he does not see the distribution problems as inseparably bound with the inner logic of capitalism, he is led to the conclusion that a change in distribution, in favour of people who are more in need of consumption, is not only desirable – on moral and economic efficiency grounds – but also possible within the capitalist framework. A better income distribution would avoid under-consumption and thus imperialism. Lenin clearly rejects this conclusion, though he does not specifically discuss the issues of distribution and under-consumption. On the whole Lenin's work has a much sharper political focus.

Both authors see imperialism in terms of colonialism, which was the historically relevant force at the time they were writing. Neither of them discusses, openly, the possibility of finding outlets for investments abroad independently of political subjugation and colonization. Hobson explicitly mentions the possibility and desirability of international trade independent of colonization, but he sees investments as bound up with political annexation. Neither, of course, could foresee the modern developments in FDI and cross-country investments. Lenin's passage on the increased socialization of production is very interesting and still applies today. Indeed the tendency towards socialization of production has increased as: (a) developed countries have been both host and home to FDI; (b) products and processes are located worldwide; (c) LDCs are becoming hosts to some manufacturing investment. We could say, in fact, that socialization has become a more relevant and worldwide phenomenon as advances in communication have made possible the global planning of production and markets.

What does this trend imply for Lenin's prediction? It is very difficult to say, of course. However, it seems to the present writer that the increased socialization in the hands of transnational monopolies has had the following effects: it has made the conflicts and issues less sharply focused along a nationalistic divide; it has led to stronger blocs of capital *vis-à-vis* nations and governments; it has contributed to the fragmentation of the labour force under the control of transnational monopolies. These themes will be reconsidered later.

In spite of the changing conditions of today's internationalization, the reader is struck by the relevance of some of the points mentioned in Lenin's pamphlet, such as the issues of monopolies, finance capital and economies on 'transaction costs' on the part of large firms. This last issue has become a major focus for the development of theories of the growth of the firm and the TNCs; the antecedents of these new developments are not, however, to be found in Lenin, but in Coase (1937). This issue is discussed further in chapter 11.

3.5   Bukharin on imperialism and world economy

In 1917 Nikolai Bukharin published an essay that had been completed for
two years. In it, he attempted to place imperialism in the context of
changes in the overall world economy and the historical development of
capitalism.

Bukharin (1917) starts his work with a disquisition on the division of
labour and particularly on the international division of labour; this is, in
his view, based on two kinds of prerequisites: natural and social. Natural
conditions lead to the production of different products in different countries and thus give scope for trade and division of labour. However,
division of labour and trade between different countries can also be the
result of 'differences in the cultural level, the economic structure, and the
development of productive forces in various countries' (p. 18) and hence
of social conditions.

The scope for international exchanges is very wide as 'Countries mutually exchange not only different products, but even products of the same
kind' (p. 24). Trade and the international division of labour lead to strong
connections between capitalists and workers in the two countries. The
growth of the world economy is accompanied by growth of migration,
trade (in both raw materials and products) and movements of capital.
The capitalist economic system has moved more and more away from
competition into monopolization, which is, however, a natural, logical
development from competition itself.

Bukharin gives pages of examples of the growth of cartels and trusts
in various advanced countries. Concentration of production can take a
horizontal or vertical form, but whichever the form, increased monopolization leads to conflicts among the different cartels. The 'process of binding
together the various branches of production' and 'transforming them into
one single organisation' goes hand in hand with a similar process between
banking and industry: 'banking capital penetrates industry, and capital
turns into finance capital' (p. 70). The binding process also links together
private enterprises and the state in capitalist systems.

Thus various spheres of the concentration and organisation process stimulate
each other, creating a very strong tendency towards transforming the entire
national economy *into one gigantic combined enterprise under the tutelage
of the financial kings and the capitalist state, an enterprise which monopolises
the national market and forms the prerequisite for organised production on
a higher non-capitalist level.* (pp. 73–4)

As monopolization increases, capitalists look for new markets and for
higher profits: 'the motive power of world capitalism' is 'the race for

higher rates of profit' (p. 84). Imperialism is then needed to secure raw materials and to secure markets for products. This second motive becomes more and more pressing with the advent of mass production and with the increasing protectionist policies of many countries that rely on high tariffs to protect their own industries.

The struggle for sources of raw materials and for markets is accompanied and greatly enhanced by the struggle for investment opportunities abroad. Capital is exported in order to gain higher rates of return abroad than could be realized at home. The export of capital is enhanced by the increasing monopoly profits and by the difficulties in exporting products because of protectionist policies; hence one of the motives given for the export of capital is the avoidance of tariffs in the 'host' country.

The export of capital is more likely to lead to struggles for annexation and wars than the export of commodities. This is because with commodity export 'the exporters risked only their goods, i.e., their circulating capital', while with export of capital and the investment 'in gigantic constructions: railroads stretching over thousands of miles, very costly electric plants, large plantations etc., etc.' the capitalists have their 'fixed capital' at stake and want to guard it closely (p. 101).

The seeds of discord, wars of annexation and wars for the division of colonies are therefore sown: finance capitalism and imperialism are inevitably linked together. Imperialism is the product of monopolization and finance capital and at the same time 'finance capital cannot pursue any other policy than an imperialist one' (p. 140). In a clear concise chapter (IX) Bukharin strongly criticizes other theories of imperialism which do not stress the historical character of this particular stage of capitalism and do not link it to finance capital. Similarly the 'necessity' and inevitability of imperialism are asserted as part of a strong critique of Kautsky's theory in a chapter devoted to this topic (XII). Kautsky's mistake is in not seeing that imperialism is the logical, inevitable development of capitalism in its high stage. According to Bukharin, Kautsky looks upon imperialism not as an inevitable accompaniment of capitalist development, but as part of the 'dark side' of capitalist development.

Bukharin also criticizes the view that wider markets could be found at home, since this could be achieved only via income redistribution. There is a major obstacle to this course as 'one cannot imagine that the big bourgeoisie would begin to increase the share of the working class, in order thus to drag itself out of the mire by the hair' (p. 79). Here, of course, there is a criticism of Hobson's view and conclusion, though Hobson is not directly mentioned. The role of trade unions in forcing changes in income distribution seems to be ignored by both Hobson and Bukharin.

Bukharin, like Lenin and Engels before him, stresses the interest that some workers in advanced countries have in imperialism. He writes:

'Super-profits obtained by the imperialist state are accompanied by a rise in the wages of the respective strata of the working class, primarily the skilled workers' (p. 165).

3.6   Some comments

Bukharin's treatment of imperialism is, in its essence, not different from Lenin's; this applies to both causes and effects as well as to its methodological treatment. Most points are developed at greater length and with more details than in Lenin's work. Bukharin's book also contains topics not (or not fully) dealt with by Lenin, such as a critique of other theories of imperialism: in particular, theories based on 'race' and on the universality of a 'policy of conquest'. In discussing this last theory he makes a very interesting methodological point when he writes that the theory 'is untrue because it "explains" everything, i.e., it explains absolutely nothing' (p. 112). In Popperian methodology this theory would be unscientific because it is unfalsifiable.[3]

There are some other areas in which concepts used by Bukharin have a 'modern' ring to them. He deals with vertical and horizontal integration and uses this modern terminology; he deals with the exchange of the same or similar products, as in modern intra-industry trade literature. On the whole, his treatment takes more account of *direct* investments than Hobson's or Lenin's treatments, where the focus tends to be more on portfolio investment and financial capital movements. Bukharin not only gives specific reference to 'fixed capital', which must be 'guarded' closely (Bukharin, 1917, p. 101), he also specifically mentions that tariffs in the 'host' country may be in the interest of the foreign investor, who will then have a protected market for the products (p. 98).

At the same time, there are areas in which Bukharin's treatment is dated and does not lead to good predictions of some modern developments. In particular, in chapter VI he stresses how developments in agriculture have not kept pace with those in industry and this has led to increased demand for raw materials and agricultural products; as supply has remained stagnant agricultural prices have tended to increase. Subsequent developments (particularly since the Second World War) have falsified his statements, as agricultural production has greatly increased for both food and raw materials, and substitutes for raw materials have led to greatly increased supplies. The end result has been a worsening of the terms of trade for the agricultural producers and traders *vis-à-vis* the producers of manufactured products. Bukharin does not see that developments in manufacturing were bound to lead to improvements in agriculture.[4]

Among the reasons for 'discord' he sees the fact that imperialist policies split 'the ruling class (the bourgeoisie)' into '"national" groups with contradictory economic interests' (p. 106). He does not see, and possibly could not have foreseen, the emergency of an international bourgeoisie with common interests developing alongside international enterprises, all with interests, to a large extent, decoupled and detached from the 'national' ones.

In spite of various mentions of the role of markets and the need for capitalists to widen their foreign markets, Bukharin's and Lenin's focus is on the need to look for higher rates of profits abroad to counteract falling domestic rates; this is, of course, in contrast to Hobson's under-consumptionist treatment. There is, however, no doubt that in Hobson, Lenin and Bukharin the main stress is on the role of finance capital and the export of capital.

3.7   Rosa Luxemburg on imperialism

In section three of *The Accumulation of Capital* (1913) Rosa Luxemburg develops a theory of capitalism that binds together indissolubly capitalist societies with pre-capitalist ones. This is a completely novel approach and it starts with a critique of Marx on two points: (a) because Marx did not give sufficient weight to the problem of realization and to the fact that, in a system where capitalists and workers are the only consumers, lack of effective demand prevents the full realization of the surplus value; (b) because Marx fails to see that pre-capitalist forces of organization of production are necessary for capitalism, and because he adheres to the principle of 'the universal and exclusive domination of capitalist production' (p. 365). The first point – the realization problem – is crucial to her overall approach.

She starts from the observation that 'The workers and capitalists themselves cannot possibly realise that part of the surplus value which is to be capitalised. Therefore, the realisation of the surplus value for the purposes of accumulation is an impossible task for a society which consists solely of workers and capitalists' (p. 350). In order to solve the realization problem – 'a vital question of capitalist accumulation' – the system needs to find 'strata of buyers outside capitalist society' (p. 351). The buyers from non-capitalist societies can absorb either consumer goods or means of production or both; the supply of products from the capitalist economy to the pre-capitalist one can take the form of sales from production in the capitalist centre or direct production in the pre-capitalist system. In practice, a combination of these various elements takes place as relationships between capitalist and pre-capitalist forces of organization unfold.

Capitalist systems need pre-capitalist organizations essentially for three reasons: (a) to increase effective demand (for consumption goods or means of production or as outlets for investments) and thus solve the realization problems; (b) to supply the raw materials needed for production; and (c) 'as a reservoir of labour power for its wage system' (p. 368). The pre-capitalist organization needed by capitalism can be part of the same national identity and boundaries, or it can be geographically dispersed and part of a different national identity. No matter where they are geographically located, capital will struggle against societies with a 'natural economy', that is, an economy 'where there are primitive peasant communities, with common ownership of the land, a feudal system of bondage or anything of this nature', where 'there is no demand, or very little, for foreign goods, and also, as a rule, no surplus production, or at least no urgent need to dispose of surplus products' (pp. 368–9).

The struggle against pre-capitalist societies aims to: (a) gain access to and possession of land and raw materials; (b) gain access to labour and involve it in the wage system; (c) introduce a commodity economy based on market exchanges; (d) separate trade and agriculture. Crafts are gradually wiped out and peasants are 'forced to buy' industrial products in exchange for agricultural ones. The struggle takes market forms as well as using coercion by force; Luxemburg gives many historical examples to substantiate her points. In all of them the building of a good network of communication and transport is essential to the destruction of the 'internal' national economy.

One immediate conclusion of her analysis is the existence of a major contradiction in the relationship between capitalist and pre-capitalist forms of organization. Capitalism needs pre-capitalist forms but it also destroys them; as the destruction proceeds and becomes accomplished, there arises the need for further expansion into other pre-capitalist systems. Luxemburg writes: 'Historically, the accumulation of capital is a kind of metabolism between capitalist economy and those pre-capitalist methods of production without which it cannot go on and which, in this light, it corrodes and assimilates' (p. 416). It is in highlighting the contradictory nature of the relationship between capitalist and pre-capitalist forms of organization that Luxemburg disagrees with Marx, for whom, in her view, 'The accumulative process endeavours everywhere to substitute simple commodity economy for natural economy. Its ultimate aim, that is to say, is to establish the exclusive and universal domination of capitalist production in all countries and for all branches of industry' (p. 417).

As time goes on, the struggle for access to, and domination of, pre-capitalist societies become more and more fierce with more and more countries joining in (including those that are gradually moving from the pre-capitalist to the capitalist stage) and with fewer and fewer pre-capitalist areas left. Eventually the systems will come to a standstill and 'For capital, the standstill of accumulation means that the development of the productive forces is arrested, and the collapse of capitalism follows inevitably, as an objective historical necessity' (p. 417).

A major medium through which capitalism penetrates non-capitalist countries is international loans. Such loans are made for armaments and the building of infrastructure, particularly railways; they accompany all stages of capitalist penetration. The loan helps accumulation of capital in various ways; particularly it serves to: (a) 'convert the money of non-capitalist groups into capital'; (b) 'transform money capital into productive capital by means of state enterprise – railroad building and military supplies'; (c) 'divert accumulated capital from the old capitalist countries to young ones' (p. 420). International loans are therefore the means by which 'capital accumulated in the old country' finds 'elsewhere new opportunities to beget and realise surplus value, so that accumulation can proceed' (p. 427).

Capital makes it impossible to have a peaceful transition from the pre-capitalist stage for those areas and societies it involves in its sphere of influence. This means that armaments and militarism are necessary to subjugate new societies and territories, and to fight against rivals. However, military expenditure financed out of indirect taxes has also specific economic functions. First, indirect taxation lowers real wages without direct confrontation between capital and labour; secondly, and most important, the support of the arms industry creates a stratum whose effective demand helps towards solving the realization problem.

3.8   Some comments

Luxemburg's main contribution is her attempt to integrate the inner working of capitalism with its links with pre-capitalist forces of social and economic organization. Indeed, for her, 'Accumulation is more than an internal relationship between the branches of capitalist economy; it is primarily a relationship between capital and a non-capitalist environment' (p. 417).

It is possible to argue, as Lee (1971, p. 854) does, about the extent to which her analysis 'implies that the colonial or imperialist relations between an industrial nation and its colony or neo-colony are symmetrical with the relation between that nation's industrial sector and its own hinterland or pre-capitalist environment'. However, the geographical location of pre-capitalist systems is, to a large extent, unimportant; what is important is the formation of a satellite relationship between these systems and the capitalist one. Luxemburg develops clearly the contradictory nature of the relationship which leads, in her view, to the final destruction of capitalism. 'Though imperialism is the historical method for prolonging the career of capitalism, it is also a sure means of bringing it to a swift conclusion' (p. 446).

Like Hobson, Luxemburg develops the realization thesis as one of the main problems of capitalism; there, however, the analogy ends. Luxemburg, in fact, sees other reasons why pre-capitalist societies are necessary for capitalism. Besides, the conclusions of the two authors are completely different. Hobson sees a way out of the problems of realization and related imperialism in the redistribution of income. Luxemburg sees imperialism as inevitably necessary and, at the same time, as conducive to the destruction of capitalism.

Unlike Lenin and Bukharin, Luxemburg does not emphasize the role of finance capital in its dominance of industrial capital, nor the cartelization and monopolization aspects. Foreign investment, helped and mediated by financial loans, has the main aim and effect of utilizing surplus financial capital in the advanced capitalist countries. Foreign investment in means of production widens the scope for capital accumulation, and loans are a way of facilitating that process. However, for Luxemburg, neither foreign investment nor trade with pre-capitalist economies can solve the realization problems in the long run. As the domain of capitalist relations spreads, so does the need to find further outlets for the utilization of the surplus.

Methodologically, like many other Marxist writers Luxemburg works on what we might call a multi-disciplinary level, in which economic analysis is supplemented by and integrated with sociological, political and anthropological analyses linked together in the context of historical case studies.[5]

Luxemburg's theory was received with great hostility in Marxist circles when it first appeared.[6] There are undoubtedly problems with her overall prediction, given the fact that more and more pre-capitalist economies have been absorbed into the capitalist sphere without dramatic ill effects on capitalism.

The growth in the volume and pattern of TNCs' activities has brought with it changes in the relationship between pre-capitalist and capitalist countries. Pockets of industrialization (mainly through export processing zones) and finance and banking links are among the changes. Luxemburg's scheme, appropriately reconsidered, might help to analyse the nature of the new relationship; attempts in this direction have been made by other Marxist writers, and we shall consider some of these works in chapter 5.

4

The Realization Problem Back in Fashion

4.1 Baran and Sweezy on imperialism

Paul A. Baran and Paul M. Sweezy begin their 'Notes on the theory of imperialism' (1966a) by summarizing the main achievements of the Marxist theory of imperialism, which they identify with the writings of Hilferding, Luxemburg and Lenin.

This theory has, in their view, achieved the aims of: (a) giving us a theory of international relations encompassing relations between advanced and underdeveloped countries and between the advanced countries themselves; (b) helping to understand the development of social and political conditions within capitalist countries; and (c) providing an explanation of economic tendencies within advanced capitalist countries. In particular, the theory helps us to understand how wealth is transferred from underdeveloped to developed countries, and how imperialism provides outlets for the surplus of advanced countries: this means that advanced countries can thus be helped to sustain their income and employment.

The rest of the paper is full of interesting points, although a clear theory of imperialism does not emerge from them. Among the points made are the following:

1 The benefits of imperialism cannot be assessed by using *ex post* data on GNP or employment but must be assessed on an *ex ante* basis.
2 The view that imperialism 'does not pay' because of the costs associated with it is based on various misconceptions: in particular, on this issue of *ex ante/ex post* assessment and, more relevant still, on the issue of class analysis. The costs of imperialism are borne by the public at large 'while the returns accrue to that small, but usually dominant, section

of the capitalist class which has extensive international interests'
(p. 16). This last point echoes similar remarks by Hobson in his theory
of imperialism.

3 The traditional Marxist theory has seen industrialists and bankers as
the dominant class. Industrialists were dominant in the first phase,
up to the last decade of the nineteenth century. Their interests in
underdeveloped countries were related to supply of cheap food and
raw materials and to outlets for markets. The second phase, from
about 1880 onwards, saw the dominance of finance capital and the
crucial role of underdeveloped countries became one related to outlets
for exports of capital. This went hand in hand with colonial expansion.

4 The more recent phase (particularly after the Second World War) has
seen a new dominant class linked to the growth of big monopolistic
corporations; the class is formed by their owners and functionaries,
who 'constitute the leading echelon of the ruling class' (p. 18). The
modern big corporation has achieved financial independence from
banks. It spreads its business in a variety of areas and countries. It
relies more and more on foreign countries for its profits. It is highly
involved in research and development. It invests abroad. However,
when full account is taken of the influx of profits, it turns out to be a
net importer of funds from other countries, in particular underdeveloped ones: 'United States Multinational Companies are on balance
massive importers, not exporters, of capital' (p. 26). From this last
point various others follow, in particular point 5.

5 'Foreign investment, it seems, far from being a means of developing
underdeveloped countries, is a most efficient device for transferring
wealth from poorer to richer countries while at the same time enabling
the richer to expand their control over the economies of the poorer'
(pp. 24–5).

6 Large multinational corporations pursue their own profit goals independently of, and often against, the interests of underdeveloped countries (or of their own home country when necessary); in this pursuit
they are helped by their size and organization. The manipulation of
transfer prices ('intercorporate prices') helps to maximize the profits
of the corporation as a whole.

7 Do giant multinational companies have any 'interests in common on
which they can unite?' (p. 29). Baran and Sweezy see two main such
interests: (a) they all desire to operate in as many countries as possible;
(b) in the countries in which they operate they want 'laws and institutions to be favorable to the unfettered development of private capitalist enterprise' (p. 29); the state in such countries should intervene
only to create a favourable infrastructure in which the multinational
companies can operate.

4.2   Monopoly capital

Baran and Sweezy's most famous work (1966b) deals more specifically with the inner workings of giant corporations and their effects on the macroeconomy. Their book develops the under-consumptionist, stagnationist approach previously introduced by Hobson, Luxemburg and Kalecki (1939, 1954), among others.[1]

Baran and Sweezy consider lack of effective demand and a stagnationist tendency to be a permanent feature of modern capitalism in its monopolistic phase. They trace the reason for such a tendency to the oligopolistic price mechanism, in which big firms are price-makers and a leader tends to fix prices that will be followed by the whole industry. In an oligopolistic market structure rivals avoid price wars[2] and competition among giants tends to take other forms, leading to sales drives and cost cutting.

The end result of all this is a tendency for the economic surplus to rise; Baran and Sweezy conclude that the law of the rising surplus has replaced the law of the falling profit rate.[3] They define the economic surplus as the 'difference between total output and the socially necessary costs of producing total output' (p. 84). The economic surplus includes profits, rents and interests; however, the rising surplus can manifest in a variety of ways, including under-utilized capacity. In theory the surplus is an *ex ante* concept and hence its full manifestation cannot be estimated via 'actual' levels of the various variables but should be estimated via their potential level. The relevance of *ex ante* concepts for the proper assessment of economic performance and the effects of various strategies is an issue that comes up in both the Baran and Sweezy works considered here.

Unless the monopolistic system can find ways of utilizing the surplus, the economy will be plunged into deeper and deeper depression. Like previous Marxist authors (Lenin and Bukharin) they rule out that, under capitalism, the increase in effective demand needed to absorb the potential surplus can be found via an increase in consumption deriving from income redistribution.

An increase in sales efforts via advertising as well as an increase in the output of other sectors which are not (or not fully) socially necessary (banking, insurance etc.) will help to absorb the surplus and utilize capacity. However, this strategy leads to an increase in surplus as the advertising and financial industries generate large profits. Baran and Sweezy's most controversial conclusion is that modern monopolistic systems have found a way out of permanent stagnation via arms expenditure. Defence expenditure and wars are therefore seen as a way of bailing the capitalist system out of the tendency to permanent depression. Here there is an echo of Luxemburg's point on the useful role of the arms industry for the absorption of the surplus. However, this particular outlet for the surplus plays a much bigger role in Baran and Sweezy than in Luxemburg.

Baran and Sweezy discuss foreign investments and their role in increasing effective demand as part of 'exogenous' investment; other 'exogenous' types of investment are those linked to population growth or new products, processes and technologies. They see little scope for exogenous investment as an overall surplus absorber. With regard to foreign investment in particular, they acknowledge its ability to raise the level of effective demand exogenously. However, foreign investment gives rise to high profits and indeed countries like the USA or the UK tend to have a much larger inflow of profits and dividends from cumulative past investment, than an outflow for current foreign investment. All in all, therefore, foreign investment generates a large surplus in its own right and hence compounds the long-term problems of absorption: 'foreign investment aggravates rather than helps to solve the surplus absorption problem' (p. 113).

4.3   Some comments

Baran and Sweezy's book (1963b) has been one of the most important and controversial Marxist works in the post-Second World War decades. They present us with a fully developed theoretical approach corroborated by empirical evidence on the behaviour of modern capitalist systems, in particular the US system. They link micro and macro elements and present us with what, at first, appear as plausible explanations for the behaviour and performance of large corporations, governments and economic systems. The fact that their theory was presented in clear terminology without formal models, added to the appeal and success of the book. The underconsumptionist theories have always had considerable appeal and their macro–micro integrated approach has proved particularly successful.

Baran and Sweezy's work has, however, aroused strong outrage in some Marxist circles and has provoked huge quantities of critical writings. The substitution of the law of the rising surplus for the Marxian law of the falling rate of profit has been one of the most heated areas of contention. Their definition of surplus clearly invites criticism as they rely on the unclear, not well defined and controversial concept of 'socially necessary cost' of production.

In terms of our specific interest, it can be concluded that their approach is very far from giving us a theory of FDI, its growth, its pattern and its effects. That under-consumption cannot explain foreign investment is quite clear and indeed accepted by Baran and Sweezy themselves. Foreign involvement by large corporations affects defence policy and military aid; however, the major economic role of military expenditure is linked to surplus absorption: 'On what could the government spend enough to keep the system from sinking into the mire of stagnation? On arms, more arms, even more arms' (Baran and Sweezy, 1963b, p. 211).

The issue of the increasing monopolization of capitalist systems and its effects has been further explored by Cowling (1982). It has recently been taken up by Cowling and Sugden (1987b) in an attempt to extend the analysis of monopolistic capitalism to the growth and workings of TNCs. This last work is considered in chapter 15.

4.4   Magdoff on imperialism

Harry Magdoff's writings on imperialism (1966) came from the same *Monthly Review* forum as Baran and Sweezy's. He was writing when feelings about the Vietnam War were running very high in the United States and when, therefore, crucial questions about the connections between that war, US foreign policy and US business abroad were becoming more widespread.

Magdoff sets out to show the interconnections between US foreign policy and US economic involvement abroad. The foreign economic involvement relevant to his analysis is spelled out by Magdoff as being related to:

1   The supply of raw materials, particularly some strategic ones in terms of defence. This supply was becoming more and more crucial as the self-sufficiency of the USA was declining in spite of the development of substitutes and in spite of the unfavourable terms of trade for the underdeveloped countries suppliers of raw materials.
2   Markets for products.
3   Outlets for foreign investment. Foreign investment bases are seen as bases for the sourcing of host countries as well as for export to countries other than the host and home ones. Magdoff therefore sees a relationship of substitution between exports and FDI. The basic motivation behind FDI seems to be a combination of the search for markets, in order to counteract a possible lack of effective domestic demand, and the search for higher profit rates; and of course these two elements are connected.

He is very critical of 'Hobson's panacea of an increase in consumer income' (p. 24) as 'unrealistic' in conditions of capitalist production. He considers it a 'sort of iffy history' (p. 23) in which, although it might be possible to conceive *in theory* of an income distribution that would give enough to the working class to increase domestic demand to the level of capacity, this is not a realistic option, given the profit motive of business activity.

Magdoff is keen to dismiss the argument that foreign economic involvement is not relevant to foreign policy because the size of this involvement is small compared with the overall size and performance of the US economy as measured by its GNP. He emphasizes the strategic elements of most foreign activities, particularly those related to FDI. What is more relevant, he shows how the overall quantitative reliance on FDI cannot be understood by using flow data on the yearly investment: unlike exports, which are fundamentally a flow concept, FDI is a *flow* which gives rise to accumulation and hence to a *stock* of capital abroad. It is the accumulation of capital stock abroad that is relevant in terms of overall wealth and interests in foreign countries and in terms of the overall income it generates. The inward flow of income from the accumulated stock over the years outstrips the flow of outward new investment. It is the stock and the related inflow of profits that foreign policy is designed to protect. The relevance of such policy and its connection with business interests are further highlighted with reference to the need not only to protect the existing stock (hence the *actual situation*) but also to keep an open door for future possibilities for FDI (hence creating the basis for *potential* expansion of foreign investment).

In more conventional economic and political literature there is a current of opinion stating that foreign policy and foreign economic development cannot be linked because the balance-sheet of overall costs and benefits for foreign involvement – particularly FDI – seems to be highly weighted against business activities abroad, when the military and related expenditures are fully accounted for. Magdoff dismisses this point by using arguments similar to those previously used by Hobson, Bukharin, and Baran and Sweezy. He stresses the need to analyse costs and benefits in class terms: the costs fall on the citizens as a whole, the benefits on big business, which is what pushes for a particular type of foreign policy. Magdoff stresses the role of foreign aid in sustaining, promoting and protecting US business interests abroad, particularly FDI.

In terms of theoretical analysis, Magdoff adds little to what had already been said by previous Marxist authors. However, his work is relevant in linking together foreign policy and economic involvement, a point on which, for example, Baran and Sweezy's book – a much stronger work from a theoretical point of view – fails, as already pointed out.

5

Some Recent Marxist Approaches

5.1 The international firm in the context of an internationalist approach to the world economy

In 1972 Robin Murray published an article which contains many interesting points, albeit not always fully developed or consistently linked together. The article is structured around some basic background elements:

1 That in analysing the development of the international firm and its impact on the economic environment, particularly in underdeveloped countries, we should take the macro system rather than the firm as the starting point.
2 That 'Rather than treating the international economy as a summation of national units, it is more helpful . . . to see it as a single, predominantly, capitalist system'. From this outlook, 'Competitive firms, particularly international firms, become the dominant units of the system' (Murray, 1972, p. 162).
3 That 'underdevelopment (or more properly uneven development) is a necessary aspect of a capitalist mode of production' (p. 187).

The first two points summarize the international stance taken by Murray. The last point has, of course, a ring of Rosa Luxemburg about it; however, the arguments used to substantiate it are quite different. For Luxemburg the satellite economies are necessary mainly as an absorber of surplus through the provision of exogenous effective demand; for Murray the uneven development and symbiosis between developed and underdeveloped countries derive from the tendency to 'agglomeration' that is inherent in capitalism. It is also worth pointing out that while for

Luxemburg the satellite economies may or may not be geographically dispersed, Murray concentrates mainly on the relationship between metropolitan and periphery areas, as exemplified by developed and underdeveloped countries.

The tendency towards agglomeration leads to uneven development; the tendency derives directly from the concentration drive, which is one of the characteristics of capitalist development. Thus material conditions lead to economies of scale, and competition among rival capitals leads to the need to realize those economies of scale. Economies of scale derive from specialization, communication, control and insurance, and they lead to corporate, sectoral and geographical inequalities.

'Specialisation leads to cost savings principally because it yields a saving of time' (p. 165). Communication and controls are more efficient within the same corporate organization than between different firms. The market can perform a communication function but at higher costs and lower speed than the single firm because firms are reticent to supply full information, even at a price, to people and institutions external to their own organization. The end result of all this is that the expansion of firms is not checked by problems and costs related to internal organization and that, on the contrary, a large size leads to various economies. Among such economies and advantages are those related to the communication and control functions.

Scale economies are also achieved via insurance and the related law of large numbers, which 'suggests that there will be economies of scale in maintaining reserves to guard against uncertain outcomes in the markets supplying inputs (raw materials, semi-finished materials, skilled labour, means of communication) and in the market receiving outputs' (p. 168).

These various scale economies lead to industrial concentration as well as geographical concentration for the same reasons, because essentially: 'Distance is the enemy of time. To cross space takes time, direct and indirect' (p. 168).

All this gives us reasons why geographical polarization and agglomeration take place: but where will agglomeration be located? 'There will be a number of poles of attraction: sources of raw materials, power supplies, market outlets, transport modes, or military bases. But the strongest attraction for agglomerative tendencies are agglomerations themselves. There is a continual reinforcement' (p. 171). There will, however, be many counter-tendencies to agglomerations because of various elements linked, for example, to the supply of raw materials or the location of markets. On the whole, Murray dismisses the view that it is possible for a periphery economy (i.e. an underdeveloped country) to develop enough counter-tendencies to the agglomeration in advanced countries to successfully embark on the development path.

Murray develops a variety of arguments to support the general thesis of a tendency towards uneven development and the formation and perpetuation of metropolitan–periphery centres within capitalism; underlying it all is the disadvantage in which the periphery finds itself in the competitive struggle of different blocks of capital. Such a struggle may take place within an industry or a sector or a geographical area; the outcome of the struggle depends on the monopoly power. Monopoly power and the way it is used lead to the reinforcement of unevenness, partly because of the high entry barriers in the metropolitan centres and partly because the monopoly power is used to extract a large surplus from the periphery and syphon it off to the metropolitan centres.

The focus of Murray's paper is on the international division of labour and uneven development. However, as this is not the focus of this book the reader is referred to the original article for more on the perpetuation of underdevelopment. Our attention will now turn to Murray's treatment of the international firm and foreign investment, on which there is a significant amount, albeit all or most in the context of underdevelopment.

Murray starts section 4 of his article by asking the following question: 'What . . . is the significance of international firms over and above the fact that they are bearers of market forces?' (p. 207). The answer is that such significance must be sought in their role as units of economic integration and as units of power.

As units of integration the firms can realize economies of scale due to specialization and also economies due to circulation and control. Economies of specialization may account for the overall size of firms, but they do not explain why firms want to expand geographically. When it comes to circulation of commodities, technology and general information, internal transfers are more efficient and speedier and this applies to the international firm as well as to the large national firm; the transmission of information about the technology of production and the control of quality both benefit from internal organization. Similarly, large and international firms are more efficient as systems of planning, implementation and control over production, partly because they have a more efficient flow of information than is available through the market. Murray concludes that 'It is the economies of specialisation taken together with those of communication and control which give the international firm significance as an institution in the international market economy' (p. 215).

There are various aspects to the issue of international firms as units of power. First is the origin of power, which is to be sought in the monopolistic position of the international firms. Second is the use to which power can be put, particularly in terms of securing the holder with 'the maximum proportion of surplus value produced by the society in which he operates' (p. 219). Monopoly power can be used *vis-à-vis* labour in order to weaken its position and reduce wages and/or increase productivity, or it can be used *vis-à-vis* rivals or states and governments.

Monopoly power comes to the international firm not only through its size but also often because it is granted to it by governments in underdeveloped countries as a *quid pro quo* for investment. Special privileges and power are also often given by the relationship with governments in the metropolitan country. Power can, of course, be restricted by decisive governmental action and by the joint action of various governments in underdeveloped countries.

5.2 Some comments

As already mentioned, the main focus of Murray's article is underdevelopment, on which I shall not enlarge any more other than by saying that his theory of uneven development is the best developed section of the paper. It is interesting to see some of Luxemburg's polarization arguments developed through the working of firms and industries.

From the theory of international firms sketched by Murray we may extract the following points:

1 There is a tendency for firms to grow and for production to become concentrated both internationally and geographically.
2 Economies of scale in specialization, in organization, and in the transmission of information and control lead to the supremacy of internal growth over market transactions.
3 Murray stresses the efficiency of internalization, that is, of intra-firm coordination and allocation of resources, as against inter-firm, market coordination. This is an area of analysis which owes much to the writings of Coase (1937), and later Williamson (1981), regarding the firm in general. Similar arguments have been used to try to arrive at a full theory of multinational firms by the authors of the 'internalization' theory, which is considered in chapter 11.
4 The monopolistic structure of modern capitalism is stressed and its consequences are explored in terms of behaviour towards rivals and governments, and particularly in terms of the power that such a structure gives international firms *vis-à-vis* underdeveloped countries.
5 The actions and activities of international firms should be considered and assessed in the context of the working of the overall capitalist system in its micro and macro aspects.
6 Control is an important element in assessing the behaviour of firms and its effects. It should, however, be stressed that the control considered by Murray is almost exclusively control over internal operations.[1]

Does all this amount to a theory of international firms; to a theory of why firms become international and why they locate in some areas rather than others? It is difficult to answer affirmatively, particularly to the first question.

The nucleus of the theory is contained in the idea that economies of scale in a variety of areas lead to the growth of firms, concentration and agglomeration. This, of course, is not a new idea. However, the main point is that this approach may explain the growth of firms, internationalization and monopolization but not why firms take the international route. The only international elements in the approach are linked to advantages in the internal circulation of funds and commodities across frontiers compared to market exchanges across frontiers. Again, this is a very well known aspect which, in itself, does not seem enough to justify the growth and pattern of activities of international firms in the past 40 years. We shall return to these points when dealing with the internalization theory.

The stress on the monopolistic structure as both cause and effect is very interesting, though again not fully developed in terms of internationalization. Similar concepts have been used by Knickerbocker (1973) to develop a theory of agglomeration of foreign direct investment (see chapter 13, this book) while Cowling and Sugden (1987b) (see chapter 15, this book) have further developed the monopolization concept. The issue of control is very interesting but again underdeveloped with regard to forms of control over labour or over other production units (as analysed in chapter 1).

In summary, we could say that although Murray has taken an international stance in analysing the effects of international firms on underdeveloped countries, the analysis of the inner working of firms in their strategic decisions does not contain enough international elements to distinguish it from an analysis of national firms.

5.3 Decentralization of production under centralized control and FDI

The internationalization trend has been developed along lines different from Murray's by authors who have approached it from a more technological point of view.

Since the 1970s there has been increasing awareness of the effects of technology on location of production. In 1975 György Ádám drew attention to what he called 'worldwide sourcing'. By this he meant the increasing tendency to plan production over many worldwide locations while keeping its control centralized. In order for this process to be implemented the following scientific and technological developments were necessary and they have now all taken place:

1   Improvements in the technology of personal communication.
2   Improvements in the technology and cost of transportation.
3   Scientific planning of production processes and their technological

implementation in such a way as to locate, efficiently, various components of the products in various countries for production purposes.

Michel Aglietta (1976) develops the theme of the relationship between technological advances and the use of different types of labour in relation to the introduction of new systems of work organization. 'The new principle of work organization is that of a totally integrated system in which production operations . . . as well as measurement and handling of information, react upon one another as elements in a single process, conceived in advance and organized in its totality' (p. 124). These changes have been made possible by electronic advances and by the 'production of instruments of measurement and control for diverse production processes' (p. 125). The resulting increase in flexibility benefits the capitalists provided they can have 'total domination of programming centres, research methods, and processing of information, and total submission of the highly skilled personnel responsible for them' (p. 127). Aglietta focuses his analysis mainly on work organization, rather than on FDI and the worldwide location of production.

The internationalization theme is taken up by Folker Fröbel, Jürgen Heinricks and Otto Kreye (1980) in a book which, though it draws mainly on the German experience, contains enough general theoretical analysis to be applicable to other advanced countries in their relationships with LDCs.[2] The main thesis of the book is that, in their search for profitable accumulation, companies are engaging in a worldwide reorganization of their manufacturing activities leading to extensive relocation of production. The result of this relocation is a 'new international division of labour meaning that tendency in world capitalism which:

(a) undermines the traditional bisection of the world into a few industrialised countries on one hand, and a great majority of developing countries integrated into the world economy solely as raw materials producers on the other, and
(b) compels the increasing subdivision of manufacturing processes into a number of partial operations at different industrial sites throughout the world' (p. 45).

The extent and direction of such relocation is determined by the following preconditions related to the labour market and the productive process:

1 A huge reservoir of 'cheap' labour power provided by the underdeveloped countries.
2 Division of the productive process into a series of fragmented operations to be carried out with very low levels of skills.
3 Developments in the techniques and costs of transport and communications as well as in the management of production; these develop-

ments allow the possibility for some or all parts of the labour process to be carried out at any site almost completely independently from the location of raw materials and/or markets.

The division of the labour process into various components is part of the application of the Babbage principle and is an essential element in the division of labour under capitalist conditions.

The developments by Charles Babbage (1832) of Adam Smith's division of labour principle led to two fundamental results, connected with both technical and social aspects of the division of labour. The first is the possibility of using 'calculating' machines to perform arithmetical operations, thus starting the development of computers. The second is the possibility of dividing the labour process into various components according to the level of skills required; this enables the capitalist to pay for each component according to the skill used and hence results in lower overall labour costs.[3]

The application of the Babbage principle under capitalist conditions is not new. The novel developments in this new phase of capitalism lie – according to Fröbel et al. – in its implementation 'through the *world-wide* organised allocation of the elements of the production process to the cheapest or most adapted labour forces which can be found' (p. 41).

Progress in techniques and lower costs of transport have led to the development of 'world market factories', usually located in 'free productive zones'.[4] World market factories process, with local labour power, raw materials or semi-manufactured products imported from anywhere in the world; the products are then exported to any country in the world (often including the country of origin of the transnational company responsible for the investment). Usually, only elementary and labour-intensive components of the productive process are located in free productive zones; almost any zone is therefore suitable for the development of world market factories provided there is a large reservoir of labour and a minimum level of infrastructure. This means that companies can choose and change sites, thus playing one site (and often country) against another with the aim of gaining extra benefits in terms of infrastructures supplied by the state, grants and/or tax concessions.

The new international division of labour produces – according to Fröbel et al. – various consequences for the advanced countries, among which are: (a) an increase in structural unemployment as parts of the productive processes are relocated away from AICs; (b) an increase in import penetration as world economies become more integrated. For the underdeveloped countries this new phase of capitalism is unlikely to lead to widespread industrialization for a variety of reasons, including the fact that these countries are usually allocated only specific elementary subprocesses of production. The availability of a cheap reservoir of unskilled labour is also likely to delay the mechanization of productive processes throughout the world.

5.4 Some comments

This new focus in the explanation of the pattern and location of FDI mirrors, to a large extent, what is happening in the real economy. Many interesting conclusions can be drawn from this new focus and particularly relevant, it seems, to this writer, is that the theory:

1 draws attention to the development of pockets of industrialization in LDCs;
2 highlights the birth of a new type of imperialism in which developed and underdeveloped countries are more and more linked together by technological advances and changes in work organization;
3 emphasizes the link between technology and product/process design as well as between technology and control of production;
4 emphasizes the increasing globalism in the planning of production and in business decisions, including decisions about technology, its development and its uses;[5]
5 can be used to highlight the increasing conflicts between institutions that plan globally (TNCs) and those that are national by their own nature or for historical reasons (state or workers' organizations);
6 emphasizes how countries (both AICs and LDCs) find it increasingly difficult to have control over technology, and the spread of its linkages throughout given industries and sectors;
7 develops Rosa Luxemburg's polarization argument between dominant and satellite economies by considering the activities of modern TNCs and the development of new technologies.

Although it is very interesting to see these trends dealt with at a more general level, we are far from having a worked out theory of FDI based on technology, centralization of control and decentralization of production. The main problem is that the writers (Ádám and Fröbel et al.) who have dealt with this topic in relation to FDI have concentrated on LDCs and have emphasized FDI in LDCs; if the theory explains anything, it explains an increase of FDI in LDCs. However, as we know, the worldwide trend has been towards an increase in the share of FDI directed towards developed countries; this leaves the approach in some difficulty as a general theory of FDI.

Conclusions on Section I

On the whole, the main focus of Marxist writers when dealing with foreign investment has not been the international firm *per se*, but underdevelopment and the impact of foreign investment on it. The classical writers clearly focus on imperialism and colonialism. However, they all connect it to the economic structure of developed countries – in particular to concentration and monopolization of the economy, to which some authors (Hobson, Lenin and Bukharin) relate the role of finance capital. Luxemburg develops the under-consumptionist approach, already present in Hobson, in a way that links together indissolubly development and underdevelopment. The under-consumptionist route has been followed up in post-Second World War writings with more concern given to the effects on advanced countries.

Some Marxist authors, such as Lenin, Bukharin, Murray and Luxemburg, stress the inevitability of imperialism, whether in its colonial phase or not, and link it to the inner logical workings of capitalism, with its tendency towards concentration, monopolization and geographical agglomeration.

The Marxist literature on imperialism and underdevelopment goes far beyond what we have been able to explore here, particularly since the Second World War. Notable authors, such as Emmanuel (1969), Amin (1974), Warren (1980), Frank (1980, 1981) and many others, could not be dealt with, as the focus of this book is not on underdevelopment. Jenkins (1987) provides a good survey of various strands on underdevelopment and of the attitudes and approaches of various theorists. He also develops an 'internationalization of capital' stance along lines similar to Murray's. He points out how some Marxist authors, particularly Warren (1980), see a positive role for TNCs in the development of Third World countries. A positive role for TNCs in the world allocation of resources and in less developed countries is also seen, of course, by neo-classical and many conventional theorists.

This issue, together with the issue of the inevitability of imperialism or the role of underconsumption in Marxist analysis, brings to the forefront the problem of demarcation between Marxist and non-Marxist theories. I shall not enter into the debate other than by saying that I am aware that Hobson's theory would not be put in the same basket with Lenin's and Bukharin's by many Marxists; none the less he belongs to the same turn of the century radical writings on imperialism.

Most authors in the Marxist tradition deal with wider social issues and not just economics: issues of foreign policy are linked to economic development not only by all the classical writers but also more recently by Magdoff. As pointed out, some authors, particularly the under-consumptionists, specifically link arms production to the economic structure.

On the whole the fact that Marxists have not dealt with TNCs and FDI independently of underdevelopment – or not to a considerable extent – is, in my view, a limitation. Essentially this is because it prevents a fully international, global stance on where modern economic systems are going and it also prevents us from properly exploring developments in trends in the past 40 years. The modern TNCs greatly affect LDCs. However, TNCs' activities are not related only or even mainly to LDCs: increasingly they have been related to AICs. As pointed out in chapter 2 the bulk of FDI not only originates with AICs but is also directed towards them.

Investments in LDCs are necessary to TNCs and to capitalist systems. Increasingly, such investments have become more and more linked to the growing foreign investments in AICs. The links come through planning, organization and control of production as well as through technology. Thus causes and effects of TNCs' activities must be seen in relation to *both* LDCs and AICs considered together.

None the less, the Marxist authors have made a considerable contribution towards our understanding of the effects of foreign investment. Their analysis has tended to be built on a firm, realistic basis, with theoretical and empirical elements reinforcing each other. The fact that most of them have worked at an interdisciplinary level has added to the realism of their analysis.

Section II
The Neo-classical Paradigm

Tout est pour le mieux dans le meilleur des mondes possibles.
(All is for the best in the best of possible worlds.)

Voltaire, *Candide*

6

Foreign Investment within the Neo-classical Paradigm

6.1 Ohlin on foreign investments

Before Hymer's seminal thesis (1960) no theory of foreign direct investment as such existed. Some of the early Marxist literature considered both financial investment and investment designed to increase productive capacity, particularly through the building of infrastructure. However, given the focus of these works – imperialism and colonization – it would be difficult to see them as full theories of FDI. A considerable amount of more conventional literature existed on foreign investment but no distinction was made in it between portfolio and direct investment; most of this literature was based on neo-classical assumptions and it ran mostly parallel to the neo-classical theory of trade developed by Heckscher (1919) and Ohlin (1933). The various models put forward are specifically neo-classical in that they, implicitly or explicitly, contain the following assumptions: perfect competitive markets, perfect knowledge, certainty. The analysis is neo-classical also in that it, usually, considers movements from one equilibrium position to another and examines, comparatively, the effects of the movements between the two equilibria. Similarly to the neo-classical theory of trade, the neo-classical theory of foreign investment also assumes that countries are differently endowed with capital and labour, that there is mobility of products across frontiers, immobility of labour and, paradoxically in some cases, immobility of capital: a point on which more will be said later.

Bertil Ohlin (1933) studied 'The mechanism of international capital movements' (Chapter XIX) using the same standpoint and type of analysis as in his neo-classical theory of international trade. All the above-mentioned neo-classical features are assumed. The analysis specifically refers to portfolio investment and no distinction is made with direct investment. Besides this, the capital movements considered are assumed to be 'autonomous' with reference to other variables related to the domestic economy. The movement of capital can, in his analysis, take place through 'reparations or gifts', and he refers, interchangeably, to 'borrowing country' and 'capital importing' country (p. 256). His analysis can, therefore, be said to contain the general assumption of capital immobility (as well as labour immobility) between two countries. However, there can be, now and then, capital movements due to entirely exogenous factors; these are the exception rather than the rule.

Ohlin's concern is to analyse the new equilibrium position following disturbances due to the capital movements. The analysis is extended to effects on exchange rates, terms of trade, imports and exports as well as variables related more specifically to the domestic economy. In the book he also considers the issue of location of economic activity and production and the various elements affecting it. Besides the relative abundance of factors of production, other elements are considered in detail, such as: the relative mobility of raw materials and finished goods; the location of raw materials and markets; differences in transportation resources and facilities; economies of scale in transportation and related costs of transport; economies of scale in production.

Ohlin's book is about *Interregional and International Trade*. International trade is the main focus and capital movements must be seen in the context of his international trade theory in terms of both assumptions and effects considered. Similarly the elements which affect the location of production are considered to be similar at both interregional and international level.

6.2 Nurkse's developments

Ragnar Nurkse (1933) took the analysis of capital movements a step further than Ohlin in that he introduced endogenous capital movements due to the 'profit motive'.

The analysis is neo-classical and all the usual assumptions and features, already mentioned, apply. The foreign investment considered is still portfolio investment; however, the movements of capital are now prompted not by exogenous factors – reparations or gifts as in Ohlin's analysis – but by interest rate differentials. Interest rates are determined, like any other price, by demand and supply: a differential in interest rates can originate because of demand or because of supply conditions.

A change in savings in one or both nations – whether spontaneous or induced by credit creation – would lead to changed supply conditions and hence affect, *ceteris paribus*, the interest rates and thus the differentials between the two countries. Similarly, technical changes in production methods that affect costs and profits, or changes in consumers' tastes that affect production and the amount of capital attracted to the various industries, might lead to changes in demand for capital and hence to interest rate differentials which will cause international capital movements.

In the final analysis Nurkse, like Ohlin, is interested in movements from one equilibrium position to another and in the effects on variables, such as terms of trade, exchange rates, imports and exports, as well as in the effects on variables related to the domestic economy.

6.3   Iversen's analysis

Carl Iversen (1935) presents us with a long detailed analysis of *International Capital Movements* based on most of the assumptions and features of neo-classical economics. Again no distinction is made between portfolio and direct investment.

In analysing geographical mobility, Iversen sees that what is moving is '*not the capital goods, but something else*' (p. 21). He sees capital and its services in terms of 'waiting' when he writes: 'The new elementary productive service, a supply of which is required in order to obtain greater future satisfaction, is waiting' (p. 22). It follows, from his analysis, that 'when capital moves from country to country . . . that *part of the supply of waiting or capital disposal in one country is put at the disposal of people in another*' (p. 23). As in previous analyses, capital movements are motivated by interest rates differentials. One of the elements that affects the level of interest rates is the risk involved: as the estimated or objective risk may be different in different sectors, we could, in fact, have different interest rate differentials in different sectors and hence we might witness a two-way flow of capital in different sectors.

On the whole, foreign investment involves higher risks than domestic investment, so lenders expect higher interest rates abroad than at home. The difference in interest rates needed to set in motion international capital movements can be taken as a measure of the cost and the extra risk of capital transfer between countries. Iversen gives us a detailed analysis of why interest rates differ between countries and sectors. As with previous authors, we are presented with an analysis of the effects of capital movements on various international and domestic variables. The analysis is, again, equilibrium analysis of the comparative static type; this means that comparisons are made between the equilibrium situation before and after the capital movements but there is no analysis of the 'interim' situation, of what goes on before the final equilibrium is reached. And, of course, equilibria may never be reached.

6.4 Diagrammatic presentation of the neo-classical analysis

A graphical presentation of the neo-classical theory of capital movements activated by interest rates differentials is given by Acocella (1975, pp. 37–9), who is, however, critical of the neo-classical approach.

In figure 6.1 the horizontal axis measures capital employed in countries A and B respectively, while the vertical axis represents rates of return or interest rates.[1] In the initial situation country A employs Oa at a rate of return ad while country B employs Ob which yields bc; as $ad > bc$, the differential is likely to prompt movements of capital from B to A; the increased supply in A and the reduced supply in B will cause changes in the rates of return in the two countries. The movements of capital will go on until the rates of return are equalized ($a^1d^1 = b^1c^1$); as only two countries are involved in the analysis, the outward movement from B must equal the inward movement to A ($b^1b = aa^1$).

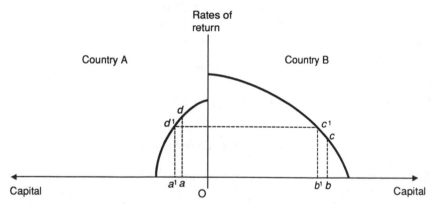

Figure 6.1. Profit rate differentials and capital movements. Initial endowments are Oa and Ob. $b^1b = aa^1$ = capital movement from B to A.

Source: Acocella, 1975, p. 38

6.5 Remarks on the more recent neo-classical literature

The post-Second World War neo-classical literature[2] on foreign investment has been concerned with the effects and welfare implications of foreign investment. Both inward and outward investment has been analysed and the effects extended to either or both home and source country. The distinction between portfolio and direct investment is not always made. The framework of analysis is usually a perfectly competitive and equilibrium one; general equilibrium analysis is specifically considered in some cases (in particular Miller, 1968). Mundell (1957) uses a neo-classical framework to analyse the relationship between international trade and factor mobility with specific reference to the effects of a trade tariff. In his analysis commodity movements and trade movements are substitutes: 'an increase in trade impediments stimulates factor movements and . . . an increase in restrictions to factor movements stimulates trade' (p. 21). A full commodity-price equalization and factor-price equalization or a tendency towards such equalizations will result, even when either factors or commodities are not fully mobile. Mundell concludes that: 'To achieve efficiency in world production, it is unnecessary that both commodities and factors move freely. As long as the production conditions are satisfied, it is sufficient that *either* commodities *or* factors move freely' (p. 30).

Using a similar analysis to Mundell's, Bhagwati (1973) and Brecher and Diaz Alejandro (1977) conclude that inward investment stimulated by a trade tariff will reduce the host country welfare if 'foreign capital receives the full (untaxed) value of its marginal product' (p. 317).

Mundell's conclusion that trade and factor mobility are substitutes is not – *prima facie* supported by the trends towards increase in both trade and FDI. The issue of substitution versus complementarity between international trade and international production is not clear cut. It is an issue that is discussed further in chapter 17.

6.6   Some comments

The neo-classical theory of foreign investment has been developed mainly as a by-product of the theory of international trade; thus some of the developments and refinements of the neo-classical theory of trade have bearings on the theory of foreign investments.[3] Methodologically, a marginalist analysis with its emphasis on marginal changes in one variable at a time can be, and has been, useful in the study of effects.

The main problem in the neo-classical analysis is linked to the unrealistic assumptions of perfect competition. A perfectly competitive environment may have been not too unreasonable as an approximation of reality when the neo-classical theory was first applied to international trade. It is, however, completely at variance with reality to apply such an assumption to the activities of TNCs, in terms of both FDI and trade, of which they now control a large share.[4]

That an analysis based on perfect competition and equilibria is unsuited to an understanding of the behaviour of transnational companies, and to an assessment of the effects of foreign direct investment or of any other feature of the modern economic system, should be quite obvious. None the less, such an influential economist as Milton Friedman (1953), writing from an instrumentalist position, has defended the methodological approach based on unrealistic assumptions. He clearly expresses the instrumentalist position: 'the relevant question to ask about the "assumptions" of a theory is not whether they are descriptively "realistic", for they never are, but whether they are sufficiently good approximation for the purpose in hand' (p. 15). For Friedman, 'The decisive test is whether the hypothesis works for the phenomena it purports to explain' (p. 30) and in general we should accept unrealistic assumptions provided we are satisfied that the real world behaves '*as if*' these assumptions were correct. Thus we can accept the perfect competition assumption provided we are satisfied that, in terms of the phenomena we are studying, the agents behave as if the system were competitive and the main economic relationships remain valid. We should, according to Friedman, assess theories for their predictive power independently of their explanatory power.

Instrumentalism as a methodological approach to science in general has been criticized by many philosophers of science; Friedman's position as regards economics has been attacked by both philosophers of science and economists.[5] On the whole, it is difficult to see how wildly unrealistic assumptions, such as perfect competition applied to the economic environment in which TNCs operate, can be useful.[6] They are unlikely to lead to theories with good explanatory or predictive power.

It is arguable that the neo-classical theory of foreign investment would, in modern economic systems, apply to portfolio investment; it is out of the question that it could possibly have either explicative or predictive power when applied to direct foreign investment. For a start, the transition from a theory of portfolio investment to one related to direct investment would imply that interest rates and profit rates can be used interchangeably, an assumption that holds in the long run under perfectly competitive markets and certainty, but not in the real world of imperfect markets and uncertainty.

The difficulty of the neo-classical theory in explaining portfolio investment and in its application to direct investment has been highlighted by Hymer (1960). Hymer points out that the neo-classical theory of portfolio investment does not provide a clear cut answer to which way capital would flow and by what amount, because of the elements of risk and uncertainty involved as well as the costs of gathering information.

Hymer's point can be strengthened with reference, for example, to Iversen's claim (mentioned in section 6.3) that the cost and risk of capital transfers can be assessed with reference to the difference in interest rates, while the theory which he is presenting would claim that the differentials in interest rates depend, among other things, on the risk involved. An independent assessment of costs and risks of transaction thus becomes necessary for the theory to have predictive and explanatory power. Hymer concludes that it is imperfections in the market that make difficult the explanation of portfolio foreign investment in the context of the neo-classical theory. However, these are the factors that make the study of direct foreign investment relevant.

In analysing the applicability of neo-classical portfolio investment to foreign direct investment, Hymer brings in some very convincing arguments and evidence to show the poor predictive power of such theory. For example the neo-classical theory based on interest rates differentials would predict that capital moves from the investing country to the countries where the investment takes place; however, this is often not the case as companies involved in direct investment can raise the capital somewhere else, including the same country in which they invest. Similarly, the neo-classical theory would predict that capital would move from a country with low interest rates to a country with high interest rates. In reality, foreign direct investment seems to follow the industry lead rather than the country lead: according to Hymer, foreign direct investment tends to concentrate in certain industries across countries, rather than in some countries across industries.

Iversen's hypothesis that industries differentials can be explained by different risks is difficult to test; his argument is indeed circular as he implies that interest rates differentials depend on different risks (and their estimates) while, at the same time, he seems to argue that movements of capital and differentials in interest rates are indicators of the amount of risk involved.

It would be difficult to explain the present, and increasingly relevant, situation of countries that are both source and host country, and in particular to explain the growing amount of intra-industry foreign direct investment (see section 2.3) using the neo-classical theory. All in all the neo-classical assumptions are clearly unsuited to dealing with the activities of multinational companies.

Section III
Prevalent Theories

---

che, non men che saper, dubbiar m'aggrata.
(that it is no less pleasing to me to doubt, than to know.)
                    Dante, *La Divina Commedia, Inferno*. XI, 93.

7

Foreign Direct Investment and Market Imperfections: the Hymer and Kindleberger Approach

7.1 The theory

Steven Hymer in his doctoral dissertation of 1960 put forward the first modern theory of 'international operations' by large companies. His work was published posthumously in 1976. Hymer's work constitutes a radical departure from the conventional neo-classical approach of the time. It opened a whole new research programme in the area of foreign direct investment. Follow-ups, refinements and new twists to the theory (whether acknowledged as such or not) are continuously coming out. The first additions to the theory are due to Charles Kindleberger, who supervised Hymer's thesis, encouraged him and helped to get his work fully recognized.

In order to understand the relevance of Hymer's contribution as well as the novelty of his approach, we must remember that, when he was writing, there was hardly any theory of foreign direct investment. There were theories of portfolio investment that were widely assumed to extend and apply to direct investment; hence there was, up to that point, no perceived need to consider direct investment as a special case.

Hymer starts by analysing portfolio investment and its determinants. The main determinant of movements of funds across frontiers is the difference in interest rates, with other elements, such as risk and uncertainty, playing a subsidiary, though important, role.

Hymer then goes on to consider the peculiarities of foreign direct investment which could not possibly be explained via interest rate differentials. In particular, he and Kindleberger (1969) later emphasized how: (a) direct investment does not necessarily involve movement of funds from the home to the host country – direct investment is, at times, financed by borrowing in the host country or using retained profits or by payments in kind (involving patents, technology or machinery in exchange for equity in a host country enterprise); (b) direct investment often takes place both ways so that both countries involved are originators and host to it; (c) direct investment tends to be concentrated in particular industries across various countries rather than in a particular country across various industries, as one might expect if the main determinant were interest rate differentials between countries. The conclusion is that, although direct investment may involve capital movements, it cannot just be equated with capital movements in its significance or effects or determinants.

One explanation for firms' direct investment abroad which is considered and also dismissed by Kindleberger is that it is all related to the growth of the firm. There are two strands to this view. The first stresses the search for markets and hence considers foreign direct investment as demand-led; it is, however, difficult to explain why the extra markets cannot be sourced through exporting products produced in the home country. The second strand emphasizes the role of internal finance; retained profits from foreign subsidiaries are best used for reinvestment in the host country. This view gives direct investment a passive role quite at variance with the large expansion witnessed since the Second World War.

Before approching the issue of determinants of foreign direct investment, Hymer considers the question of what is special about FDI and what differentiates it from portfolio investment. The answer is that the special feature of direct investment is the fact that it gives the investor *control*, thus making the investment safer. Both Hymer and Kindleberger assume that direct involvement abroad is costly and risky and that, if firms decide to engage in it, there must be strong counterbalancing advantages; the *control* acquired by the investor, via direct investment, allows the exploitation of such advantages.

According to Hymer the high costs of direct investment abroad are due to:

1 Costs of communication and of acquisition of information in general; these costs are linked to the different cultural, linguistic, legal, economic and political background in which the firm will have to operate in the host country.
2 Costs due to less favourable treatment given by host countries' governments.
3 Costs due to exchange rate risks.

The counterbalancing advantages all derive from the existence of *market imperfections* and their potential increase. One, and indeed the main, motivation for direct investment and control of business abroad is, therefore, collusion and the general weakening of competition in the expectation that this will lead to larger profits.

The second motivation is also linked to market imperfections and is related to the fact that firms differ in their abilities and advantages in any particular industry. Firms that have particular *advantages* in production and/or marketing will find it profitable to use that advantage to produce directly in another country. They can, and sometimes do, market their advantage via licensing; however, licensing is usually less profitable than direct production and involves risks of poor control over the product or inability to keep a monopoly over patents and similar technological advantages. This means that any explanation of foreign direct investment in terms of lower production costs in the host country is not tenable because it does not explain why production is not undertaken by the local firms. It is with reference to special advantages and market imperfections that we can explain why the foreign firm is able to engage in productoin rather than the local firm.

A third, 'minor', reason for foreign direct investment on the part of large firms is given by Hymer as the drive towards *diversification*.

So the main message of Hymer and Kindleberger is that, for direct investment to thrive, there must be market imperfections that create conflicts. By investing directly and by thus reducing competition, the firm aims to reduce or eliminate the conflicts. The market imperfection can be due to:

1 imperfections in the goods markets;
2 imperfections in the factors markets;
3 internal and external economies of scale (the last linked to vertical integration);
4 governments' interference with production or trade.

Firms' advantages in the goods markets (e.g. special marketing skills), in the factors market (advantages in raising capital, superiority of management or special patents and general superiority in technology) or in economies of scale, are, of course, linked to market imperfections and can lead to direct foreign investment.

Later in his short life Hymer moved towards a more Marxist approach in which he stressed conflicts and contradictions of the internationalization of production. In his 1971 article he begins by analysing the historical development of the firm and the links with its internal organization, which were discussed in chapter 1.

His later analysis leads to the conclusion that on the one hand the multinational company is a strong progressive force which enables the planning and organization of production on a worldwide scale and leads to an increase in productivity and to the spread of new technology and new products. However, the MNCs, with their large size, power, hierarchical structure and spread of activities into many sectors and countries, also contain the germs of considerable conflicts and contradictions. In particular, the functional and geographical division of labour leads to conflicts within the corporation, within a single country and between countries; this is because development and opportunities spread unevenly, thus creating tensions.

The main contradiction arises out of the formidable planning power of TNCs. The system operates as fully planned at the *micro* level but unplanned and unstructured at the *macro* level where all is left to the vagaries of the market. The lack of plans and structure at the macro level creates difficulties for the business world itself. This is the more so since economic policies – and demand management policies in particular, which were fashionable when Hymer was writing – are difficult to harmonize internationally.

According to Hymer, the gap between micro planning and macro anarchy may eventually turn against the TNCs themselves as people will come to realize how efficient the system could be if the planning, so far applied within firms only, were to be applied between them, in a comprehensive regional or national set up.

7.2 Some comments

Hymer's theory was pathbreaking in both a backward and a forward looking way: because it developed a fully coherent approach and theory in a field where nothing existed, and indeed foreign direct investment was not even considered in the economic literature as an autonomous category needing explanation; and in a forward looking way because his approach has led and still is leading to follow-ups. In particular the Reading school (with Buckley and Casson's (1976) internalization theory and Dunning's (1977) eclectic theory of international production) has followed Hymer's lead and made relevant additions to his theory of international operations.

One major element of Hymer's theory is his stress on the *control* which foreign direct investment, in contrast to portfolio investment, allows firms. The issue of *control* as relevant for understanding wider business operations has recently been taken up by Cowling and Sugden (1987a), as highlighted in section 1.4. Cowling and Sugden (1987b) develop the 'collusion' aspect of Hymer's theory in a new interesting direction. The relevance of market imperfections and monopolization is acquiring a new global dimension with the spread of international joint ventures (as mentioned in section 2.10).

Hymer's theory is developed as a departure from the neo-classical approach and in many ways it is put into the straightjacket of being developed as a comparison with it; it is a departure from the portfolio investment theory and it is a departure from the perfect competition case. Both Hymer and Kindleberger are preoccupied with the issue of why it is the MNC (usually from the USA) that invests in the foreign country rather than the local national firm. They thus overlook the issue of many big MNCs competing to get into a particular host country and the issue of special advantages of the successful firm compared with the others. This issue is further developed by Dunning (1977) and it also leads to the interesting results of Knickerbocker (1973), who finds that direct investments in a particular country tend to bunch-up (chapter 13).

Hymer and Kindleberger (and later Dunning) consider fully the issue of licensing versus directly investing for any particular big firm. The relevance of internalization and Coase's analysis is, however, overlooked. Coase's article (1937) is not mentioned in Hymer's thesis, although it is mentioned in his later works.[1]

By concentrating mainly on the relationship between direct investor and local firm in the host country, Hymer misses the issue of globalism and the advantages and disadvantages that firms (as well as countries and governments) derive from the fact that direct investments are spread over many countries; indeed Hymer starts from the assumption that the foreign investor is at a disadvantage and he looks for counterbalancing elements in market imperfections. However, one could as easily consider advantages of multinationality *per se*. There are many areas in which transnationalism gives special advantages (on which more in chapter 14). In fairness to Hymer, one should consider that the advantages of transnationalism have been increasing with its spread, and they were not as high as they are now at the time he was writing.

8
The Product Life Cycle and Foreign Direct Investment

8.1 The technological gap theories of trade as background

The 1960s saw the development of a new set of theories of international trade around the basic concept of *technological gap*.[1] Posner (1961) analyses how an initial product innovation in one country leads to cumulative technological advantages and to trade advantages. The extent and duration of the trade advantages will depend on the extent of the cumulative advantages for the innovating firm, on the speed with which demand for the new product spreads and on the speed with which other domestic and foreign firms start imitating the new product.

According to Posner, a strong contribution to cumulative advantages is made by the development of 'dynamic economies of scale'. He writes (p. 329): 'Where technical progress occurs, unit costs for a particular firm are lower today than they were yesterday . . . because this particular firm can now draw on its experience of yesterday's production.' It is the experience of past production that gives rise to dynamic economies of scale in Posner's view.

Hufbauer (1966) develops further the technological gap theory of trade in the context of an application to synthetic materials. He introduces two main developments from Posner's theory. First, he modifies the learning function and the related lag to take account of the length of time the firm has engaged in the new production and not just the volume of past production. Secondly, he takes account of differences in relative wages in the trading countries. Hufbauer highlights the speed and the process with which the manufacture of new products spreads from one nation to another. The threat that the new product poses for existing products acts as an incentive to its quick spreading. Similarly, the lure of high profits to be made by moving into the new product will increase the speed with which the manufacture of the new product will spread. Hufbauer concludes (p. 32) that: 'The two spreading mechanisms therefore usually ensure that high-wage countries imitate more rapidly than low-wage countries.'

Meanwhile, other researchers – and in particular Simon Kutznets (1953) – had been linking the growth of demand for products to the cycle of the product's life from invention to growth to maturity. The growth of demand tends to be slow in the innovation phase of a product then to accelerate and finally to slow down again. Seev Hirsch (1965, 1967) analyses the phases of the product's life in relation to the technology and scale of production, to the type of labour skills needed and to the countries' competitive advantages. He applies his product life cycle hypothesis to the production and trade pattern of the US electronics industry.

The product requires skilled and high-cost labour (engineering, scientific) in the initial phase; capital expenditure tends to be kept relatively low in this introductory phase. The ratio of labour to capital is reduced in the subsequent growth phase, when mass production and mass distribution are introduced; the product becomes, in fact, more capital-intensive in this phase; at the same time, the availability of skilled managerial labour is essential. In the last, mature, phase the product becomes standardized; both scale and technology are stable, the need for skilled labour is reduced and more unskilled labour is required. The mature phase tends to be very capital-intensive, indeed more capital-intensive than the previous phases. Hirsch writes on the manufacturing process during the various phases (1965, p. 94):

> We would expect the 'growth' sectors to employ more skill intensive methods; we would expect the 'mature' sectors to be more capital intensive now than they were when in the growth phase. . . . What the product cycle view suggests is that for any particular product the ratio of the capital stock to value added will be higher in the mature than in the growth phase.

Hirsch, like Posner and Hufbauer, analyses the trade effects of technological gaps between countries. However, the cumulative effects of technology and dynamic economies of scale we saw in Posner's and Hufbauer's works are played down in Hirsch's analysis. Instead, we have effects on competition and trade deriving from the various phases of the life of the product. According to Hirsch, in the first phase of the product's life developed countries have an advantage as they can provide the engineering and scientific skills required. He argues (1967, chapters II and V) that this is a phase suited to both small advanced countries (e.g. Britain, Switzerland and Israel) and the USA.

Hirsch concludes also that the US competitive advantage is to be found in the growth phase of the product. This is because in this phase large amounts of capital are needed for mass production, as well as inputs of skilled managerial labour for the organization and management of large-scale production. The USA loses competitiveness in the last phase when the product is standardized and its high unskilled labour intensity favours locations with relatively low wages. In this last phase, the less developed countries are found to be more competitive.

It follows from this that, according to Hirsch, the product cycle approach to the explanation of international trade throws light on the 'Leontief paradox'. This 'paradox' has its origin in the factor proportions theory of trade, according to which countries relatively abundant in capital will export capital-intensive products while labour-abundant (low wages) countries will export labour-intensive products. This prediction of the theory was falsified by the findings of Wassily Leontief (1953, 1956). In a study of the structure of US domestic production and foreign trade, Leontief found that, contrary to expectations based on the comparative costs theory, the USA appeared to export products that were less capital-intensive than those imported. A similar paradox, the other way around, was found for Japan.[2] Hirsch explains the apparent paradoxes by analysing the relationship between trade and the phases of the product. He writes (1965, p. 97):

> The growth products, in which the United States is likely to be most competitive, are not necessarily produced in a highly capital-intensive way; indeed their main characteristic – judging from the electronics industry – is their high skill content. The mature products, in which Japan has considerable export success, tend to have high capital–output ratios; but their skill content – in the widest sense – is relatively low. It is in engineering and scientific skill and managerial ability, rather than in capital, that the United States has the greatest competitive advantage.

From the contributions of the technological gap theories and the product life cycle theory the following points can be highlighted:

1 Technological advantages lead to competitive advantages.
2 Technological advantages are likely to be cumulative for various reasons, including dynamic economies of scale, learning-by-doing and a tendency towards a cumulation of inventions.
3 Competitive advantages change during the phases of the product: a country which has an advantage at the innovative phase of the product is unlikely to maintain the advantage when the product reaches maturity.
4 Imitation effects – in terms of demand and production – are very relevant and likely to be stronger in countries with high incomes.
5 The mechanisms and speed of imitation in production are linked to the market structure in which firms operate.

6 The product life cycle linked the technological gap approach to the factor proportions theory via the various phases of the products and the different labour skills required during them.

8.2 Vernon's theory

It was against this background that Raymond Vernon used the product life cycle approach to develop a theory of foreign direct investment. The origin of his work is in the technological gap theory as well as in the literature on the life of the product. However, while most previous researchers had been concerned with the effects of technological gaps and/or life of the product on international trade, Vernon (1966) put particular emphasis on international production, although links with international trade are also present in his article. Vernon's work is concerned with: where new ideas and technology for new products are likely to originate; where the production of new products is likely to begin; what circumstances lead to the location of production abroad; where and what are the consequences for the flow of FDI and for international trade.

He begins 'with the assumption that the enterprises in any one of the advanced countries of the world are not distinguishably different from those in any other advanced country, in terms of their access to scientific knowledge, and their capacity to comprehend scientific principles' (p. 306). However, equal access to knowledge does not mean an equal probability of application of such knowledge; there is a large gap between the knowledge of a scientific principle and the embodiment of the principle in a marketable product. It is the consciousness of opportunities and the responsiveness to such opportunities that vary from one entrepreneur to another. Such consciousness and responsiveness are associated with the market conditions in which entrepreneurs operate; this makes knowledge inseparable from the decision-making process about its use. Therefore knowledge is not an exogenous variable.

The US market offers unique opportunities for the exploitation of knowledge and its embodiment in new products. This is because of the following characteristics of the US market:

1 It is a market in which consumers have high average income per capita.
2 It is a very large market; hence even minority tastes are likely to provide a fairly large market.
3 It is characterized by high unit labour costs and a large supply of capital; it is, in other words, a market abundant in capital and scarce in labour.

The first two characteristics mean that new products requiring high incomes are more likely to have a market in the USA. The same is true for products designed to save labour at the consumption or production levels, or both.

An entrepreneur in the USA is more likely to spot opportunities for markets in products designed to save labour and requiring high per capita income. Spotting the market is likely to lead to the idea and conception of a new product. Is it, however, likely that the production of the new product will be located in the country where the market has first been spotted (in Vernon's analysis, the USA)? Vernon's answer is affirmative. In his view the new product will be located in the USA, in spite of its high production costs, essentially for the following reasons. In the early stages of its introduction the product is unlikely to be standardized, but will instead come in a variety of models. This has many implications, in particular:

1   At the initial stage producers are interested in flexibility and freedom in adapting the product and changing inputs as necessary.
2   It is useful to have not only flexibility in the adaptation of the production process but also, and paramount, flexibility of adaptation to the requirements of consumers and to their criticisms. For this second issue, proximity of production to the market is essential to ensure swift and effective communication between producers and consumers.
3   The product enjoys, in its early stages, a high degree of differentiation and a monopolistic position. This means that the price elasticity of demand is likely to be comparatively low, thus freeing the producers from excessive worries about costs.

The result of this analysis is that, if the favourable market conditions are in the USA, not only will the product be conceived and developed in the USA, but it will also be produced there in its initial stage. However, as demand for the product grows, a certain standardization will occur. This has locational implications because:

• the need for flexibility and proximity to customers declines – mass production will replace short production runs;
• concern about production costs is likely to start replacing concern about the characteristics of the product.

While demand spreads at home, there is also likely to be a spreading of demand overseas in advanced European countries. It is the countries with high incomes that are likely to accept the new product. The demand from Western European countries will, at first, be met by exports from the USA. However, a variety of factors may soon support a strategy based on direct foreign production rather than exports. Among such factors are: the threat of rivals beginning imitations of the product in European countries; lower production costs in European countries; the threat of import controls by European governments.

Gruber et al. (1967) explore this issue further. There are two additional points made in relation to foreign investment and technological gaps. The authors point out how overseas direct investment usually follows involvement via exports. This means that the 'marginal costs' of setting up production are reduced because the basic information regarding the country and the market are already available to the company. Besides, the research-intensive industries tend to be oligopolistic. 'In the oligopoly industries . . . individual firms are likely to consider foreign investments as important forestalling tactics to cut off market preemption by others' (p. 31). The firm may also start sourcing other markets in Europe or elsewhere from production in the particular European country(ies) in which it has invested. It is also possible that, if production costs outside the USA are low enough to outweigh transport costs, the product will be imported into the USA.

As the product becomes more and more standardized it will require high capital intensity and unskilled labour. In this phase imitation becomes easier, competition will increase and cost-cutting will become necessary. This may lead to a strategy of location of production in LDCs in search of low labour costs. Imports into the USA will continue to increase. The USA will gradually lose its competitive advantage as a location.

The effects of the product cycle on trade and location of production have been illustrated by Vernon in a clear diagram reproduced in figure 8.1. The time lag between foreign production and domestic innovation depends on many elements, among which are: the speed with which demand for the new product spreads; the market position of the innovating firm in European countries; the comparative costs of production in the USA and Europe. The spread of demand, the spread of production and the spread of technology from the USA to Europe go hand-in-hand.

The spreading sequence and mechanisms highlighted by Vernon are supported by the findings of the Organization for Economic Cooperation and Development (OECD, 1970). There is evidence that many innovations originate in the USA and later spread to Western Europe; there is also evidence that the main mechanism for the spread of technology was – up to 1970 – direct production by US companies through their foreign investment in Europe. The same study finds that the USA tends to show a lead in terms of diffusion of newer innovation (nuclear power, computers); the levels of diffusion for more mature products (man-made fibres and plastics) tend to be similar for the USA and European countries.

The general pattern of trade and FDI emerging from the product life cycle is also supported by Gruber et al. (1967). In this work the technological gap and the innovative tendencies in various industries are assessed by looking at research and development efforts.

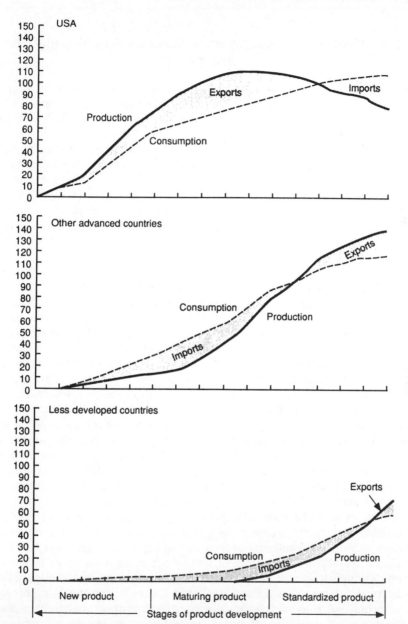

Figure 8.1. Production, imports and exports, and stages of product development, in various countries. © 1966 by the President and Fellows of Harvard College. Published by John Wiley and Sons, Inc. The Quarterly Journals of Economics vol. LXXX n. 2

Source: Vernon, 1966, p. 200

8.3   Vernon on location of production and oligopolistic structures

In his 1974 paper Vernon develops further the link between location of production, multinationality and oligopolistic structures. Is location of production affected by the fact that decisions are taken by MNEs rather than national firms?

According to Vernon the answer is affirmative for various reasons, including the following. The MNE buys and sells throughout the world, so the factor costs considered are not only those where the subsidiary is located (or to be located) but the costs in other parts of the world as well. Capital can be borrowed anywhere, some labour can be transferred from other countries, components can be moved. MNEs operate in oligopolistic markets to a larger extent than national enterprises, so considerations of oligopolistic equilibrium will play a large role.

In linking MNEs' decisions to oligopolistic structures Vernon identifies three stages of oligopoly. An *innovation-based oligopoly* is one in which the innovator acquires barriers to entry due to the new technologies used, whether in products or in processes. The first location of production of the new products is likely to be the country where the research takes place and this is likely to be the country where headquarters are located. In a *mature* oligopoly, 'the basis for the oligopoly is not the advantages of product innovation but the barriers to entry generated by scale in production, transportation or marketing' (p. 97). The overwhelming concern in such an industry is with stability; this concern is reflected in both pricing and location strategies. On this last issue, Vernon's conclusion is that 'there is a hint in support of the proposition that the search for stability in the mature oligopolies leads to a geographical concentration of investment which could not be explained on the basis of comparative costs' (p. 102). He reaches similar specific conclusions regarding location of production by MNEs and writes: 'there is a strong possibility that the existence of multinational enterprises in the mature industries tends to concentrate economic activity on geographical lines, to a degree that is greater than if multinational enterprises did not exist' (p. 104).[3]

There are oligopolistic situations in which economies of scale are not strong enough to act as barriers to entry and thus maintain oligopolistic stability; in these cases enterprises may use other methods to prolong equilibrium, such as cartels or product differentiation. Sometimes these strategies are successful, at other times they are not; in any case the equilibrium is fragile and enterprises may start looking for costs advantages. This is the situation of what Vernon calls '*senescent oligopolies*'.

Many consumer durables markets are characterized by a fragile equilibrium: in spite of 'considerable product differentiation and brand differentiation, cross-elasticities are still uncomfortably high from the producer's viewpoint' (Vernon, 1974, p. 105). In these markets the barriers to entry may not be high enough to maintain oligopolistic stability. Producers will often be seeking cost cutting as barriers to entry. Cost reducing locations can be sought at the national or international level. The MNEs are particularly well placed to scan for low-cost locations, particularly in LDCs.

8.4   The product cycle in a new macro-environment

Interestingly enough, Vernon himself has come out with a critical review of his own theory in a paper which analyses 'The product cycle hypothesis in a new international environment' (1979). His self-criticisms are related mainly to the changed environment in European countries. In this paper he analyses two main elements in order to derive conclusions as to the applicability of the product cycle theory in the late 1970s and 1980s. The two elements are related to (a) the degree of internationalization and new products diffusion and (b) changes in the European macro-environment.

Vernon starts by pointing out that there has been a considerable increase in the spread of the geographical network of MNCs' operations. His analysis of the geographical spread of activities is based on the results of the Harvard Multinational Enterprises Projects; a version of the results presented by Vernon was considered in section 2.1 (point 7). From these it appears that, in the earlier periods, US multinationals would start by locating in familiar countries (Canada, the UK) and only at a later stage would spread to less familiar locations (such as Asia and Africa). Vernon writes on this point:

> For product lines introduced abroad by the 180 firms before 1946, the probability that a Canadian location would come earlier than an Asian location was 79 percent; but for product lines that were introduced abroad after 1960, the probability that Canada would take precedence over Asia had dropped to only 59 per cent. (p. 259)

As TNCs engaged in more and more global planning, not only the spread of their operations increased, but the overall lag between the appearance of a new product in the USA and its introduction and spread in other locations diminished considerably. The two trends reinforced each other as firms with established subsidiaries abroad would tend to spread new products in the locations of their operations more and more quickly.

The findings of the OECD (1970) support Vernon's ideas on this point. The OECD finds that 'there is a tendency for the time lag between the initiation of production in the United States, and production of the same commodity abroad, to diminish' (p. 259).

The second big change considered by Vernon is that in the macro-environment; this is connected to those just discussed. As we moved from the early 1960s to the late 1970s and 1980s quite a few changes occurred in Europe which closed the gap between Europe and the USA. The differences in per capita income, cost of labour, size of markets and consumer tastes between Europe and the USA have narrowed considerably. This has made the product life cycle theory less applicable than in the 1950s and 1960s. Essentially TNCs have become more and more global scanners and, at the same time, many products have become standardized (computers, pharmaceutical products etc.). This means that the environment which generated the product life cycle is disappearing and the theory is less applicable.

There are still some areas in which there is scope for the application of the theory. First, it still applies to innovative activities of smaller firms which are not global scanners and cater for smaller markets and non-standardized tastes. Secondly, the theory may still be able to explore the spread of innovation between developed countries and less developed ones; it might also apply within LDCs themselves for certain specific products, and between NICs and LDCs. Besides, one must remember that MNCs are not perfect global scanners; to the extent that they are not, there is still scope for cautious behaviour and thus for the trial of some products on home ground with subsequent spread to other developed countries, in a product life cycle sequence.

8.5 Some comments

The product life cycle theory has been the most quoted, anthologized, used and misused theory in the study of international business. It has also been one of the most criticized ones. The theory is very interesting for a variety of reasons. First, it is very dynamic. Secondly, it blends elements related to the market with production elements. Technology and knowledge are considered as endogenous and their development is linked to the economic environment of the country considered (the USA) and to market conditions. There is a strong interplay between the role of consumers, the role of producers and the market structure. Conflicts between capital and labour, and between rival blocks of capital for market shares, are brought in, although in a role subsidiary to that of consumers and markets. Trade and FDI are examined together, their pattern emerging from the life cycle of the product and from the technological gap between various countries.

As in Hirsch's analysis, the technological gap theory is linked to the factor proportions theory of trade via the phases of the product's life. As the product matures and becomes standardized, relative costs and wages become more and more relevant. The step from a theory of trade to a theory of both international production and trade is made by Vernon through the incorporation of oligopolistic elements as well as comparative costs in the two locations.

The excessive concentration on the product and its life constitutes a weakness of the theory; the firm loses proper focus in favour of the product. By thus focusing attention, Vernon's theory loses considerable elements linked to multi-product firms and diversification strategies that are often related to multinationality strategies.

The original technological gap theories emphasized the cumulative aspects of technological advantages deriving from cumulative production and/or the length of time for which the firm has been engaged in the production of the new product(s). Cumulative advantages for the firm, the industry and the country also derive from the tendency for inventions to cumulate and thus for new products and processes to emerge. Some of these cumulative elements are lost in Vernon's analysis. This is partly because of his excessive concentration on demand, relative to production, and partly because the emphasis on the phases of the product's life tends to highlight shifts in advantages between countries rather than cumulation. Concentration on the product rather than the firm prevents a proper analysis of the spread of technological (as well as managerial and marketing) advantages from one product to another.

None the less, the stress on foreign direct investment linked to the technological gap constitutes a considerable advancement on previous theories. International production becomes a strategy to prevent rivals from imitating the product, but it is also the strongest mechanism for the spread of new technologies to other countries, as highlighted in the OECD report (1970).

Vernon's (1979) own critique of his theory is not only courageous but also very interesting and valid. However, it raises some problems. First, it seems a pity that, having gone into an analysis of the causes and effects of the geographical spread of operations, he has not felt the need to plunge into the product spread and examine the effects on his theory on diversification. Secondly, his excessive concentration on consumers and markets leads to another missed opportunity: the analysis of the effects of global scanning on the production process and labour, on which there is more in chapter 14.

Vernon (1979) ends his self-criticism by listing situations in which the product life cycle theory is still applicable. We might add one more case to his list: the possible involvement of advanced Western countries and East European ones in a product life cycle sequence.

9

Currency Areas and Foreign Direct Investment

9.1 The theory and its background

Robert Z. Aliber (1970) developed a theory of direct investment based on currency areas. His theory is concerned with explaining when and why foreign markets are sourced by domestic production through exports, by host country production through licensing agreements involving local firms, or via direct foreign production by the source country's firms.

He starts by assuming that direct foreign investment involves extra costs and disadvantages related to the management of enterprises at a distance; there is therefore a need to look for compensating advantages. A theory of direct investment must analyse the source of such advantages while explaining the pattern of FDI with particular reference to the following characteristics:

1 The fact that a substantial part of FDI worldwide originates in the USA.
2 The considerable differences in the FDI pattern across industries.
3 The existence of FDI through takeovers of foreign firms.
4 The existence of cross-hauling, i.e. the fact that a country engages in outward FDI while also being the recipient of inward FDI.

Aliber rejects explanations of FDI based on superior managerial skills as, in his view, any such types of superiority should be reflected in costs and exchange rates. Similarly, he does not accept explanations based on industrial organization of the Coasian type because such theories, based on advantages of internalization, may explain the growth of firms in general, but not their internationalization. He also rejects the Hymer and Kindleberger explanation.

In approaching the internationalization issue he sees the need to look for explanations that refer to the 'foreignness' of FDI: 'The "foreignness" of the investment reflects the movement across the boundaries between customs areas and between currency areas. In the absence of such boundaries, the distinction between foreign investment and domestic investment disappears' (p. 21). The existence of multiple customs areas affects the prices of products exported from one area to another; the existence of multiple currency areas affects the interest rates on securities issued by borrowers from different areas, reflecting different risks owing to movements in exchange rates.

Aliber assumes that the firm in the source country has a monopolistic advantage which he calls 'the patent'. This can be a general advantage of any type: technological, managerial etc. 'The value of the patent is the capitalized value of the difference between production costs before and after the patent is used' (p. 22). The firm owning the patent has three choices open to it, if it wants to source a foreign market: it can produce domestically and export; it can license its patent to a foreign firm that will produce for the local market; or it can produce directly abroad.

Aliber then goes on to develop his argument by first assuming a situation of unified currency areas within separate customs areas, and then assuming the opposite.

The first assumption leads to a situation in which it is advantageous to satisfy demand from local production rather than from foreign production, as foreign production will be subject to tariffs on importation. Economies of scale would favour production in the domestic economy, and the sourcing of foreign markets via exports; however, the existence of tariffs makes it less costly to produce in the country where the market is, and avoid the tariff. There is a trade-off in domestic versus foreign production between reduction in costs due to economies of scale and reduction in prices due to tariff avoidance. The switch-off point on the quantities produced at home or abroad depends on the costs of production (and thus on economies of scale) and on the height of the tariff, which affects the price of import in the foreign country. However, foreign production using the same monopolistic advantage (the patent) can take place in two different ways: via licensing to a local firm, which will then become the producer, or via direct production by the source country's firm.

The patent produces a stream of incomes whose capitalized value will be different in the three cases: exports of domestic production, licensing and direct investment. The pattern of income streams and capitalized values in the three cases will determine the quantities of production at which the crossover between the three cases occurs.[1] The capitalization ratios and hence the interest rates will be crucial in the three choices.

Aliber then develops his model under the second assumption: unified custom areas and separate currencies. The single custom area means that production will tend to be unified to take advantage of economies of scale. The crucial question now becomes whether foreign production will be carried out by the host country firm (through licensing) or by the source country firm: 'the decision whether the source-country firm or the host-country firm exploits the patent abroad depends on the costs of doing business abroad and on national differences in capitalization ratios and not on the height of the tariff' (p. 27).

Income streams of different countries' firms will be capitalized at different rates for various reasons, including the fact that they belong to different currency areas. The theory would therefore predict that 'Source-country firms are likely to be those in countries where the capitalization rates are high; host-countries firms are those in countries where capitalization rates are low' (p. 28). The market applies different capitalization rates to assets denominated in different currencies for two reasons. The first is as a premium against exchange risk. The second reason – which is in fact more of a hypothesis – is 'that the market applies a higher capitalization rate to the source income stream generated in the host country when received by a source-country firm than by a host-country firm' (p. 30). This last point would explain why direct investment, rather than licensing, takes place in the exploitation of a certain patent.

According to Aliber different capitalization rates attached to different currencies explain the geographical pattern of FDI. Countries with strong currencies (the USA, the Netherlands, Switzerland) tend to be source countries as their currencies carry high premiums. Countries subject to a low currency premium will, on the contrary, tend to be host countries. The dispersion in capitalization rates is one of the elements that affects the pattern of FDI. Other elements are 'the size of the host-country's market, the value of the patents, the height of tariffs, the costs of doing business abroad in a particular industry' (p. 31). In Aliber's view his theory predicts that FDI will be larger in more capital-intensive industries, 'since the disadvantage of host-country firms is larger, the larger the contribution of capital to production' (p. 32) and similarly for research-intensive industries.

Takeovers across countries can be explained by the difference in capitalization ratios. Cross-flows of investment – or intra-industry FDI – are explained by Aliber partly by historical reasons; partly because inward investment in the USA comes from a very small number of firms (Shell, Unilever, Phillips, Bayer etc.). However, he is still left with the problem of why these firms produce in the USA rather than export. His answer is that: 'If the price offered for a patent is very low, then the firm may invest in that country rather than license, even though its profit rate will be lower than the profit rates of host-country competitors' (p. 33).

In conclusion, Aliber's theory tells us that the division of the world into different currency areas leads to the market putting a higher premium on certain currencies than on others depending on its estimate of the risk. This premium affects the capitalization value of the income streams deriving from 'patents' and hence 'determines whether a country is likely to be a source country or a host country for foreign investment' (p. 34).

While his main theory stresses the role of currencies and currency areas (and hence monetary policy affecting them) in MNEs' decisions, in a subsequent article Aliber (1971) focuses on the effect that MNEs' activities may have on exchange rates and monetary policy. In this paper Aliber emphasizes the advantageous position in which MNEs find themselves regarding movements of funds into various currencies. Their advantage over 'national' firms derives from the fact that they can have more immediate information on interest rates in various countries in which they have subsidiaries. At the same time the geographical spread of subsidiaries gives them a useful multiplicity of contacts with banks and credit systems. Thus MNEs tend to react quickly to actual and expected changes in exchange rates and/or interest rates by switching funds from currency to currency. From this and other related elements, one could draw the 'plausible inference . . . that the volume of funds which are shifted in response to an anticipated change in the exchange is increasing' (p. 56). In Aliber's view this puts pressure on the monetary systems of various countries and 'One possible consequence is a widening of interest rate differentials' (p. 56).

9.2 Some comments

The currency areas explanation of FDI is quite ingenious, but unfortunately it is not very effective in its explanatory and predictive power. It is a classic example of using much to achieve little: the 'much' used is in terms of the complicated presentation and the large number of assumptions that are made. The achievement is the conclusion that: (a) in a world of custom areas there comes a point where firms who want to source a foreign market will find it more advantageous to produce in the country either directly or through a licensee, rather than produce domestically and export; and (b) in a world of different currency areas, countries with strong currencies will tend to be source countries and countries with weak currencies will tend to be hosts to FDI.

Point (a) is a fairly uncontroversial, obvious and a quite well known conclusion. Point (b) is not satisfactorily corroborated by Aliber and its conclusions cannot be accepted. More will be said on this point below. Aliber starts by overemphasizing the difference between his approach and the market imperfections approach of Hymer and Kindleberger. However, in reality, as Dunning (1971) points out, Aliber's theory could be reduced to a special case of market imperfections as, in the last analysis, his explanation is in terms of imperfections in the market for currencies.

Methodologically the theory seems flawed for the following reason: the conclusion about the relationship between source and host countries and strong and weak currencies (the crux of the matter, in fact) crucially depends on the market applying a higher capitalization rate to the same income stream when received by a source country firm than by a host country firm. If the capitalization rates applied were the same, there would be no incentive for foreign investment. No clear reasons are given for the different valuation, nor any evidence for its existence. Indeed the whole reasoning may be circular in that while Aliber's theory implies that differences in capitalization rates are responsible for determining which country is likely to be source and which host, he seems also to argue that one can assess the difference in capitalization rates by considering whether a country is source or host to FDI.

He tries to explain (1971, pp. 52–3) the differences in the capitalization rates as due to source countries' firms being more efficient in hedging exchange risk, or to the fact that they provide the investor with a diversified portfolio. However, this cannot be considered as evidence to back his crucial assumption of differences in capitalization rates, but rather as an explanation with reference to the host–source country situation. Besides, while he argues that superior managerial skills and similar advantages cannot be used to explain the pattern of FDI (1970, pp. 19–20), he does not use the same argument in considering firms' efficiency in terms of exchange risk hedging or portfolio diversification; would this type of efficiency and advantage not be reflected also in costs and exchange rates just like managerial advantages?

With regard to the predictive power and the explanation of the pattern of FDI, the theory is in great difficulty, in spite of Aliber's claims, particularly when it comes to explaining cross-hauling or intra-industry FDI. Aliber minimizes the extent of this type of FDI in both his articles (1970 and 1971). The phenomenon is, however, quite a large one and has been growing, as mentioned in section 2.1, point 3.

It is difficult, in general, to explain with the currency areas theory the situation of countries which are both, and to a large extent, source and host countries. Aliber quotes the Netherlands, besides the USA, as a country which is heavily involved in outward FDI and whose currency is strong. However, the Netherlands also has high and increasing ratios of inward investment. The average ratio of inward FDI to gross domestic fixed capital formation (GDFCF) has been 3.6, 4.4 and 6.2 for the 1960s, 1970s and 1980s respectively, well above the average for the developed market economies. Similarly the UK is, and has been, a country heavily involved in both inward and outward FDI. The inward flow as a percentage of GDFCF was 3.3, 3.9 and 6.7 for the 1960s, 1970s and 1980s; the outward flow as a percentage of GDFCF during the same periods was 4.8, 7.7 and 14.1. These figures, taken from table 18.1 (p. 192), give a marked contrast to the corresponding average figures for the 12 developed market economies considered; table 18.1 shows, in fact, that the average outward ratios for the 1960s, 1970s and 1980s, respectively, were 1.9, 3.0 and 5.4 while the corresponding inward ratios were 2.9, 2.8 and 3.2.

One noticeable feature is that currencies' strengths tend to change through time and a strong currency may become weak for a time and then strong again; yet the flow of FDI tends to show a pattern that is more long-term. This is, in a way, as expected since direct investment involves long-term strategies and commitments. I would like to suggest that issues related to currency fluctuations, their premiums and related effects on interest rates and capitalization rates are more likely to affect short-term than long-term investment.

One useful and realistic point made by Aliber (1971) relates to the effect of MNEs' activities on currencies and exchange rates and hence on monetary policies of national governments and related interest rates. His basic theory implies that interest rates affect the pattern of FDI; his subsequent additions imply that MNEs' activities in general, and particularly those related to short-term investment, affect interest rates. Although I do not accept his main theory as a satisfactory explanation of FDI, I find that this type of interaction between MNEs' activities and the environment in which they operate is very realistic and clearly typical of oligopolistic structures.

Most of the problems of Aliber's theory stem from the fact that he concentrates on a surface phenomenon and does not bother to consider the world of production. His reference to 'foreignness' as a custom areas phenomenon may be a useful one; however, we could also refer to such areas in relation to other institutional arrangements. For example, nations or regions may be designated by areas of union organizations; different 'areas' have different workers' organizations and allegiances; firms may be prepared to forgo advantages linked to economies of scale in order to move from strong trade union areas to weak trade union areas. Indeed, the process may be a dynamic and interactive one in that the ability of firms to locate production in different 'trade union organization areas' may have effects on the power of workers and their trade unions.

Increasingly, international production has become vertically integrated across national boundaries. This has tended more and more to make countries both source and host countries according to the various components and stages of the production process considered. Aliber's identification of the host country as the country where the market for the product is, may be too simplistic. In the real world the location of production may or may not be the same as the location of the market; we can even have situations in which some products or components are produced abroad and then re-imported by the source country's firm into the source country.

Clearly, these are developments which can only be understood with reference to the organization of production and not with reference to currencies. Currency and currency areas may, however, be useful in the understanding of short- and medium-term capital movements.[2] These movements – as noted by Aliber (1971) – can in their turn affect the behaviour of the monetary authorities and hence the economic environment in which MNEs operate.

10

Horizontal and Vertical Integration, Diversification and the MNE: Caves's Approach

10.1 The main theory

Richard E. Caves (1971) begins his analysis by pointing out that foreign direct investment: (a) 'ordinarily effects a net transfer of real capital from one country to another; and (b) it represents entry into a national industry by a firm established in a foreign market' (p. 265). His analysis concentrates on the industry characteristics of the investment and on some structural features of the markets in which MNEs operate. Firms' expansion in a new geographical environment can involve horizontal and vertical extension or conglomerate diversification.

Through horizontal expansion the MNE extends its operations abroad by producing the same product in new countries. Vertical integration implies that the firm becomes directly involved in other stages of the production process (whether backward or forward stages or both) connected with the product(s) it already produces. When the integration takes place across national boundaries we have the vertically integrated MNE. Foreign investment that involves neither horizontal nor vertical integration is said to be conglomerate.

Why do firms engage in horizontal integration across national boundaries? Caves looks for an explanation in the possession of special assets by the firms, which would have the character of a public good within the firms, i.e. an asset that once acquired can be used for additional activities at little or no cost. The asset conducive to FDI has an opportunity cost that is low relative to the return which can be obtained by employing it on FDI. Furthermore, 'the return attainable on a firm's special asset in a foreign market must depend at least somewhat on local production' (pp. 269–70).

These special characteristics of the asset must give the foreign firm an advantage over the host country's firm, which, operating in a well-known market, would in normal circumstances have a greater advantage. The particular features of the market structure in which such characteristics for assets are likely to be found are those that involve product differentiation. Differentiation of products leads to different profit rates according to the degree of success in differentiation. 'Here is the link to the basis for direct investment: the successful firm producing a differentiated product controls knowledge about serving the market that can be transferred to other national markets for this product at little or no cost' (p. 271). This result is true whether the differentiation takes the form of patents or brand names, or is simply the result of a successful advertising campaign. A successful marketing campaign for a particular market produces considerable intangible assets for the firm. They are the result of spill-over information from one market to another as well as of the acquisition of knowledge of a particular market (including foreign ones).

Caves's theory would predict that horizontal FDI is to be found in industries with considerable product differentiation. Industries in which FDI takes place tend to be very research-intensive; as a considerable amount of research is directed towards new products and product development, this feature fits – in Caves's view – with the theory that FDI and product differentiation go hand in hand.

The transmission of knowledge via licensing of intangible assets is rarely a satisfactory solution; this is partly because of uncertainty about the value of the knowledge and partly because of difficulties in transmitting it in isolation from 'entrepreneurial manpower' (p. 273). This is the reason why, according to Caves, large firms tend to shy away from licensing agreements in favour of direct investment in servicing a market. Conversely it is relatively small firms that get involved in licensing agreements.

'The motives for vertical investments among the industrial countries seem to turn heavily on the avoidance of oligopolistic uncertainty and the erection of barriers to the entry of new rivals' (pp. 276–7). In situations in which both buyers and sellers of raw materials are few in number, uncertainty over long-term supplies *and* prices can be eliminated by backward integration. Besides eliminating uncertainty, vertical integration can also achieve the objective of raising barriers to entry: a producer that controls the supply of raw materials is a very formidable competitor for a new entrant into the industry. Industries where vertical integration takes place will therefore tend to be characterized by high seller concentration, which will give incentives to eliminate uncertainty and to raise barriers to entry.

The overall result of Caves's approach is that foreign direct investments tend to be specific to certain sectors and they generate a tendency – in conjunction with entry barriers – 'to equate rates of return between countries in a given industry but not between industries in a given country' (pp. 285–6).

10.2   Caves's later developments

In a later work (1982) Caves reiterates the main thrust of his theory regarding the determinants of FDI but introduces a few modifications and additions that are worthy of consideration. Horizontal integration across countries is still motivated by excess capacity in intangible assets, which yields a special rent and which can be used across frontiers at relatively low cost. Compared with his 1971 work, there is more emphasis on the transactional advantages of operating under common ownership across frontiers and less on marketing skills and successful advertising as the source of intangible assets.

The main divergence in his analysis is to be found in his treatment of diversified MNEs and of FDI motivated by strategies of vertical integration. In 1971 the main features stressed by Caves, in order to explain vertical FDI, were sellers' concentration, oligopolistic structures and barriers to entry. However, his 1982 work plays down these features in favour of transactional explanations. Vertical integration means internalization of the market for intermediate products and it occurs 'because the parties prefer it to the contracting costs and uncertainties that would mar the alternative state of arm's length transactions' (p. 16).

Suppliers of raw materials have knowledge about their products and their supply which would be very useful to the buyers, but which, nevertheless, it is not in the sellers' interest to pass on fully. Uncertainty and the cost of acquisition of knowledge can be reduced if the seller buys up the raw materials supply.

An additional feature of his 1982 work is Caves's analysis of vertical integration that depends 'not on natural resources but on subdividing production processes and placing abroad those that are both labour-intensive and footloose' (p. 20). It is transactional costs that determine whether different components related to the subdivision of the production process are produced internally or externally to the firm across frontiers. Vertical and horizontal integration are often combined, as subsidiaries can be involved in both producing components and selling final products to the local market.

The diversified MNE invests abroad in sectors other than the one in which it is involved at home. Diversification in general is usually undertaken in order to minimize risks. By diversifying internally a firm may spread the risks deriving from problems common to various sectors in the same macro-environment; for example, problems stemming from economic policies.

10.3   Some comments

One good feature of Caves's analysis is the fact that his work is placed in the realistic environment of an oligopolistic structure; it is a pity that his later work seems to move away from oligopoly, entry barriers and product differentiation. His departure from such realistic market structures, and his later emphasis on transactional costs and internalization, moves the theory more and more away from a 'strategy' and towards an 'efficiency' approach.[1] The emphasis is too much on markets and marketing rather than on production, a feature, in some respect, similar to Vernon's analysis.

His attempt to consider vertical integration due to the subdivision of production processes adds a note of realism to the treatment. However, a central point is missed: the MNEs themselves are responsible for the technology of the division of production processes into stages – a point on which I say more in chapter 14. In general neither this feature of vertical integration nor diversification on an international basis is fully explained.

Caves's writings, in general, have many interesting remarks regarding the behaviour and structure of firms. However, they are less satisfactory at the explanatory level. In all the cases considered one might accept his theory as an explanation of growth strategies of firms. However, what is not clear is why such strategies are applied internationally; in other words, the internationalization aspect is not satisfactorily dealt with.

Finally, it should be mentioned that Caves's analysis shows similarities with Knickerbocker's (1973), on which there is more in chapter 13.

11
Internalization as an Explanation for International Production

11.1 Introduction

An approach that has proved popular and successful with followers of the international business literature is the one based on internalization. One of its contributors recently referred to the theory of internalization as 'the modern theory of the multinational enterprise' (Rugman, 1982, p. 9).

The internalization approach to the theory of the firm is, in fact, not new. R. H. Coase in his seminal paper (1937) brought to the attention of economists the inconsistency between the assumption that, in market economies, resources are allocated via the price mechanism, and the assumption or reality that, within the firm, such allocation is done by planning and organization rather than through arm's length transactions. He writes:

> Outside the firm, price movements direct production, which is co-ordinated through a series of exchange transactions on the market. Within a firm, these market transactions are eliminated and in place of the complicated market structure with exchange transactions is substituted the entrepreneur–co-ordinator, who directs production. (p. 333)

Coase therefore sets for himself:

> The purpose . . . to bridge what appears to be a gap in economic theory between the assumption (made for some purposes) that resources are allocated by means of the price mechanism and the assumption (made for other purposes) that this allocation is dependent on the entrepreneur–co-ordinator. (pp. 334–5)

The gap is bridged by analysing, from the firm's point of view, the costs of carrying transactions through the market against the costs of organizing the internal allocation of resources; the latter costs will, among others, set a limit to the size of the firm. In Coase's words: '. . . a firm will tend to expand until the costs of organising an extra transaction within the firm become equal to the costs of carrying out the same transaction by means of an exchange on the open market or the costs of organising in another firm' (p. 341).

Coase's approach therefore explains the existence and growth of the firm in terms of costs and benefits of internal transactions – and therefore of internal allocation of resources – versus the costs and benefits of external transactions and therefore of allocation of resources through the market.

Coase's article has sparked off a very large amount of literature. A recent criticism by Auerbach (1988) focuses on the disjointed way in which Coase and his followers see firms and markets, in particular the 'presupposition of the existence of markets and the failure to see the role of firms in the *making* of markets' (p. 121).

Williamson's comprehensive article (1981) owes much to Coase's approach as well as to the works of the economic historian Chandler (1962). He starts from the premise that 'the modern corporation is mainly to be understood as the product of a series of organizational innovations that have had the purpose and effect of economizing on transaction costs' (p. 1537). He uses economizing on transaction costs to analyse not only the growth of the firm, but also the evolution of the internal structure of modern corporations and the issue of ownership and control within it. He thus interprets the whole of business history, with its internal and external effects, in terms of economizing on transaction costs. The development of TNCs is thus seen as the product of benefits of internalization across frontiers, coupled with developments in internal organization that have made possible the control of operations across many countries.

The approach based on transaction costs economizing sees the growth of the firm as a positive, efficient process, since it leads to private and social cost economizing. This is contrary to the neo-classical approach, which, by focusing on markets and competition, saw growth and large size as socially harmful because of their market power implications.

There are important policy implications from Williamson's approach: if internal growth is the product of economizing and if the economies are not only privately but also socially beneficial, then any anti-trust regulation ought to assess the various cases not only in the light of market power but also in the light of benefits deriving from transaction costs economizing. It could be that any negative social effects due to excessive market power are counterbalanced by positive social effects due to economies of trans-action costs. Williamson (1984, p. 116) writes on this point: 'The inhospitality tradition within anti-trust owes its origins to this view of firm and market organization.' The view he refers to is one that stresses power and neglects the complexities of internal organizations and the striving towards efficiency of such organizations.

11.2 Buckley and Casson's long-run theory of the MNE

Peter Buckley and Mark Casson (1976) made use of Coase's internalization approach to arrive at 'A long-run theory of the multinational enterprise'. The basic assumption behind this approach is the existence of market imperfections, which generates benefits of internalization. Thus the approach is in line with other explanations of multinational activities based on market imperfections, such as those of Hymer and Kindleberger, Vernon, and Caves.

Buckley and Casson develop their long-run theory of the multinational enterprise by starting from the following simple postulates (p. 33):

1 'Firms maximise profit in a world of imperfect markets.
2 When markets in intermediate products are imperfect, there is an incentive to bypass them by creating internal markets. This involves bringing under common ownership and control the activities which are linked by the market.
3 Internalization of markets across national boundaries generates MNEs.'

The main groups of factors relevant to the internalization decision are the following:

1 Industry-specific factors related to the nature of the product and markets; they lead to the internalization of markets for intermediate products and thus to vertical integration.
2 Region-specific factors.
3 Nation-specific factors.
4 Firm-specific factors, which reflect the firm's ability to organize and manage efficiently internal markets.

The two most important areas of internalization are markets for intermediate products and markets for knowledge.

Before the Second World War the major factor that contributed to the emergence of MNEs was demand for primary products, leading to vertical integration across frontiers and to internalization of intermediate markets. Since the Second World War the major factor has been the growth in demand for knowledge-based products coupled with the difficulties of organizing efficient external markets for knowledge. Buckley and Casson stress one point already present in Caves's analysis (see chapter 10): the character of knowledge within the firm. They write: 'Knowledge is a public good within the firm' (p. 35), and thus its costs of transmission are low and it then becomes easily internationalized.[1] The growth of MNEs has also, according to Buckley and Casson, been made easier by the 'steady reduction in communication costs, and the increasing scope for tax reduction through transfer pricing' (p. 36).

Why do firms internalize? What are the limits to internalization? There are benefits of internalization and there are also costs; the balance between the two will determine the limit to internalization. The benefits of internalization stem from market imperfections, in particular from the following situations of market imperfections:

1   When there are long time lags between initiation and completion of the production process and, at the same time, future markets are non-existent or unsatisfactory.
2   When the efficient exploitation of market power over an intermediate product requires discriminatory pricing of a kind difficult or impossible to implement in an external market, though possible to implement internally.[2]
3   When imperfections would lead to bilateral concentration of market power and thus to an unstable situation under external markets.
4   When there is inequality in the position of buyer and seller regarding knowledge on the value, nature and quality of the product; the resultant buyer uncertainty may encourage forward integration.[3]
5   When there are imperfections deriving from government intervention in international markets such as the existence of *ad valorem* tariffs, restrictions on capital movements, discrepancies in rates of taxation.

In certain markets the incentive to internalize is particularly strong; this is the case of markets for knowledge. In fact R&D is a market showing all the above types of imperfections since it is characterized by:

● long implementation lags;
● monopoly power over results of R&D;
● the likelihood of the prospective purchase being a monopsonist and thus a sole buyer for the fruits of R&D;
● difficulty on the part of the buyer in assessing the true value and quality of the 'knowledge' to be acquired;
● an ideal situation for transfer prices manipulation since the price of the knowledge being transferred is difficult to assess.

The costs of internalization may derive from problems related to internal communication and organization. In the case of internalization across national boundaries there may also be costs due to discrimination against foreign producers by the governments of the host countries.

So much for internalization; how does this lead to a theory of the MNE? An MNE implies internalization across national boundaries. Buckley and Casson (1976) write on this issue:

> There is a special reason for believing that internalisation of the knowledge market will generate a high degree of multinationality among firms. Because knowledge is a public good which is easily transmitted across national boundaries, its exploitation is logically an international operation. (p. 45)

Buckley and Casson (p. 51) stress that their R&D concept is very broad and includes marketing-orientated R&D as well as technical R&D.

So the conclusions seem to be that imperfect markets generate incentives to internalize; the market for knowledge is highly imperfect, so there are strong benefits in internalizing it. Knowledge is a public good within the firm: this means that it can be used in various branches of the firm at little or no extra cost. Knowledge is easily transmittable across national boundaries, so transmission of knowledge will tend to generate internal markets across frontiers and therefore to generate MNEs. Another relevant conclusion of Buckley and Casson's analysis is that the characteristics of MNEs are not attributable to multinationality *per se* but rather to their internalization drive and to the fact that they operate in industries and markets where there are strong incentives to internalize (such as markets for knowledge and for intermediate products).

Buckley and Casson explain the post-Second World War pattern of FDI, in particular large cross-investment between developed countries, with reference to the market for knowledge and its internalization. Firms would tend to invest in countries where they can use and exploit their knowledge by adapting it to the countries where there are the necessary labour skills for the processing of that knowledge and where there are consumers who are sophisticated enough for the knowledge-based products.

11.3 Some comments

The internalization theory has proved very successful and indeed has led to the spread of the 'internalization–externalization' vocabulary, which is useful in itself. It is a very interesting approach which stresses efficiency as a primary motor in decision-making. However, the theory suffers from a number of problems. For a start the whole approach can be no more than a tautology: internalization is another way of expressing the fact that firms exist and grow, and hence it cannot be taken as an 'explanation' for the growth of the firm.[4]

Market imperfections are supposed to help break away from the tautology. However, at the level of very large firms it is not clear to what extent market imperfections lead to growth of firms or growth of firms leads to market imperfections: market imperfections cannot be taken as an exogenous variable when we are dealing with big corporations. It has already been mentioned that the market imperfections feature is shared with Hymer's approach; however, the 'internalization' theorists use it in a different way. For Hymer, market imperfections are an assumption and part of the environment in which MNEs operate, but also a creation of MNEs; MNEs aim to increase their market power and their level of control and in acting to achieve these aims they generate imperfections which then become endogenous to the real world and to the theory. In the basic internalization theory, imperfections are taken to be exogenously given. The conclusion that internalization is an efficient process and that MNEs are efficient allocators of resources can only hold if we take market imperfections to be exogenous: a clearly doubtful assumption given the size and power of MNEs.[5]

The main problem with the internalization approach is that, if the theory explains anything at all, it explains the growth of the firm in general, not why firms decide to take the multinational route in the course of their growth. Firms could, after all, internalize and grow at home and source foreign markets by exports: why do they choose to internalize by spreading activities in many countries? The purely multinational elements in this internalization approach seem rather weak (transfer pricing advantages and government regulations of transactions across frontiers).

Considerable relevance in the theory is given to R&D and to the fact that MNEs tend to operate in knowledge-based industries. The link between knowledge and multinationalization is located by Buckley and Casson in the fact that knowledge is easily, cheaply and risklessly transmittable internally but not externally. This makes it easy to transmit across frontiers internally but not externally to the firm. However, while this may explain why big firms prefer direct production to licensing in their foreign operations, it does not explain why they prefer to service foreign markets through international production rather than by exports and thus through domestic internalization. The overall lack of analysis of the full range of options open to large firms (domestic production and exports, international production, licensing) is one of the drawbacks of the theory.

Another serious drawback is the authors' failure to analyse multinationality *per se*; indeed they seem to deny that there are advantages of *multinationality per se* or that they play a role in shaping the characteristics of TNCs. This lack of a multinationality perspective stems from their strong concentration on internalization, from which it follows that internationalization is seen as a by-product of internalization. This outlook constrains their analysis and prevents them from realizing that the two issues of internalization and internationalization are not always part of the same package and, in particular, that internationalization cannot be simply viewed as an extension of the internalization process since there may be cases in which it should be viewed as a reaction to problems created by internalization.

The last serious drawback is the lack of analysis of labour and of the relationship between labour and capital. Coase's approach in terms of costs and benefits of internal transactions makes no specific reference to labour other than indirectly through a brief reference to 'variations in the supply price of factors of production to firms of different sizes' (p. 342). Since he was writing in 1937, his oversight may have been justified. However, in considering nowadays the costs and benefits of internalizing, it is not justified to overlook the effects that the firm's expansion has on labour.

Buckley and Casson point out that by concentrating on knowledge transmission within the firm they can explain FDI across developed countries and its increase in recent decades. Essentially firms look for locations where knowledge-based products can find the required sophisticated, high-income, consumer markets and the labour skills suitable for the processing of such products. It is not, however, fully clear in their approach why such large parts of FDI across countries are also intra-industry.

In conclusion I feel that the theory is not fully successful in explaining international production, partly because the 'efficiency' approach has put it in a straightjacket. Decisions about international production, whether related to the location or to the type of involvement, are strategic decisions; although efficiency elements may play a role, the strategic ones are more likely to be prominent. However, Buckley and Casson's approach has proved useful in giving a theoretical framework for analysing locational decisions and assessing them on the basis of efficiency.

12

Dunning's Eclectic Approach

12.1 The theory

John Dunning (1977) develops a 'systemic' theory to explain international economic involvement by various countries. He begins by considering the nature of a country's economic involvement with other countries. He analyses two types of involvement. The first is related to those economic activities that take place within the national boundaries – and thus use national resources – but concern goods and services directed towards foreign markets; similar are imports of resources and/or products from other countries. The second type of involvement is related to the activities of national economic agents that use resources located in a variety of countries to produce goods and services, in order to supply foreign markets. The first type of involvement falls within the domain of conventional international trade theory, the second within the domain of international production and foreign direct investment. Dunning's first perceptive insight is in realizing that these two activities must be seen as part of the same process and that any realistic theory of international economic involvement must attempt to explain them both. Essentially, in terms of a country's involvement, one has to explain *why* and *when* foreign markets are sourced through FDI and international production rather than domestic production and exports. In terms of a company's strategy one has to explain *why* it decides to produce abroad directly (rather than produce at home and export or rather than license to other enterprises) and *where* the FDI is likely to be directed.[1]

Dunning's approach consists of an attempt to analyse the *why* and *where* decisions in terms of *ownership*, *locational* and *internalization* advantages. Ownership advantages are those that are specific to a particular enterprise and that enable it to take advantage of investment opportunities abroad. Locational advantages are those advantages specific to a country which are likely to make it attractive for foreign investors. Internalization advantages are all those benefits that derive from internal markets and that allow firms to bypass external markets and the costs associated with them.

In some cases a country will have a locational advantage which will favour domestic production; in other cases its own enterprises will have special ownership advantages which will favour them in producing in other countries. 'Foreign production then, implies that location-specific endowments favour a foreign country, but ownership endowments favour the home country's firms' (p. 399).

In his 1980 article Dunning identifies three conditions for FDI to take place:

1 The enterprise concerned must possess 'net ownership advantages *vis-à-vis* firms of other nationalities in serving particular markets' (p. 275).
2 The enterprise must have benefits from internalizing the use of resources in which it has an advantage rather than selling them on external markets, e.g. via licensing.
3 The country where the FDI takes place must offer special locational advantages to be used in conjunction with those deriving from *ownership* and *internalization*.

Location specific advantages are external to the enterprise, while ownership-specific endowments are internal to it.

Dunning identifies three types of ownership advantages. The first type comprises standard advantages which any firm can have over another producing in the same location; they are benefits of (a) access to and usage of raw materials and markets, (b) size and (c) monopoly power. The second type of advantages which a branch of a national enterprise may have over a *new* enterprise relates to all those economies and benefits deriving from belonging to a larger pre-existing organization (cheaper inputs, knowledge of markets, R&D at zero or low marginal costs, etc.). The third type of advantages is that deriving from the multinationality of the enterprise; this means that a company operating in many countries is in a better position than a national firm to take advantage of different factor endowments and market situations.

A country's overall competitive situation depends not only on its locational advantages and on the ownership advantages of its enterprises, but also on 'the desire and ability of these enterprises to internalise the advantages resulting from this possession' (Dunning, 1977, p. 402). The incentive to internalize derives from the existence of market imperfections that confer special advantages to internal markets as opposed to external ones. The market imperfections generating advantages of internalization may be *structural* (such as barriers to competition) and *cognitive* (linked to imperfect knowledge on the part of the seller or buyer about products or processes). Public intervention is likely to increase market imperfections and thus is likely to lead to further internalization.

Lack of common policies among countries and, generally, lack of harmonization create incentives for internalization across frontiers (to take advantage of differential tax rates or expected movements in exchange rates). Dunning points out the interrelationship between ownership and internalization advantages by noting that internalization helps enterprises to acquire or increase those assets that give them an ownership advantage.

One question that Dunning asks is: 'given the ownership endowments, is the location of production by MNEs likely to be different from that of non MNEs?' (1977, p. 409). The answer is affirmative because the MNE is in a better position to exploit fully the advantages of internalization in many countries. Such advantages may derive from a full analysis and global resourcing of locations as well as from government intervention in the various countries. The same question is asked by Vernon (1974), who arrives at similar conclusions as was highlighted in chapter 8.

Dunning (1980) develops a detailed dynamic analysis of the effects of a country's *characteristics* on the ownership advantages of firms, on the tendency towards (and benefits deriving from) internalization and on the development of locational advantages.

The essence of the eclectic approach is in considering the advantages of ownership, location and internalization all together and in applying them to both international trade and production. This means that the approach can be seen more as a synthesis of other approaches that concentrate on trade or international production separately, on the possession of superior technology (for the explanation of either international trade or international production) or on imperfect market structures. For example, the distinctive feature of technology highlighted in Dunning's approach is not just the possession of superior technology but such possession (ownership advantages) combined with its internalization, which gives an advantage to foreign direct investment over licensing in the use of spare resources in knowledge and technology.

Dunning calls his theory *systemic* because 'it relates to the way in which the enterprise coordinates its activities' (1977, p. 406).

12.2 Some comments

Dunning develops the application of the 'market imperfections' line to the explanation of internationalization a step further than previous authors. He does so by attempting to interpret elements specific to firms together with elements related to the macroeconomy and with some elements related to market structures. This leads him not only to attempt to integrate micro and macro elements, but also to try to explain international trade and international production within the same analytical framework. This attempt constitutes a great strength of his theory. So does his dynamic approach, in which ownership, locational and internalization advantages interact with each other. Locational advantages and countries' differences may create incentives to internalize; at the same time internalization creates further ownership advantages. Curiously enough in this dynamic analysis of interrelationships, he seems to miss the possible effects of ownership advantages, particularly size and monopoly power, on the macroeconomy and thus on locational advantages. His analysis concentrates on the effects of the macroeconomy on enterprises but not vice versa; however, the 'vice versa' cases may be quite relevant when we consider very large and powerful enterprises. The effects of TNCs' activities on market structure and the macroeconomy have been considered by Cowling and Sugden (1987b) and their work is analysed in chapter 15.

By concentrating on countries' characteristics and their effects on ownership–location–internalization advantages, Dunning (1980) seems to conclude that 'countries with low labour costs and/or natural resources tend to have an above average inward investment because of their locational attractions, while rich industrialized countries have an above average outward direct investment, because their factor endowments favour mobile ownership advantages' (p. 288). However, this approach cannot explain the case of countries (especially the UK) that are heavily involved in both inward and outward FDI and the fact that the largest (and increasing) share of FDI is directed towards developed countries (besides, of course, originating mainly with developed countries).

The inclusion of locational advantages in his analysis allows Dunning to go a step further than Buckley and Casson in that it allows him to take into consideration the issue of exports versus foreign direct investment in the choice open to TNCs. Buckley and Casson's excessive concentration on internalization led them to see the dichotomy and choice only between internalization across frontiers via foreign direct investment and licensing. Unlike Buckley and Casson, Dunning explicitly considers advantages of multinationality *per se*, albeit briefly.

The theory does undoubtedly have some strong points which have made it very successful indeed; any conference on international business is, usually, likely to have at least a couple of papers using Dunning's taxonomic reference. It has certainly been successful in introducing the taxonomy of OLI (ownership, location, internalization) advantages. It is interesting, for example, that the latest UNCTC (1988) work on TNCs adopts both Dunning's eclectic scheme and terminology and the internalization ones.

The main doubt about this approach is whether it can go any further than a classificatory analysis. Dunning himself acknowledges the problem when he writes: 'In presenting the systemic theory, we accept we are in danger of being accused of eclectic taxonomy' (1977, p. 406). The danger is certainly there: in a nutshell the approach is helpful as a descriptive and classificatory device but much less so as an explanatory theory. The explanatory, and hence the forecasting, power of the theory is impaired not just by the concentration on taxonomy. The main problems are, in this writer's view, caused by the fact that the number of elements and variables emerging from the three OLI classes of advantages and used to 'explain' international involvement are very large and susceptible to endless addition. In his 1980 article Dunning lists at least 20 possible ownership advantages, at least 11 internalization incentives advantages and at least 16 location specific advantages; in each case the list can increase when sub-categories are considered.

Any *ex post* study of FDI is bound to find that it fits with at least some of the above characteristics; this means that the eclectic theory can always be applied without fear of falsification. However, in terms of scientific methodology this point, rather than constituting a strength, may be a major weakness. This is a point clearly and concisely made by Bukharin, as mentioned in chapter 3 section 3.6. Popper (1963) considers this issue at great length. He writes with reference to theories that 'appeared to be able to explain practically everything that happened within the field to which they referred' (p. 34): 'It was precisely this fact – that they always fitted, that they were always confirmed – which in the eyes of their admirers constituted the strongest argument in favour of these theories. It began to dawn on me that this apparent strength was in fact their weakness' (p. 35). Popper ends his section with the following: 'One can sum up all this by saying that *the criterion of the scientific status of a theory is its falsifiability, or refutability, or testability*' (p. 37).[2]

Section IV

Strategic Approaches

Human knowledge and human power meet in one; for where the cause is not known the effect cannot be produced.
Francis Bacon, *Aphorisms Concerning the Interpretation of Nature and the Kingdom of Man*. III.

Introduction to Section IV

Hymer's dissertation was seminal in the sense that many modern works on international production develop ideas which can, to a smaller or larger extent, be traced back to his work.

First is the idea of control over operations; this has recently and fruitfully been developed by Cowling and Sugden (1987b) as noted in chapter 1. The idea of the advantages of large TNCs is further and very well developed by Dunning under his ownership advantages rubric. One aspect of Hymer's thesis that has been relatively neglected is the issue of *strategy*. In Hymer's work international production is the result of firms' strategies towards competitors and markets.

A considerable amount of the literature on international production of the 1960s and 1970s concentrated on issues of efficiency rather than strategy. This has been unfortunate because, although efficiency issues are likely to be relevant, particularly in the short term, it is by looking at firms' overall long-term strategies that the real causes of internationalization are likely to be found.[1]

In the next three chapters we shall consider three works that look at international production as a result of strategic decisions. It is in the emphasis on strategies that the similarities between the three works lie, as well as the similarities between each of them and Hymer's work. Another similarity could be the fact that none of these works is fully developed.

In the first and third works (chapters 13 and 15) the strategies considered are mainly those towards rivals and the market; in this sense the theories presented in these two chapters address strategic issues similar to those of Hymer's dissertation. In the second work (chapter 14) the strategic elements emphasized are those towards labour. Thus the similarity with Hymer's work is in the strategic focus, not in the actual elements towards which the strategy is directed.

The three works presented here are not the only ones dealing with strategies.[2] The decision about which theories to include in this section was a difficult one, particularly since some of the works presented in section III contain fairly strong strategic elements, particularly Vernon's and Caves's works. The demarcation line between sections III and IV was drawn partly on the basis of the extent of strategic elements present in the theories, and partly on the basis of whether the theories would be considered 'prevalent' by the academic community involved in the study of internationalization.

An issue developed by Hymer in his later works (1970 and 1971) is that related to 'conflicts and contradictions', particularly conflicts generated by TNCs' activities and behaviour: conflicts with labour, conflicts between developed and developing countries, between managers in many countries, between different managerial layers, between rivals. My own work, presented in chapter 14, considers the 'conflicts' aspect with regard to labour. Chapter 15 presents Cowling and Sugden's theory, which deals with various types of conflicts, particularly conflicts between rivals, as well as conflicts between capital and labour.

13

Oligopolistic Reactions as an Explanation for Foreign Direct Investment

13.1 Knickerbocker's theory

In 1973 Frederick T. Knickerbocker published a book on a theory of foreign direct investment which was the outcome of his doctoral dissertation at the Harvard Business School.

His work consists of: (a) a theoretical 'informal' model containing the *a priori* reasons why certain firms' behaviour should lead to FDI and how such behaviour is linked to the market structure; (2) the testing of the model; and (3) conclusions regarding findings and expectations for the future. The *a priori* model should, in theory, be applicable to the behaviour of firms from any advanced Western country, although there are some possible restrictions (on which more below). However, the testing is done specifically for the USA. Twelve industries are considered and the source of the data is the 'Multinational Enterprise Study', a survey of international expansion by major firms, conducted between 1966 and 1971 at the Harvard Business School.[1]

The testing of the theory is done for the period since the Second World War. The study starts with three preliminary observations, which are confronted by the evidence contained in the source data: (a) in the post-Second World War period firms have tended to become more and more international; (b) firms in a number of US industries have tended to locate their outward foreign direct investment in the same countries; (c) firms involved in international expansion belong to industries characterized by oligopolistic structures.

Knickerbocker starts by defining FDI as the capital flow resulting from investment by an enterprise 'in assets outside its home country in order to control, partially or fully, the operation of these assets' (p. 2). He then defines as '*aggressive* investment' the establishment of the first subsidiary in a given industry and given country and as '*defensive* investment' the establishment of subsequent subsidiaries on completion of the first one.

Knickerbocker's empirical study is concerned mainly with defensive investment. Its aim is to find out the following: (a) whether the forces that induced aggressive and defensive behaviour were the same or whether defensive behaviour was influenced by forces additional to those that prompted the first move; (b) whether, in fact, defensive behaviour was induced by reaction to aggressive FDI; (c) why and how the pattern of defensive FDI varies according to industries and countries.

The author then goes on to develop his informal *a priori* model based on oligopolistic structures. The term oligopoly defines a structure characterized by: (a) few sellers; (b) products that are close substitutes; (c) 'substantial market interdependence among the competitive policies of these firms' (p. 4). The third characteristic means that oligopoly is defined in terms of both the market *structure* and the *behaviour* of firms. Although the term oligopoly should strictly refer to a market situation, economists often use it with reference to an industry; Knickerbocker uses it in both meanings.

In an oligopolistic structure the interdependence of firms means that their behaviour leads to a pattern of action and reaction, move and countermove, as in a game of chess. Each oligopolistic firm combines moves to improve its own position with moves to offset aggressive policies by its opponents. An aggressive move may be prompted by special opportunities to seize a market or new technologies or sources of raw materials. The advantage that the aggressor may gain in the long run could be highly detrimental to its rivals, who therefore have to react in order to minimize risks; such reactions lead to their defensive policies.

Firms are well aware that, in a situation of roughly equal strengths, aggressive moves are likely to lead to defensive ones and thus to the risk of mutually destructive competition. Since they all want to avoid this, the end result is the following: first, price warfare is avoided in favour of the more peaceful, market-enhancing competition via advertising; secondly, in industries that do not change or grow rapidly, the oligopolistic equilibria tend to be maintained and aggressive policies are unlikely to be used. The oligopolistic equilibrium is defined by Knickerbocker as a state of affairs among sellers such that, 'all rivals having roughly the same competitive capabilities, there is little reason for any one rival to expect that it can, with impunity, improve its market position at the expense of others' (p. 7).

In fast-growing industries, where technologies and markets change, individual firms may see very profitable opportunities deriving from aggressive behaviour that make it worthwhile to run the risk of defensive attacks by rivals; the oligopolistic equilibrium is, therefore, more likely to be disrupted in fast-changing, fast-growing industries. However, Knickerbocker himself is aware that oligopolistic reactions in themselves cannot explain why the first firm made the move and why the move took a particular form; in our case, why the move took the form of FDI. There is also the need to explain, within the same theoretical framework, divergences between different industries. Knickerbocker sees, therefore, the need to place his theory in a broader context that would allow him to explain why oligopolistic moves and countermoves take the specific form of FDI.

He sees the need to answer three sets of specific questions and to establish links between them. The questions relate to: the reasons why US manufacturing industries have extended their activities abroad; why the bulk of such activities have taken place in industries with oligopolistic structures; and why, under oligopolistic conditions, firms have tended to match each other's moves in FDI.

The fundamental inducement towards FDI is to be found in the analysis of the product cycle model. Vernon's model is at the basis of Knickerbocker's theory, and indeed Vernon was supervisor to Knickerbocker's thesis. The product life cycle theory tells us how the US economic environment created opportunities for a continuous stream of labour-saving, high-income products and generally for product development; how – to begin with – such products were more likely to be developed and produced at home rather than abroad. This meant that US producers developed special capabilities for: (a) developing a stream of new products and managing the organization of the related R&D needed; (b) producing these new products for large markets and managing the organization of production and the necessary continuous adaptation needed in the first stage of the life cycle; (c) selling new products by developing sophisticated marketing techniques and using them vigorously. They became skilled at 'pioneering' products. The development of special skills in such a variety of areas (production, R&D matching laboratory development with marketing skills and developments) is the direct result of the evolution of the economic environment of the USA; the end result is that this process has given US firms an advantage over foreign firms, who could not match such skills and capabilities. European markets and economies lagged behind those of the USA ones. However, after a few years, Europe was ready to receive the labour-saving, high-income products. Exports of US products were followed by FDI, which, in some cases, was preceded by licensing.

US firms had disadvantages in producing abroad deriving from the foreign environment, from less preferential treatment by governments compared with domestic firms, from difficulties and costs of gathering information etc. However, the great advantage they had in the accumulated knowledge of managerial, marketing and organizational skills, combined with the lower costs of inputs in European countries, meant that US firms had an overall advantage over domestic European enterprises.

'In a few words, U.S. product pioneers stormed foreign markets with competitive weapons forged at home' (p. 17). Other circumstances may also have pushed US firms towards FDI rather than exporting or licensing. Knickerbocker mentions, in particular, the existence of tariff and non-tariff barriers in European countries, and the fact that producing near the market allowed firms to offer after-sales services and to adapt the product to the requirements of local customers. However, these circumstances acted only in a subsidiary role; Knickerbocker's conclusion is, in fact, that for foreign direct investment 'the product cycle model suggests that the fundamental consideration underlying such undertaking has been the desire of U.S. businessmen to exploit overseas the novel skills that their firms acquired in the course of satisfying U.S. demand' (p. 18).

There is a link between product pioneering, and therefore the product life cycle, and oligopolistic structures. Firms that operate in fast-changing industries and are therefore involved in new products and new developments are also likely to experience various advantages. These advantages will, in the long run, lead to few producers and sellers as scale economies eliminate smaller producers and act as entry barriers to new ones.[2] The advantages are due to scale economies but also to the special skills accumulated in the course of developing and managing new products, their production and marketing. These skills help in both the domestic and foreign environments. 'The nub of the case being made here is that the special technological and organizational capabilities acquired by these firms first invested them with market power at home and, at a later date, invested them with market power abroad' (p. 20).

So, in a nutshell, the product life cycle can explain why the first firm pioneer in a product will want to expand its activities abroad via FDI; the forces that lead to the development of new products will lead to an oligopolistic structure at home and to the search for FDI opportunities abroad. What now remains to be explained is why rivals follow the move of the first firm and engage in defensive foreign investment, thus leading to a 'bandwagon effect' and to an overall pattern of FDI that exhibits 'bunching up' in terms of countries, industries and timing.

Investment in a foreign country involves a considerable amount of uncertainty; this is particularly so for the product-pioneering firm that is launching a new product, is using new technologies and is moving into a new country. However, the firm learns with each move and improves its abilities to scan the world and reduce uncertainties. A rival firm also faces uncertainties in investing abroad. However, it faces risks if it does not invest: the risk that the rival firm would gain considerable advantages from its aggressive move and then use the advantages against its rivals.

For businessmen, countering was a form of insurance. The premium firms paid to insure the perpetuation of the competitive balance was the cost involved in making a matching move. One reason firms were prepared to pay the premium was that its costs tended to go down since the marginal costs of each additional step into the international market place tended to go down. But the fundamental reason for paying the premium was that its costs were at least partially predictable whereas the costs to a firm, if it did not counter the moves of a rival, were often unpredictable and could, very possibly, far exceed those of countering. (Knickerbocker, 1973, pp. 25–6).

The advantages the first firm – which makes the aggressive move – could gain are in production or marketing or both. Advantages of large-scale production, of the use of new productive process, of vertical integration and general access to cheaper inputs, can all result in cost reductions. Similarly, marketing abroad can give advantages to a firm in both the international and the home markets. The further organizational, managerial and marketing skills acquired from the first move can then be used for further aggressive policies. All these advantages acquired – whether in the production or marketing or management areas – can then be used to change the competitive equilibrium and gradually eliminate rivals. The other firms want to avoid such risks and that is why they follow up with their own foreign investment. Ultimately, therefore, Knickerbocker explains the *bunching up* of FDI as the result of firms' *defensive policies*, which are designed to minimize *risks* in an *oligopolistic environment*.

Kickerbocker claims that his empirical findings support his informal model. Entry into certain foreign markets has tended to be concentrated in peak years. Entry concentration appears to be positively related to industry concentration; this means that firms pursued a more active defensive policy on foreign investment in industries with high sellers' concentration than in industries with low sellers' concentration.

Firms involved in narrow product-lines have tended to respond with defensive foreign investments more readily than firms dealing in wide product-lines. This is explained by Knickerbocker on the basis that firms involved in many products have wider defensive strategic choices.

Leaders in each industry, i.e. those firms 'that react swiftly to one another's moves, tend to ignore scale considerations when they invest abroad' (p. 195). Followers have tended to give more consideration to scale. 'The profitability of overseas manufacturing industries is positively related to entry concentration' (p. 195). Causation here could, however, go both ways, as Knickerbocker points out: high profitability could lead to high entry concentration or vice versa. On the whole the clustering behaviour varies between industries and markets: in some industries it has occurred more than in others, in some countries more than in others.

13.2 Some critical comments

Knickerbocker's theory is very interesting. It puts right at the centre of analysis a realistic oligopolistic structure in which the agents of international business operate. It attempts to deal with uncertainty and risk – indeed risk avoidance is the essential determinant of the clustering of FDI. It is dynamic, as it is all about reactions and counter-reactions, changes in the oligopolistic balance, the devising of strategies. However, a close look at Knickerbocker's analysis leaves us with the uneasy feeling that, although the work is a very good start, as the author himself stresses his theory does not explain the first move: why firms choose FDI as an aggressive policy. Knickerbocker's main concern is with explaining 'bunching-up' and he does this with reference to risk avoidance strategies. However, risk is difficult to quantify and risk avoidance difficult or imposs- ible to assess: a point already stressed by Hymer (1960) in his critique of the neo-classical theory of foreign investment and its emphasis on risk, as highlighted in chapter 6.

Knickerbocker brings to our attention, and gives systematic quantifi- cation to, the tendency towards clustering of FDI and the relationship between entry concentration and sellers' concentration and their industry differences. This in itself is very useful, although there may be doubts about the degree of corroboration these findings offer to the theory.

Knickerbocker's theory takes Vernon's (1966) product life cycle as its starting point. However, Vernon himself has, to a considerable extent, repudiated his first theory in his 1979 article. The product life cycle approach to FDI is linked to bunching-up, in that they are both the expression of oligopolistic behaviour and aim to explain the first, aggress- ive move, via Vernon's theory, and the following defensive FDI, by Knickerbocker's theory. We might be led to conclude that a rejection or reassessment of the product life cycle approach to FDI might bring the same fate to Knickerbocker's theory. However, I am inclined to think that Knickerbocker's theory might still hold because it is a theory of bunching-up only. A necessary condition for the theory to hold is the existence of an oligopolistic structure; there is no doubt that such a structure is present both in the real economic world and in Knicker- bocker's model. It is the behaviour of oligopolistic rivals that leads to the clustering of FDI, independently of whether the oligopolistic structure is or is not linked to the product life cycle. In effect Knickerbocker explains bunching-up independently of the product life cycle and therefore his theory could, in principle, be accepted even if one rejects Vernon's theory. There is another advantage in 'decoupling' Knickerbocker's theory from Vernon's: the product life cycle theory is strictly applicable to the USA in a particular historical period; the changed environment in Europe has thrown doubts on its wider applicability to the USA and Europe. Knickerbocker's theory is not linked very closely to the US conditions but only to the existence of oligopolistic structures; this means that the part of Knickerbocker's theory that is independent of the product life cycle (the bunching-up) has a more general applicability than Vernon's theory. However, as already explained, it is here felt that the risk minimization explanation, though interesting, is not fully satisfactory as an explanation of the clustering pattern of FDI.

There is another point that might be worth raising with regard to Knickerbocker's analysis. He rightly stresses the role of moves and countermoves in oligopolistic strategies; however, he then confines himself to moves and countermoves *within* FDI. In reality firms' strategies can have many dimensions and relate to issues such as strategies towards development and use of technology, towards diversification, towards production in other countries, towards sourcing markets in other countries, towards vertical integration, towards labour, towards the supply of components (internal production or acquisition through market transactions or mixed strategy via sub-contracting), towards cooperation with other firms (licensing, joint ventures), towards expansion (greenfield plants or acquisitions) and so on. A move towards FDI by one firm could involve a chain of events different from that envisaged by Knickerbocker. First, rivals could react by implementing countervailing strategies, not necessarily in terms of FDI but in terms of other variables and dimensions; for example, in reaction to firm A's investment in country X, firm B could buy up a source of raw materials to acquire a countervailing advantage. This move might make sense because as firm A's resources are engaged in producing its product(s) abroad, it is less likely to be able to invest in raw materials as well; it would also give B a counterbalancing advantage without the risk of excessive competition in the country where A has invested. Knickerbocker briefly touches on this point when he mentions a possible divergence in strategies between firms involved in narrow or wide product-lines. Wide product-lines offer firms opportunities for a variety of strategies and hence lead to lower levels of clustering; however, Knickerbocker seems to overlook the fact that other aspects of firms' activities also give scope for a variety of strategies. Secondly, in a world of many possible strategies and a fairly continuous sequence of moves and countermoves, it is difficult to distinguish between aggressive and defensive behaviour; firm A may be the first to invest in country X but this move may have been induced as a defence against other firms' strategies in technology, in sub-contracting, towards labour or in terms of moving into new product lines.

Essentially what I am saying is that aggressive and defensive moves cannot be seen and assessed in isolation within a single type of strategy, but must be seen in the context of multi-strategic behaviour by oligopolistic firms.

The end result is that Knickerbocker's theory cannot be used to predict the behaviour of firms and the pattern of FDI in various countries and industries, essentially for two reasons.[3] First, its emphasis on risk makes it difficult to quantify the variables; secondly, there is a possibility that firms use a variety of strategies and can move into a country via FDI for a variety of reasons. The continuous spread of transnational activities, in terms of countries, industries, sectors, types of activities and contractual arrangements (sub-contracting, joint ventures, licensing, etc.), gives wider and wider scope for different strategies and hence for behavioural patterns that move away from the narrow field envisaged by Knickerbocker.

The stress on oligopolistic structures and reactions is the strongest point in Knickerbocker's approach. It is interesting that just after the publication of this work, Vernon (1974) produced an adaptation of his product life cycle to explicit oligopolistic conditions.

There are also analogies between Caves's (1971) analysis and Knickerbocker's.[4] In both cases firms may invest abroad in order to utilize spare capacity in 'intangible' assets in organizational, managerial and marketing areas; these assets are 'public goods' within the firm and can be used abroad at little cost for the firm as a whole. This point of the analysis is applied by Knickerbocker to the first firm that invests abroad: the product pioneering one that acquires a variety of skills, including technological skills, in the course of developing, producing and marketing a new product. In Knickerbocker's analysis there is a certain emphasis on marketing, though much less pronounced than in Caves's analysis. Both Knickerbocker and Caves stress uncertainty and oligopolistic structures. However, in spite of these similarities between the theories of these two authors, the main thrust of the argument is different: Caves stresses efficiency and the minimization of transaction costs as a motive for FDI; Knickerbocker stresses the strategic objectives *vis-à-vis* rivals, whether FDI is done for offensive or defensive reasons.

14

Transnational Corporations and Strategies towards Labour

14.1 Background

In chapter 2 we considered various trends in internationalization. One of the striking features – which is also one of the less known ones in the popular or semi-popular view of internationalization – is the extent of TNCs' involvement in developed countries (section 2.1, point 3). Other very relevant, and perhaps surprising, features are the extent of involvement in both inward and outward FDI by many DMEs, and the related large amounts of intra-industry FDI (section 2.1, points 2 and 5). All these are also points that are difficult to explain by a conventional, comparative advantage type of theory.

The reason they are difficult to explain is that insufficient weight has been given by the standard literature on international production to strategic elements in the internationalization decision and in particular to strategic elements towards labour. Some Marxist writers have emphasized labour relations and strategic elements towards labour, but usually with regard to the exploitation of labour in LDCs; thus the location of production in LDCs has been given paramount attention and the aim of such location has been seen to be the pursuit of low wages and low costs of production.[1] However, as the largest, and an increasing, share of FDI not only originates with TNCs located in AICs but is also located in other AICs rather than in LDCs, any theory that predicts large and increasing involvement in LDCs is in difficulty.

I feel that labour is a crucial strategic element in the internationalization decision. However, strategies towards labour are not related just to comparative wage levels and indeed wages are only one of the elements of labour costs;[2] other elements (for example, productivity or employment subsidies) affect unit costs. Besides, there are other long-term elements that enter only indirectly in the determination of costs but that are essential to long-term strategic decisions, such as the location of production. Among such elements are the overall power of unions, not only with regard to wages and costs but also with regard to such elements as flexibility of contracts and conditions of work in general.

The argument is developed here by stressing two strategic factors: the fragmentation and externalization of labour.[3]

14.2 Internalization, multinationalization and labour

The problem of looking for explanations of the growth and pattern of international production is approached by asking the following questions:

1 Are there problems created by further and further internalization at home that are not present, or are attenuated, by internalization in a multi-country context?
2 Conversely, are there specific advantages and benefits to be gained by internalizing in a multi-country context that are not to be found within domestic internalization?

The answer to both these questions is affirmative. In developing the arguments leading to such answers, the focus is on globality, multinationality and geographical spread of activities as key elements rather than on nationality of the investor, direction of the FDI flow or characteristics of specific locations.

As the firm grows and more and more resources are allocated through internal transactions there is – *ceteris paribus* – also an increase in the labour force employed internally by the firm. Such an increase has also led – historically – to an easier internal organization of labour, with resulting stronger unions. The outcome for the expanding firm has often been higher costs, deriving not just from wages but also – and in some cases mainly – from the ability of unions to extract more favourable conditions of service and more permanent positions for their members.

As part of the internalization process, capital has, therefore, had clear benefits but it has also, gradually, come to be confronted by a stronger and, often, more militant labour force whose strength was achieved to a large extent because of this internalization process. I therefore see the main problems created for capital by internalization at home as lying in the opportunity for labour to organize itself better when working within the same national and ownership context.

Transnationalization can then be seen as an attempt, on the part of capital, to retain the advantages of internalization while avoiding the problems it creates in the sphere of labour conflicts. This is achieved, essentially, because transnationalization of production generates a situation in which labour – although working under the same ownership umbrella – is more dispersed and fragmented and thus finds it more difficult to organize itself, compared with a situation in which internalization takes place in the domestic environment, whether within the same plant or on a multi-plant basis. This process is linked to the application of new electronic technology to the planning and controlling of the production process, as discussed in chapter 1.

In a discussion of the problems and technological conditions of neo-Fordism, Aglietta (1976) touches, among other things, on two important issues: the new division of the production process and its relationship to geographical decentralization, and the related effects on the balance of class forces.

> Automatic production control divides up the production processes in a new way, linked on the one hand to a centralization that permits direct control of production by long-distance transmission of information, and on the other hand to a rearrangement of the segments of a complex labour process to allow for important savings in transfer time, quality control and the preparation of production programmes. A far more advanced centralization of production becomes compatible with a geographical decentralization of the operative units (manufacture and assembly). . . . The capitalist class can benefit from this in two ways. On the one hand, a far greater flexibility in the installation of production units allows it to break up large working-class concentrations and create an environment that minimizes convergence of struggles at the point of production. (Aglietta, 1976, p. 127)

The advantages of multinationalization *vis-à-vis* labour can be looked at from a micro and a macro point of view. From a micro point of view the single company retains the advantage of organizing and controlling production worldwide while facing a more fragmented and less well organized labour force. From the macro point of view, for any one particular country, we can compare (a) the situation arising out of expansion of production via domestic internalization on the part of existing domestic firms, against (b) the case in which the expansion of production occurs – partly or mainly – through the inward foreign direct investment by foreign TNCs. In the case (a) the internalization process corresponds with an expansion of labour employed by existing firms, and hence with a situation in which a larger section of the labour force finds itself under the same ownership or management umbrella. In the case (b) the increase in employment by large firms takes place under different ownership or management and, in particular, under foreign management. From the point of view of the overall strength and organization of labour in any particular country, case (b) leads to a weaker position for labour than case (a), for the following reasons:

1   Trade union links are very strong, nationally, within the same company even if plants are spread over many sites; links are, however, rather weak between different companies, let alone countries. This means that, within a particular national context, union power is greater when labour is under the same ownership or management umbrella than when it is working for different companies, particularly when one of them is a foreign newcomer.
2   There is less or no initial struggle over new technology: the foreign newcomer usually arrives with a given technology; in the long-established firm the new technology has to be negotiated with existing unions.
3   Very often union practices are part and parcel of the initial agreements, in a 'take it or leave it' situation.

While recognizing that labour militancy does not depend just on internalization and size of firms, I feel that, on the whole, the geographical dispersion and the ownership and nationality fragmentation of production put labour in a weaker position *vis-à-vis* capital.

In summary, the view put forward here is that the expansion and pattern of international production, far from being explained by internalization, can, to a considerable extent, be explained as a reaction to, and an attempt to minimize, the problems created by internalization in the sphere of labour conflicts.

There are many advantages for TNCs in investing in developed countries. They derive from proximity to markets and avoidance of protectionist measures, to the availability of a skilled labour force, infrastructure, research facilities, and so on. There are also serious problems related to labour that might have pushed international production more towards LDCs. However, by following a strategy of fragmentation and geographical spread of production, TNCs have managed to attenuate the problems, thus accentuating the trend towards location in developed countries, albeit in a more spread out form.

Undoubtedly, other variables play a very important role in the explanation of the growth and pattern of FDI. However, focusing on the labour fragmentation effects of multinationality helps towards explaining the geographical and sectoral pattern of foreign direct investment.

14.3   The externalization of labour

The geographical fragmentation of production through increased multinationalization is – according to the approach presented in section 14.2 –
one of the reactions of capital to the increasing power of organized labour.
It is not, however, the only reaction and strategy. Other developments in
international capitalism can be considered as part of the same trend and
general strategy: the segmentation of labour with a view to weakening its
power.

In section 2.1, point 9, stress was laid on the tendency towards increased
non-equity involvement by TNCs, in particular via licensing and sub-
contracting. Recent trends towards increases in sub-contracting arrangements, homework and putting-out must be seen as a response on the part
of big capital to the growing pressures of organized labour that have
resulted, to a large extent, from the internalization developed in the past
few decades. Large firms are indeed more likely to contract out than
small ones.[4] For capital, sub-contracting is basically a way of *externalizing*
labour costs and risks while internalizing products, technology, revenues
and the control of production in general. Sub-contracting thus helps to
remove – for big capital – the labour constraint to further expansion.[5]

There are many advantages, for capital, in externalizing labour via sub-
contracting arrangements. The sub-contractors are often small units that
are geographically dispersed; their small size makes it difficult for labour
to achieve internal organization within each unit. At the same time, the
ownership and geographical dispersion makes the organization of labour
between various units very difficult. Sub-contracting can take place at the
national or international level and, hence, the geographical dispersion can
in some cases be very large indeed. In relation to sub-contracting in the
motor industry, Friedman (1977, p. 120) writes:

> The major advantage of maintaining sub-contracting relations with these
> relatively inefficient firms appears to be lower wages which these smaller
> firms pay their workers. Evidence from various sources suggests that the
> differential is in the order of 25 per cent to 50 per cent. . . . This is primarily
> because worker organisation is much weaker in the small supplier firms.

Solinas (1982) gives evidence on a similar increase in the decentralization
of production in the Italian knitwear industry, and on the issue of weaker
labour organization in smaller units than in larger enterprises. He writes
on this last point:

> In the smaller enterprises the picture is totally different: most have no shop-
> floor union organisation, the legislation against unfair dismissal offers no
> protection in firms engaging less than fifteen persons, and workers are laid

off at the first signs of a crisis. In many instances agreements between individual worker and the employer take precedence over collective contract, welfare norms are evaded, and variations in the workload and in working hours occur more frequently than in larger firms. The homeworking sector is even less well protected. (p. 334)

The advantages for big firms of sub-contracting are not just in costs. Many authors have stressed the advantages for capital of 'flexibility'.[6] The flexibility can be *vis-à-vis* laying off the labour force or choosing sub-contractors and switching from one to the other, or *vis-à-vis* the trade cycle.[7] 'Cyclical flexibility' means, of course, that big firms even out fluctuations in output and employment by passing on the fluctuations to smaller units in the advanced countries or in less developed countries (whenever international sub-contracting takes place in LDCs). The other advantage for large corporations is the low capital risk; this is particularly relevant in the case of international sub-contracting. Michalet (1980, p. 59) explains this particular issue very clearly in the following passage:

By expanding international sub-contracting, firms can avoid having to make more investments abroad or to increase the size of existing facilities without forgoing the opportunities offered by growing markets. In more specific terms, the volume of capital exposed to the risk of asset-freezing or, worse still, of nationalisation is limited to a relatively negligible amount, while the profit-earning capacity remains unaffected.

'Flexibility' is not, of course, given only by sub-contracting. Any contractual arrangements designed to create core–periphery elements in the labour force are likely to weaken the power of labour; the core–periphery structure with regard to labour can refer to contractual arrangements (full-time, permanent versus part-time, temporary contracts) or to the location and the industry (workforce in core locations and/or industries versus workforce employed in areas and/or industries of high unemployment). Unlike periphery workers, core workers are usually in a strong position in negotiations for pay and conditions of service. Core-periphery elements and the related creation of dualism can also be detected within capital itself: the strong core of powerful firms surrounded – and indeed often creating and controlling – large numbers of small, weak units subject to bankruptcies.

There is a very considerable amount of literature on the core–periphery issue, with doubts being cast on its existence, its extent and its usefulness as an analytical scheme.[8] Without getting involved in this debate, the point to be made here is the following. Capitalist economies have been moving towards greater segmentation of labour, which is being achieved via multinationalization of production, via externalization of labour (through sub-contracting arrangements) and via the introduction of some 'flexibility' elements in contractual arrangements.

The increase in sub-contracting and similar arrangements designed to externalize the allocation of labour undoubtedly creates different problems for capital. Among such problems are less stability, difficulties of coordination and quality control.[9] However, the advantages deriving from externalizing labour transactions far outweigh these disadvantages and should be considered as the prime mover for the recent increase in sub-contracting. These advantages are both micro – for the individual big firms – and macro: the overall level of union organization, militancy and related conflicts, in any particular country, may diminish as labour becomes, *ceteris paribus*, more fragmented geographically and structurally. The geographical fragmentation is achieved through international production; the structural fragmentation is achieved through the allocation of labour to a combination of large and small productive units.

In summary, the growth and pattern of international production and the growth of sub-contracting arrangements can, to some extent, be explained as reactions on the part of capital to the problems created, in relation to labour, by internalization. These are spontaneous strategies on the part of capital and are directed towards the fragmentation and segmentation of the workforce. Such fragmentation is taking place in a number of ways:

1   Via geographical dispersion of production. Geographical dispersion weakens labour because, while capital has been able to plan and organize the control of production over many countries, labour has been, so far, unable to counteract this trend with multi-country organization.[10]

2   Via ownership dispersion within the same country. The activities of many firms within the same sector render labour organization and solidarity weaker, compared with a situation where, *ceteris paribus*, labour is employed by a few companies.

3   Via structural dispersion; this is a by-product of the trend towards externalizing labour risks and costs via sub-contracting and similar arrangements.

14.4   Conclusions

This chapter has stressed strategic elements in decisions about the internationalization, location and organization of production by TNCs. The strategies emphasized are mainly those towards organized labour; the results are geographical and structural fragmentation of labour with production spread in many countries and increasingly allocated to sub-contractors. The increasing involvement of sub-contractors means that big corporations manage to achieve 'externalization' of labour, their most problematic factor.

This externalization of labour and its geographical fragmentation, via the location of production in many countries, is achieved by TNCs while they retain control over production. This has been possible through the widespread use of high technology, as argued in chapters 1 and 2.

The emphasis on strategies of fragmentation and externalization helps to explain some of the more puzzling elements in the internationalization trends and their combined presence; in particular it helps to explain:

- the large and increasing share of FDI going to DMEs;
- the fact that some developed countries are both host and originator of FDI and that this trend is increasing;
- the growth of intra-industry FDI;
- the apparent increased geographical spread of the network of TNCs;
- the increase in non-equity forms of involvement by TNCs, and in particular sub-contracting.

Although it is felt that consideration of strategic elements is of vital importance in looking for explanations of international production, it is not here claimed that the strategy towards labour is the only relevant element to be considered. Other strategic elements are found to be relevant as well. For example, the increasing political instability and uncertainties in the Third World may have contributed to the desire on the part of TNCs to avoid increasing commitments in them. At the same time, the growing potential markets in AICs may have acted as a pull towards investing in them. The question then is: how can growing shares of investments be directed towards AICs while mitigating the problems related to the increasing power of labour? Geographical and structural fragmentation of labour seems to have been the answer. Strategies towards rivals may also, of course, play a part. Similarly, efficiency and strategy should not be seen as opposite poles; on the contrary, appropriate strategies are likely to lead to higher long-term efficiency. It should also be remembered that the relationship between international production and labour is very complex and likely to involve causes and effects going both ways. Labour strength, militancy and conflicts are likely to have an effect on the location of production, on technology and product design, on the emergence and spread of new arrangements between big capital and small productive units. These developments lead to geographical, ownership and structural dispersion of production which, in turn, has profound effects on labour organization and strength.

15

Transnational Monopoly Capitalism

15.1 Cowling and Sugden's approach

Keith Cowling and Roger Sugden (1987b) start their analysis with a definition of firms and TNCs based on control rather than legal ownership of assets (see section 1.4). They then argue that the profit maximization objective of firms rules out a perfectly competitive environment; the contradiction between this objective and the assumption of perfect competition is obvious as:

> . . . firms in perfectly competitive markets merely achieve normal profits, which they will undoubtedly find unsatisfactory. Clearly, then, they will attempt to avoid such competition; i.e. they will try to dominate product markets and, in the extreme, obtain pure monopoly profits. Moreover if they succeed the competition view is misplaced. (p. 17)

Cowling and Sugden therefore start by placing TNCs firmly in a realistic oligopolistic framework in which collusion and rivalry coexist (see also Cowling, 1982). Rivalry means that firms must be in a position to both '*defend* against rivals (i.e. prevent others gaining profits at their expense) . . . and *attack* (i.e. improve their profits to the detriment of rivals' (Cowling and Sugden, 1987b, p. 18); in this game the existence of retaliatory power becomes crucial. Firms will seek strategies that give them high retaliatory power; in fact they can use their worldwide production and resources to retaliate against a given rival. The end result is that 'firms will become transnationals to pursue profits in a rivalry and collusion environment, an environment which follows from the profit maximising assumption' (p. 21).

TNCs have great *detection* power because of their ability to collect, process and use information to their advantage; this helps them to secure high price–cost margins and high monopoly power. The desire to monopolize markets leads to transnationalization and, similarly, transnationalism leads to more and more monopolization; here Cowling and Sugden point out how the presence of both foreign and domestic TNCs in a particular country increases monopolization.[1]

Firms become transnational 'either because of the risks which lead them to defend against rivals, or because of the advantages which cause them to attack' (p. 61). One way of defending themselves against attacks from rivals is to secure lower labour costs. Hence transnationalism is linked to the search for cheaper labour and for a divided labour force – therefore for a labour force with less bargaining power.

There are clearly some analogies between this part of Cowling and Sugden's work (1987b, chapter 4) and the views presented in chapter 14 here.[2] However, there are also differences. Cowling and Sugden's analysis mainly stresses strategies towards rivals and sees the 'divide and rule' strategy as a by-product of the search for advantages over rivals, while in chapter 14 we saw labour as the main focal point of TNCs strategies. Cowling and Sugden, by focusing primarily on cost-cutting, are led to emphasize the location of TNCs' activities in LDCs. They write: 'In short, then, our analysis leads to the so-called "new international division of labour"' (p. 69). However, as already pointed out in various parts of this book, although it is true that some manufacturing does take place in LDCs it is also true that by far the largest share of FDI is directed towards DMEs and that this share has been increasing. Thus the emphasis on the location of manufacturing in LDCs is not the strategic relevant factor; the relevant strategy seems to be location in many countries, both developed and less developed, with a view to fragmenting the labour force.

Cowling and Sugden dismiss the claim that the divide and rule hypothesis is untenable – as claimed by many economists – because, after all, 'transnationals appear to pay wages at least as high as their rivals and they therefore cannot be founded on a division of the workforce to lower labour costs' (p. 70). They point out various fallacies in this argument, including the fact that wages are only one element in labour costs.

Cowling and Sugden see an increase in monopolization owing to the presence and the overall activities of TNCs for the following reasons:

- international trade does not act as a competitive element in a particular country (e.g. the UK) because trade itself is controlled by TNCs;
- the power structure is moving more in the direction of capital and away from labour;
- transnationalism is spreading throughout the world in both advanced and less developed countries;
- the increase in the number of small and medium-size firms cannot be

seen as a move towards a more competitive environment as many such firms are controlled by large TNCs; this is a point in their analysis that was examined in chapter 1.

Cowling and Sugden see the effects of these trends manifesting in the following:

1   A tendency towards stagnation as a high degree of monopoly leads to a lack of effective demand; this argument follows Baran and Sweezy (1966b), Kalecki and Steindl as well as Cowling's previous work (1982). In this last work the links between the degree of monopoly, under-utilization of capacity, lack of effective demand, and the gap between potential and actual profits, all leading to long-term stagnation, are spelt out in detail by Cowling.
2   This lack of effective demand may also lead to low *actual* profits in spite of the high *potential* profits that monopolization could generate.
3   De-industrialization in some advanced countries is not necessarily followed by industrialization and growth in less developed ones. Relocation strategies by TNCs result in a negative-sum game; this is because 'the allocation of production and investment is not guided primarily by questions of efficiency' (p. 98) but is motivated by issues of control over production, the labour process and distribution.
4   Distribution away from labour and related curtailment of the power of unions will further strengthen the stagnationist tendencies.
5   At the same time demand management policies aimed at full employment will become less effective, given the presence of corporations operating transnationally.

While recognizing that TNCs are innovative institutions, Cowling and Sugden express doubts about the directions and use of innovation. If the innovation is in products, TNCs will use the advantage to achieve further monopolization leading to further stagnationist tendencies. If the innovation is in processes, it is used to control the work process and to push down wages, again leading to curtailment in aggregate demand and hence to stagnation.

Cowling and Sugden see the solution in a higher level of democracy and participation as well as in state intervention designed to achieve coordination between various industries and sectors. The overall result will be a higher level of control of TNCs, avoidance of the problems connected with transnational capitalism, including the stagnationist tendency, and a higher level of efficiency partly enhanced by a higher level of participation.

15.2 Some comments

There are some very good points and insights in Cowling and Sugden's analysis, in particular:

1 The novel view of the firm based on 'control'.
2 The development of a theory of transnational capital based on strategic decisions and thus a move away from the restricting framework of advantages and efficient markets. Their strategic approach, though related mainly to market power and strategies towards rivals, is quite different from, and indeed much more developed and sophisticated than, either Hymer's or Knickerbocker's analysis.[3]
3 The incorporation of labour issues within the overall framework of strategies towards rivals and market power.
4 The attempt at merging together macro and micro elements through the links between monopoly power, degree of monopoly and macro analysis.[4]

However, Cowling and Sugden's work is not without problems. The all-embracing approach, though interesting in many parts, leads to superficiality in some chapters, particularly those dealing with de-industrialization, democratic processes and policy recommendations.

That further monopolization in the system may lead to stagnationist tendencies is a thesis already worked out in previous literature, including Cowling's own (1982). However, the case for claiming a growing degree of monopolization owing to TNCs is not corroborated.[5] Transnationalism has certainly increased but does this lead automatically to increased monopoly power? Cowling and Sugden's case rests mainly on the high 'detection' power possessed by TNCs and their use in defence and attack towards rivals. However, high detection power is, to a large extent, connected to progress in the technology of communications and data analysis (considered in chapter 1) and to some extent many firms have benefited from it; we have, in fact, witnessed an increase in small and medium-sized TNCs. Why should detection power lead to a higher degree of monopoly when all firms have access to new technologies and presumably all large corporations have high and increasing detection power?

The extra contradictions and conflicts come not so much between corporations, because after all most of them have access to technology giving detection power and all of them are increasingly planning on a transnational basis. The main contradictions and conflicts are likely to be between institutions that are truly transnational (TNCs) in their planning, strategies and operations, and institutions or groups that, by their own nature and for historical and other reasons, cannot rely on a transnational infrastructure, such as trade unions, consumers and governments. It is over these institutions that TNCs have particular advantages, and they can use their global scanning, detection power and all other sources of power to further their advantage. It is not here maintained that issues of market power and strategies towards rivals are not relevant, but that it is in the contrast between the power of transnationalism and the power of non-transnational institutions that we are likely to see major contradictions and conflicts; it is in order to turn this contrast to their maximum advantage that TNCs use strategic planning.

Besides, the focus on market power, by emphasizing market relations, distracts attention from the main area of planning, which is production and its processes. For all these reasons it is here felt that a stress on strategies towards labour should be at the forefront of any analysis of transnational activities.

Conclusions on Part II

Marxist and non-Marxist approaches to economics tend to be non-commensurable paradigms. There is no reason, in principle, for the non-commensurability, as each theory could be assessed for its explicative and predictive power. None the less, in practice the two paradigms tend to be kept separate in a variety of ways: the concepts and the language used to describe them tend to be different; the two camps often ignore the full extent of the 'opposition' literature. But what is very relevant is that the subject matter dealt with is often non-overlapping. In the area we are considering, it is clear that Marxists, on the whole, have been interested in TNCs and foreign investment mainly in connection with imperialism and thus with the relationship between developed and underdeveloped countries.

The relevance of most of the Marxist theories presented in section I for the explanation of international production in modern day capitalism tends, therefore, to be limited; this is because an increasing share of FDI has been directed towards other developed countries. This does not mean denying the relevance of the activities of TNCs in LDCs or the imperialist relations between DMEs and LDCs. It just means that a full understanding of the growth and pattern of international production must take account of the overall growth in TNCs' activities in both developed and less developed countries.

The neo-classical approach has been presented here mainly for the sake of completeness and for the advantages that the reader may derive from comparisons with other theories. The basic unrealistic assumptions underlying this paradigm make it unsuitable for dealing with TNCs and their activities.

There is no doubt that the theory of FDI and TNCs was born with

Hymer's seminal doctoral dissertation. Most of the other theories presented in the previous pages can be traced back as developments of some of the points made by Hymer. There are three main points that emerge from Hymer's work and that are relevant to subsequent developments; these are all crucial elements in explaining the extent and pattern of international production in Hymer's theory. They are:

1 the advantages of large TNCs in general and *vis-à-vis* domestic firms in host countries;
2 market imperfections;
3 control.

Stress on element 1 by subsequent authors has led to emphasis of the role of internal advantages, such as the existence of superior managerial, marketing or technological skills, and, in general, of 'intangible' assets; the desire and opportunity to exploit any excess capacity in such assets leads to FDI. Theories developed along these lines are characterized by:

(a) an internalist, inward looking approach in which explanations emerge mainly or entirely by looking at internal characteristics of firms and their development;
(b) the assumption of market imperfections as an exogenously given environment in which firms operate and which gives further scope for internal advantages;
(c) an efficiency approach to FDI in which the investment decision is linked to the desire to arrive at a more efficient use of the firm's resources and to economies in transaction costs.

Many of the theories presented in section III concentrate on developing point 1 of Hymer's work. It should, however, be emphasized that the fact that these theories have a common root and approach does not mean that they are necessarily the same or even very similar; each has been developed along its own lines and each has some important contribution to make. This overall approach has been very useful in bringing to our attention the role of internal advantages, their origins, manifestations and effects. Where the approach has failed is in integrating TNCs' operations with the environment, and in fully developing the internationalization side. Efficiency criteria, which stress the best use of excess capacity in intangible assets, may explain why firms want to, and can, expand but not necessarily why they take the international route or the FDI route in so doing. In considering the points made here, the reader will have to take into account the differences between various theories: for example, Vernon does consider the economic environment; similarly, Aliber's and other theories (internalization and eclectic ones) do contain 'international' elements. Vernon's and Caves's theories contain many strategic elements, as already pointed out.

On the whole, therefore, it is on the first element of Hymer's theory that many prevalent theories have concentrated; there is nothing wrong (and indeed a lot of good) in developing that element. It is, however, a pity that the theories have not done so in *conjunction* with developing the other two elements, particularly market imperfections, to which we now turn.

In terms of interaction between firms and their environment, we could almost trace a continuous spectrum from theories that look entirely inwardly to the firm for an explanation of foreign involvement, to theories that consider the interaction between firms and external elements; such interaction can be considered from various points of view and to varying degrees. The firm can be considered as interacting with other rival firms, with other productive smaller units, with labour, with states and governments, with the overall macro-environment.

Many non-Marxist writers have tended to stick to a micro analysis in which either the firm is largely inward looking or it interacts with the environment in terms of the market structure in which it operates. Elements of market structure are present in most of the theories discussed in sections III and IV.

Market imperfections play a double role in Hymer's work. They form the environment in which firms operate but they are also the outcome, the 'creation', of firms' behaviour. For Hymer, it is the desire to remove or reduce competition that forms the main motivation for FDI and for direct control of business abroad. This is the most radical part of Hymer's theory and stress on this element leads to the following characteristics:

(a) an externalist, outward-looking approach in which firms fully interact with their environment in a two-way process;
(b) 'endogenously' determined market imperfections where firms are 'creators' of imperfections and not just 'takers';
(c) a 'strategy' approach rather than an 'efficiency' approach in terms of firms' objectives; this means that firms are driven by long-term strategies rather than (or at the same time as) by the objective of arriving at a more efficient use of resources.

Strategies can take a variety of forms and deal with various aspects of firms' behaviour. However, there are some strategic elements that are of particular relevance for our discussion and they are the strategies towards the external environment: towards the competitive environment and therefore rivals, towards labour and towards governments. Hymer's and Knickerbocker's theories, as well as Vernon's later developments, consider the firms' desire to influence the competitive environment by their international activities. Indeed, in their analyses, FDI is determined by the firm's aim to improve its position in the oligopolistic market structure.

Cowling and Sugden explore the effects of transnationalism on the competitive environment and conclude that TNCs' activities tend to increase the degree of monopoly in modern capitalism.

Labour, of course, figures prominently in the literature on TNCs in terms of employment and industrial relation effects. It is, however, noticeable that prevalent theories have very little explicit reference to labour as part of the strategic decisions by TNCs. Some of the recent Marxist approaches presented in section I, in particular Fröbel et al. (1980) and Ádám (1975), specifically refer to labour in advanced countries and LDCs. In the analyses of these authors FDI is seen as determined by strategies designed to utilize different types of labour available in different countries. This approach emphasizes the role of TNCs in utilizing labour in LDCs. In chapter 14 we considered strategies towards labour as one of the determinants of the growth and pattern of international production.

The interaction between the state and TNCs is dealt with at great length in the literature on the effects of the TNCs' activities. Many theories consider the effects of government policies and intervention on the location of FDI. In some theories, the government is, indeed, seen as disturbing the competitive environment and thus creating further scope for internalization: grants, trade barriers, monetary policy can all change the competitive environment. Some authors consider the effects of TNCs' activities, behaviour and pressures on state intervention. Murray (1971) explores the interlinks between state and transnational capital in terms of state functions and the territorial sphere of influence of TNCs and state.

The issue of *control* figures prominently in Hymer; however, it is rather neglected in subsequent authors except Cowling and Sugden. Another distinguishing feature of the Cowling and Sugden approach is their attempt to deal with the micro and macro environments together. This feature is also present in Murray's approach (see chapter 5 of this book). When firms are transnational, very large and powerful, developments in the firm and the economic system are bound to interact very strongly and therefore the two ought to be considered simultaneously.

The theories presented in sections III and IV have points in common and differences. Some of the economists considered in section III write with the US example as reference and some theories seem to have been tailored to that country (for example, the product life cycle theory). We can also note that a few (and only a few) theories incorporate uncertainty in their analysis. Many other distinguishing features could be found, including the fact that some theories emphasize the organization and structure of industry, some (and indeed most) markets and demand, and very few the production side of TNCs' activities.

All in all, in the past 20 years three theories have emerged as the most widely accepted in the literature on international business: the product life cycle, the internalization and the eclectic theories. No conference on international business or new book on the subject fails to refer to them;

it is part of their success that the language of 'product life cycle', 'internalization' and 'ownership–location–internalization' advantages has become a
matter of everyday international business terminology. It is unfortunate
– and no doubt against the original authors' intentions – that often the
subsequent use of these theories has tended to stress their terminology
and descriptive aspects rather than their attempts at putting forward
scientific hypotheses to be tested.

Part III
Effects

For by proving the cause you at once prove the effect, and conversely nothing can exist without its cause.

Aristotle, *Rhetorica*

16

Methodological Issues

Though this be madness, yet there is method in't.

Shakespeare, *Hamlet*. II.2

16.1 Introduction

There is a considerable amount of literature on the effects of international production and foreign direct investment.[1] Writers include not only economists but also experts in other fields; this is how it should be, since the effects go well beyond the domain of economics. In spite of the large amount of literature on effects, the methodological issues involved in assessing them are not given much attention.[2] This chapter discusses some of these 'methodological issues'.[3]

The most obvious issue is whether to take account of strictly economic effects only, or to include other related effects as well. Any major effect in the *economic sphere* is bound to have repercussions in some or all of the following: *politics, culture, ecology and society in general*.

Related to this is the issue of the *time period* over which the effects should be assessed. Not all the effects are felt within the short run; some may take a very long time to manifest themselves. This is a fairly important point, particularly as the short- and long-term effects may, at times, go in opposite directions rather than reinforce each other in the same direction. For example, the balance of payments effect of inward investments is very likely to be positive in the short run if funds for investments enter the country, but negative in the medium and long run, as profits and dividends may leave the host country.

This chapter is based on a paper presented at a conference on 'East–West International Business' in Toruń, Poland, 6–8 June 1990.

16.2 Assumptions on alternatives

Another relevant methodological issue is linked to the assessment of *alternatives* and assumptions about what might happen if FDI were not taking place. This question is closely linked to the issue of whether FDI is a substitute for, or additional to, domestic investment in the host country, and whether it is a substitute for or an addition to home investment.

Hufbauer and Adler (1968) organize the various alternatives into three sets of assumptions: *classical, reverse classical* and *anticlassical*. Under the classical and reverse classical assumptions the total world volume of capital expenditure remains the same whether FDI takes place or not. Under the anticlassical assumption the total volume of capital expenditure increases because of FDI.

The classical hypothesis assumes that FDI adds to the host country productive capacity and detracts from home country investment. The end result is a territorial shift in investment and productive capacity: the home country is deprived of productive capacity while the host country's domestic firms are not crowded out of investment opportunities. The reverse classical hypothesis assumes that foreign investment does not deprive the home country of productive capacity since other firms will supplement and take up the investment opportunity; however, FDI makes no net addition to the productive capacity of the host country because it crowds out domestic capital. The anticlassical hypothesis assumes that no substitution takes place at home or abroad; therefore FDI increases productive capacity in the host country without decreasing it at home.

These three hypotheses are clearly crucial in the assessment of balance of payments, employment and growth effects in the host and home countries. In spite of the clarity with which they have originally been expressed, they are not easy to handle in practice. This is because each of them involves a full set of sub-assumptions about, for example, the availability of funds and investment opportunities in the host and home countries, the behaviour of other investors in the two countries, methods of financing the FDI, market power, level of employment and capacity utilization in the two countries. No *a priori* generalization can be made regarding the applicability of the three assumptions; each case – country and sector – must be considered individually and the plausibility of each assumption must be assessed according to the prevailing conditions.

Russell (1978) points out how conclusions on the effects of inward FDI on the balance of payments and on the net real income of the host country are also linked to a basic underlying assumption about the 'efficacy and speed of working of the market mechanism' (p. 198). The speedy and efficient working of the market is assumed when conclusions are drawn on the low social costs of adjusting a balance of payments deficit by changing prices at home relative to overseas. Changes in relative prices might require a monetary policy that involves production and employment costs. The better the market mechanism works, the less the need to intervene with macroeconomic policies to support employment and production. Thus, according to Russell, conclusions about the effects of FDI are linked to assumptions about:

1 the working of the market mechanism;
2 the efficacy of macroeconomic policies;
3 the economists' degree of knowledge of the relevant macroeconomic relationship to be used as a guide for forecasting and policies.

16.3 Social versus private effects

One important question to ask ourselves in terms of methodology is: *effects on whom*? When dealing with international issues it is common to consider effects on various nations; this implies taking 'the nation' as the most important unit of analysis and, particularly, it implies considering the 'nation' as a homogeneous block of common interests. In reality there are conflicts of interests between workers and capital and within each of these categories: workers in different sectors or categories may have conflicting interests; similarly, the interests of national capital may not coincide with the interests of international capital. Conflicts may also arise between industrial and finance capital or between managers and shareholders of a particular company. In dealing with TNCs there is a strong tendency to identify companies, their activities and interests with those of the country of origin of the TNC; thus expressions like American, Japanese or British multinationals are used all the time with the underlying implication that what applies to, say, British TNCs applies, automatically, to Britain. In reality, the interests of TNCs as single entities or as a group may not coincide with the collective long-term interests of the nation, with the interests of single groups and classes within it, or with the objectives and strategies of the government of the day.

Connected with this is the related issue of *private versus social costs and benefits*. This is a general issue in the economics of imperfect markets. However, in the international context it may also mean that the pursuit of private benefits leads to a territorial transfer of gains from one country to another.

MacDougall (1960) develops a theoretical framework for assessing the costs and benefits of inward foreign investment on the macroeconomy. He starts with a set of ten assumptions related to employment, labour force and taxation policy as well as to market structure, economies of scale, international trade and the balance of payments. He analyses the effects of a change in inward investment by releasing the various assumptions one by one. The study is done with the Australian economy as a background and relates to inward investment. None the less, the clear, general, methodological approach is applicable to other countries as well, and to both inward and outward investment. Indeed, a similar methodology was followed later by Reddaway (1967, 1968) and Hufbauer and Adler (1968) in studies related to the UK and USA economies respectively.

A purely neo-classical approach, with related assumptions about competitive market structures, leads to the conclusion that the social effects of international production are positive as such production contributes to the efficient allocation of resources on a worldwide scale. However, Frankel (1965) reaches opposite conclusions although he works within a broadly neo-classical framework. He considers the effects of FDI on the home country and starts from the assumption that the social returns on outward investment are not equal to the private returns to the company responsible for the investment. This is because one act of investment in a given country generates a series of positive repercussions and multiplying effects on the economic system, which lead to social returns higher than the private ones. It follows that, if an amount of investment is withdrawn from the domestic arena and directed towards a foreign country, the home country undergoes a loss of social benefits that is not counterbalanced by the private returns that the investing company and its shareholders receive.

In his analysis Frankel assumes substitution between outward foreign investment and domestic investment, thus adhering to what, a few years later, was classified as the 'classical assumption' by Hufbauer and Adler (1968), as was mentioned earlier in this chapter. Frankel sees a methodological problem arising because economists tend to analyse issues of efficiency and allocation of resources within the micro sphere and issues of economic growth at the macro level without attempting to link the two. The need to integrate micro and macro issues and effects is particularly prominent when the 'micro' refers to the activities of companies which are very large and powerful. Some micro–macro issues will be considered below.

The integration of micro and macro issues, even if it were fully possible, would not exhaust the methodological problems related to multinational activities and host/home nations. The very large literature dealing with the effects of the activities of transnational companies usually separates the effects on home and host countries. Methodologically, the focus seems therefore to be on 'nations', the geographical direction of flow of FDI and the nationality of the investor.

However, this focus seems inadequate for an analysis of the effects of activities and institutions that are, by their own nature, transnational and whose focus and context are not national but international. The next chapter deals with effects without using the traditional host/home country division; the reasons for this approach are given in the next two sections of this chapter.

16.4 Globality and assessment of effects

It is the specific characteristic of many transnational companies to be able to plan 'globally'. *'Globality'* creates its own methodological problems when we come to assess the effects of TNCs' activities, for the following reason.

Some effects of international production are linked to *the direction* of the flow of investment (inward or outward), such as some balance of payments effects and direct employment effects. Conclusions on these effects can be drawn by looking separately at trends in inward and outward FDI, appropriately processed. However, there are many other effects which are linked to the fact that activities of TNCs *are planned and spread globally over many countries.* These include: effects on the effectiveness of economic policies and, in general, the power of governments *vis-à-vis* TNCs; some effects on trade; effects on the power of labour *vis-à-vis* capital; effects on technological developments; effects on market power. On each of these there is more in the next chapter.

Globality of decisions has been stressed by many authors, including Ádám (1975), Fröbel et al. (1980) and Vernon (1979), as highlighted in chapters 5 and 8. In chapter 5 we considered global planning by TNCs in relation to linkages between the location of production worldwide and labour; these linkages will now be reconsidered briefly in relation to global scanning by TNCs.

Global scanning has often been considered in relation to the location of production and the sourcing of markets. Related to all this there is, however, another area in which global scanning is of paramount importance: the internationalization of the production process. Increasingly the production process is organized in such a way that components can be sited in different countries, matching labour availability and skills in one country with the type of processing required. At the micro level this leads to cost minimization by allowing firms to locate components requiring low skills in countries abundant with such labour, and vice versa.

At the macro level the internationalization of the production process generates the following general effects:

1 Specialization of different countries by components rather than whole products. This produces effects on the industrial structure of the economy, on the spread of technology, and on the level and pattern of trade (see chapter 17).

2   A new international division of labour in which LDCs develop pockets of manufacturing activities in components.
3   A fragmentation of the product and production process. As a result of this fragmentation only the TNC that plans and coordinates its production has control over the *entire* product: single countries do not have such control.

As existing transnational firms spread the geographical boundaries of their 'scanning' wider and wider, and as more and more companies from more and more countries join the multinational league, the scope for 'globality' of decisions increases so that the need to analyse the effects of globality also increases.

What is being emphasized here is that the increasing tendency towards globalization produces not only *quantitative* change (some bigger transnational companies, larger numbers of them, larger numbers of countries in which they operate) but also considerable *qualitative* changes which need new tools of analysis.

16.5   On host and home countries and effects

As already mentioned, in the literature on FDI and international production it has been customary to deal with the effects by dividing them into effects on the home country and effects on the host country. The analysis of host country effects is very often carried out with reference to LDCs. However, excessive emphasis on home/host country is not satisfactory for various reasons, in particular:

1   Home and host countries are not the only two countries involved in the game. Third countries, where a given TNC already has production facilities, are likely to be involved in the overall strategy regarding sourcing of markets, production of specific components and supply of raw materials. What is meant here is the following: let us assume that company Z, originating in country A and with existing production activities in countries B, C and D, decides to invest in country X (where X could be any country (including A, B, C, D); the effects of this decision will be felt – in a variety of ways – not only in the host and home countries (X and A) but also in all the other countries in which the company already has production facilities (B, C, D). With the increase in the spread of TNCs' networks, the need to account for effects on 'third' countries is becoming more and more prominent.
2   Many effects are linked to the globality of operations rather than the direction of the flow of investment, as already argued in the previous section.
3   Increasingly the financing of the outward FDI does not necessarily

involve the exit of funds from the home country. It may involve borrowing on international financial markets or using profits from other subsidiaries (thus involving third countries as in 1 above) or the reinvestment of profits realized in the host country.

4   The explicit or implicit identification of host countries with LDCs, often found in the literature, is misleading from the point of view of 'representative' host countries. As some 75 per cent of FDI is directed towards AICs, it is obvious that the representative host country is not an underdeveloped country but an industrialized one. The effects on the two sets of countries – LDCs and AICs – as hosts can be different and hence need to be analysed separately.

For all the above reasons, in considering the effects of international production the traditional host/home country divide will not be used here; the effects will, instead, be analysed by economic category. Some social and political problems are touched on when appropriate. For each economic category, when applicable, the different effects on home, host and third country are considered, as are some differences in LDCs and AICs as host countries. All this is dealt with in the next chapter, where we shall consider in some detail effects on trade, balance of payments, technology, labour, the effectiveness of economic policies, growth and de-industrialization.

17

Effects

---

e qui basti l'effetto
(and here let the effect suffice)

Dante, *La Divina Commedia, Paradiso*. XXXII.66

17.1 Trade

'How important are TNCs in foreign trade?' asks the UNCTC (1988, p. 89) and it gives the following summary answers:

> ... TNCs account for well over three quarters of their home countries' trade flows.
>
> Intra-firm transactions account for between 30 and 40 per cent of these home countries' trade.
>
> TNCs are particularly important in world trade in manufactures and, over the years, they have tended to shift their production and trading activities to foreign affiliates.

There is no doubt that TNCs are responsible for a considerable amount of world trade; given this situation two questions spring to mind.

1   What characteristic(s) of TNCs lead to trade effects?
2   What is the relationship between international production and international trade? Are they complements or substitutes?

With regard to 1 what we may want to know is whether the large amount of trade generated by TNCs is a characteristic of their size, or technological bias in the sectors they operate in, or whether it is their 'transnationality *per se*' that generates trade.

The need to try to explain international production and trade together has been felt by many authors: for example, Dunning's eclectic approach (discussed in chapter 12) contains trade elements. Notably, Vernon's product life cycle theory (chapter 8) sees both trade and production moving along through time and countries as the product develops through its various phases. The full interrelationships between trade and production are far from being properly worked out at either the theoretical or the empirical level. Some points will, however, be made here on a particular aspect of this interrelationship; these points help towards answering questions 1 and 2.

A large amount of the literature dealing simultaneously with international production and trade concentrates on the issue of *sourcing of markets*. Do companies decide to source a particular market via exports or via relocation of production? The relationship between international production and trade has, therefore, been looked at mainly from the *demand* side. However, together with *demand* side effects there are effects on trade deriving from the *production* side. These have been rather neglected.

If we consider the link between international production and international trade to be mainly on the *demand* side (e.g. sourcing of markets) we may come out with a relationship of *substitution* between exports and direct production. Markets are sourced either via exports or via direct production. However, if we look at the *production* side we may come out with a relationship of *complementarity*. On the production side, the main effects on trade are linked to the design of products and processes, to their division into various components or stages and to the related worldwide relocation. Both the *volume* and the *structure* of trade are likely to undergo considerable changes as a result of the location of production of components into various countries for the following reasons.

1   The movement of components around the world for processing and assembling leads to a significant *increase* in the *overall volume* of trade and also to a larger increase in trade than in value added. This helps to explain the relationship between growth of trade and growth of production worldwide (see section 2.2).

2   The movement of commodities for foreign processing could, in theory, result in either market transactions or transactions internal to a particular TNC. In practice, however, it is likely to lead to internal transactions and indeed the incentive to relocate components may actually come from expected advantages that are typical of the structure of a transnational corporation (e.g. advantage from transfer prices manipulation). Many TNCs are vertically integrated production organizations, and this means that the scope for internal transactions across countries can be very wide. This forms the base for the considerable amount of and *increase* in *intra-firm* trade; this is, at times, two-way trade as commodities are sent abroad for processing and then back to the home country as finished product or for further processing. Fröbel et al. (1980,

p. 134) report examples of 'trouser material . . . cut in Federal Germany, sent to Tunisia for sewing into trousers, and finally shipped back, in made-up form, to the home market in Germany.'

3   One expects considerable impact on the *geographical* as well as the sectoral structure of trade because of foreign processing as components are relocated in different countries.[1]

4   Further effects on the geographical structure and pattern of trade may be linked to the manipulation of transfer prices. The factors that lead to such manipulation may also lead to changes in the geographical structure of trade as TNCs may follow trade routes leading to their overall profit maximization, in conditions of tax-rate differentials between countries or exchange rates instability. The factors favouring the manipulation of transfer prices will also favour intra-firm trade against market inter-firm transactions.

5   A tendency towards increased import penetration in industrial countries may result, partly from the increase in intra-firm trade in general, and partly from the relocation of the production of whole products or components in new countries.

6   The types of transactions that arise under the relocation of production due to foreign processing are such that both imports and exports fall under the same industrial sector. They are therefore likely to form *intra-industry* trade (IIT) as well as *intra-firm* (IFT). The overlap between IIT and IFT comes about in two ways.

(a)   Intra-firm imports between related group A (affiliate to affiliate or parent to affiliate within ownership group A) and intra-firm exports between related group B. For example, let us consider Ford to be group A and Rover to be group B. Let us assume that Ford UK imports from Ford Germany, while Rover UK exports to Rover France. Both transactions are intra-firm and, given the classification system, they are likely to be intra-industry. However, let us consider a third group C (say ICI) exporting on an intra-firm basis; these exports cannot be considered together with the transactions of group A to form IIT since the products belong to two different industrial groups.

(b)   Intra-firm intra-industry transactions: group A simultaneously imports and exports. Ford UK imports some components and exports others. The components are likely to fall within the same industrial classification and hence are likely to be IIT as well as IFT.[2] The movement of components can be, say, between the UK and two or more foreign countries or between the UK and one single country.

Since many TNCs are diversified we could have a two-way intra-firm trade that is not, however, intra-industry trade; this would happen in the case of a firm whose products are so diversified as to fall within different industrial categories.[3] However, given that the concept and measurement of IIT is highly dependent on the type and level of classification or aggregation one could envisage the two-way transaction of 'diversified' commodities on an intra-firm basis to form IIT under one classification or aggregation but not under a different one.

In practice, there can be a considerable amount of overlap between intra-industry and intra-firm trade.[4] The determinants of intra-industry trade are hotly debated in the current literature.[5] It is very likely that the movement of components for worldwide processing is one of the determinants of a high level of intra-industry trade; however, there are, no doubt, other relevant determinants as well.

It can, therefore, be concluded that the worldwide planning and location of production by TNCs and the related worldwide location of components and stages of the production process are likely to generate the following:

1   An increase in world trade and an increase in trade for both home and host countries; both imports and exports are likely to be affected.
2   Effects on the trade of 'third' countries, i.e. countries which are neither home nor host to international production; generally, effects on the geographical structure of trade.
3   Increases in both intra-firm and intra-industry trade.
4   The relationship between international trade and international production is likely to be complementary whenever trade is generated by the movements of components from country to country.

The effects on trade just highlighted are connected with the fact that transnationality creates links between various countries which give rise to trade. The trade effects can be generated equally by both inward and outward activities as they do not depend on the direction of the investment flow or the nationality of the investor, but on the creation of production links between units of the same company in various countries. This is one of the situations in which *globality of planning and control leads to cumulative effects* (of both inward and outward investment) rather than to compensating effects of the flows going in opposite directions.

Not all trade generated by TNCs is related to movements of components; after all, many TNCs are diversified companies and each of them may be moving different products around the world besides – or instead of – components of the same products.

What can we say about TNCs and trade other than components trade? The transnationality of operations gives advantages to firms in terms of both knowledge of markets for products and sources of raw materials and intermediate products. This means that the global scanning extends not only to production possibilities but also to selling and buying possibilities; thus – *ceteris paribus* – TNCs are more likely than domestic firms to engage in trade (both imports and exports). Indeed we should not forget that in many cases it is the trade-orientated domestic firms that may be induced to start investing abroad in order to internalize supplies of raw materials and intermediate products and/or produce near the market(s).

In terms of the *substitution–complementarity* issue between international production and trade we can give the following conclusion. Whenever international production is used for sourcing foreign markets, the relationship between production and trade may be one of substitution; however, in all the cases in which international production involves relocation of components there is likely to be a strong relationship of complementarity.

Kojima (1978) looks at the substitution–complementarity issue from a different perspective from the one considered here. He works within the framework of a neo-classical scheme and reaches the following conclusion:

> Direct foreign investment that is released from a comparatively disadvantageous industry in the investing country and finds its way into the industry with overt or potential comparative advantage in the host country will harmoniously promote an upgrading of industrial structure on both sides and thus speed up the expansion of trade between the two countries. This is what I call 'Japanese-type' (in contrast to 'American-type') direct foreign investment. (pp. 14–15)

Let us assume that a particular country (A) starts by exporting a product to another country (B) and then the producers decide to locate production in B; for this particular product and for country A, we have a case of substitution in the sourcing of market B between exports and international production. However, according to Kojima, the long-run situation will be one of new comparative advantages in which the host country (likely to be a LDC) will export the products (e.g. textiles) produced with foreign (Japanese) capital and import other products on which the developed country (Japan) retains a comparative advantage.

Looking at the situation in a dynamic and long-term perspective, we are led to conclude that, on the whole, transnationality in itself leads to complementarity of trade and international production and thus we should not be surprised to find that TNCs are responsible for very large shares of trade and that they exhibit high propensities to export and import.

17.2 Balance of payments

The balance of payments is obviously affected by FDI in a variety of ways. First, there are the direct effects of capital outflows and inflows destined to finance the outward and inward FDI. It should, however, be remembered that an outward FDI does not necessarily involve outflow of funds from the home country; there are other ways of funding direct investment, such as borrowing on international markets and using profits from foreign subsidiaries. Other direct effects are connected with the outflow and inflow of profits and dividends related – respectively – to past inward and outward FDI. For countries with long traditions of FDI these incomes effects can be very large. At one end of the spectrum we can have countries like the USA and the UK, whose net inflow of income from capital invested abroad has, in many years, outstripped the net outflow of capital in spite of new large acquisitions of foreign assets. At the other end of the spectrum we have many less developed countries where the outflow of profits and dividends to foreign investors far outstrips the inflow of new inward investment. Magdoff (1966, p. 198) illustrates this point with reference to US investment during the period 1950–65. The outward investment in Latin America was US $3.8 billion while the related income flowing from Latin America to the USA in the same period was $11.3 billion. This net inflow of funds into the USA was achieved in spite of the growing amount of foreign assets being acquired. Rowthorn and Wells (1987) illustrate the same point for the UK. They report, for example, that in the years 1953, 1963 and 1973 the *net inflow* of interest, profits and dividends into the UK was, respectively, £229, £398 and £1257 million, while the *net outflow* of long-term investment for the same years was £194, £155 and £518 million (Rowthorn and Wells, 1987, p. 80, table 4.2). In 1983 the opposite situation resulted from the large outflow of investment following the abolition of exchange controls: the net inflow on interest, profits and dividends was £1948 million against an outflow for long-term investment of £5504 million. No doubt this large net outflow will produce a big increase in profits, dividends and interest in the future.

The immediate effect on the UK balance of payments of large inflows of income from British capital overseas is obviously positive. However, the balance of payments effects can have profound effects on the real sector of the economy that are not always beneficial. Rowthorn and Wells refer to such effects in relation to net incomes from net foreign investment as the 'wealth trap' and this is considered in more detail in section 17.6.

We have already considered the trade effects of FDI; these will obviously produce corresponding balance of payments effects, which will be in addition to the direct effects just highlighted. As the trade effects are not related simply to outward and inward investment but are also related to the overall global position and spread of activities, the indirect balance of payments effects due to such trade effects cannot simply be classified into effects due to inward or outward FDI. The manipulation of transfer prices also has effects on the balance of payments. The invoicing of internal transfers at prices different from those of arm's length transfers distorts the balance of payments accounts. Indeed, very often the manipulation of transfer prices is motivated by the desire to take advantage of actual or expected changes in exchange rates or by the wish to transfer profits where legal impediments exist to such transfers.

17.3 Technology

A detailed study by the Organization for Economic Cooperation and Development (1971) stresses the interconnections between inventions, innovations and the diffusion of technological progress. They write (p. 19):

> The distinction between invention, innovation and diffusion is particularly important when considering the macroeconomic effects of technological progress. *Invention* is the idea of how science and technology could be applied in a new way, *innovation* consists of bringing invention to its first successful commercial use and *diffusion* consists of the spread of the use of the innovation amongst its potential population of users.

The role of TNCs and FDI in the diffusion of innovation was highlighted in a previous OECD report (1970), the links between FDI and the product life cycle theory are considered to be very strong.

The original formulation of the product life cycle theory stressed the diffusion of innovation from the USA to European countries. The OECD study is also concerned with the diffusion of technology between developed countries. However, most of the literature on international business has been concerned with the diffusion of technology from developed to less developed countries. The role of TNCs in technology has usually been discussed in relation to their involvement in LDCs and hence in relation to the *transfer* of technology from AICs to LDCs, and to the '*appropriateness*' of the technology being transferred for LDCs.

The issue of 'appropriate' technology is seen in relation to the factor endowment of the host country; as LDCs are abundant in labour and scarce in capital the appropriate technology would seem to be one that uses labour-intensive techniques. TNCs usually originate in capital-abundant countries and hence will tend to develop capital-intensive techniques; indeed TNCs are known for using high technology to a greater extent than 'national' firms. Capital-intensive techniques may be inappropriate as they cannot absorb the large pool of labour and as they may intensify income inequalities and the tendency towards dualism.

This is clearly a key issue in the debate on development and is, in many ways, outside the scope of the present work.[6] However, it is worth making a few remarks. First, there may be a case for TNCs' high technology activities in LDCs on the basis that they may initiate, in those countries, an imitation effect in relation to technology and to managerial and marketing techniques in the LDC. More relevantly, the so-called 'appropriate' technology with 'appropriate' equipment for a labour-abundant country may no longer exist. The use of high technology may, however, be seen as creating unfair competition and barriers to the development of indigenous enterprises.

The issue of appropriate technology is usually seen in relation to capital and labour endowment 'in a given country'. However, the operations of TNCs are, by their very nature, multi-country. This means that although a capital-intensive technique can be blamed on the count that it does not lead to the appropriate utilization of the abundant factor (labour), it cannot be blamed for excessive use of the scarce factor (capital), since this factor is transferred from another country where it is abundant. This shows the difficulty of applying static, 'nationally' based models to situations that are dynamic and multi-country. This again points to the issue of 'globality' of planning by TNCs. In earlier chapters the links between the development of technology, planning and location of pro-duction worldwide, and decomposition of products and processes have been discussed. This leads on to the fact that high technology may be used by TNCs to design their products and processes in such a way as to locate labour-intensive components in labour-abundant, low-labour-cost countries. This would point to a model of production planning and allo-cation that is much more sophisticated than the one that considers pro-duction techniques and factor-endowment on the basis of single nations. This model would be characterized by a dynamic close interaction and interdependence between capital-abundant and labour-abundant coun-tries; in it the type of technology developed and the possibility of developing certain products and processes depend on the possibility of operating in labour-abundant, low-skill, low-labour-cost countries as much as on capital-abundant, high skill, research-intensive countries.

The recent opening up of Eastern European countries brings a new 'third' partner into the game. Most Eastern European countries are characterized by a skilled and educated labour force, although wages are relatively low. This will introduce new variables into the global planning process of TNCs and the next decade may see considerable changes in the strategies for location of products and components by companies. There are, however, considerable obstacles to a large-scale relocation of production in Eastern Europe by TNCs. Among these are the poor communications and transportation infrastructure of many of the countries and the risks connected with possible political instability. The strategy currently pursued by some Eastern European governments is to try to attract FDI on the basis of low wages. However, low wages are not the attraction for TNCs; low costs are. Production costs in countries with poor communications and transportation can become quite high – in spite of low wages – as delivery times for components and products become erratic. A low wages strategy can also, of course, be a deterrent for TNCs that want to explore new markets.

Ádám (1975) is very sceptical about the possibility that global planning of production – or worldwide sourcing as he calls it – might lead to permanent advantages for LDCs. He sees the main problems in the fact that the manufacturing pockets created by TNCs in LDCs make the host country very closely dependent on particular components for which there is one single buyer. The TNCs are in a position to move their production facilities. The dependence on the home country's foreign policy may be considerable. Inward foreign investments may be very costly as LDCs compete with each other in offering incentives to the 'dowry' chasing TNCs and as the social costs of the investments are born by the host country. Ádám concludes (p. 102): 'Summing it up: instability, dependence, "over-kill" of incentives, the lack of linkages, etc., makes worldwide sourcing a doubtful tool in the longer term for solving the problems of the Third World, despite some job creation and export earnings.' The advantages for AICs are also limited: manufacturing jobs may be lost while 'managerial, clerical and professional occupations' may increase as a result of worldwide sourcing.

It all points towards the need to take a 'global approach' in assessing the causes and effects of technology, and the need to move away from the dichotomy of developed countries versus less developed countries, essentially for two reasons. (a) The two sets of countries may be closely interlinked in the development and adoption of technology via the 'global' planning of TNCs; and (b) the Eastern European countries are now introducing a 'third' party into the game.

A number of works have highlighted the negative effects of the *loss of linkages* between products and/or processes on the growth and diffusion of innovation as well as on the utilization and enhancement of the related labour skills. Radice (1984) analyses the effects of the spread of technological links across nations – via the operations of TNCs – on an advanced country: the UK. Radice concentrates on links between suppliers of equipment and machinery and their customers and on how new needs and improvements in one part of the chain of suppliers and customers can lead to the spread of new technologies. When the various links in the chain (or most of them) are national, the technological improvements will soon spread vertically and diagonally (to related sectors using the same or similar equipment) *within the national economy*. However, when most of the operations are in the hands of TNCs, the technology spread and its benefits – including benefits related to the development of labour skills – are likely to be lost by the national economy.

Worries about the effects on AICs of TNCs' activities are also expressed by Best (1986) in an analysis that considers the micro and macro links across countries.[7] Best's view is that advanced countries and companies within them have been, for some time now, in a new competitive era based on products rather than price competition. Product competition requires attention to innovation, quality, design and all the usual non-price factors. Product development is more likely to come forward in situations in which: (a) there are links and coordination between people working on different products and components so that all the products can benefit from exchange of information and cross-fertilization; (b) there are coordination and linkages between the people responsible for the overall planning and those responsible for production. Best thinks that the modern TNC organized around products divisions is unsuited to the new product competition as its organizational form is not conducive to the links in (a) and (b).

At the micro level he advocates organizational forms more conducive to cross-fertilization of ideas and programmes and to closer links between planners and 'doers'. At the macro level he advocates industrial policies designed to facilitate links between product and process development in various products within the same industry and between various industries.

It may be worth noting that, if Best's analysis is correct, countries which are highly dominated by large TNCs are more likely to lose the potential benefits from cross-fertilization. Cross-fertilization in innovation does not only span between products and processes separately, it also spreads across products and processes; there is indeed a tendency for process and product innovation to go hand in hand. There is a complementarity between the two: new processes are likely to lead to new products; new components and the division in different processes are likely to require new equipment for producing and/or assembling them.

Complementarity in technical innovation extends much further than the single product or industry. As Rosenberg (1982) has highlighted, there is considerable complementarity in the diffusion of technology. In the area we are dealing with, the complementarity tends to involve products and processes spread within and between industries and between various countries.

The issue of the diffusion of technology from product to product and industry to industry, and the related advantages, is also stressed by Porter (1990). He writes:

> The presence in a nation of competitive industries that are related often leads to new competitive industries. Related industries are those in which firms can coordinate or share activities in the value chain when competing, or those which involve products that are complementary (such as computers and applications software). Sharing of activities can occur in technology development, manufacturing, distribution, marketing, or service. (p. 105)

Porter discusses the fallacy of nations relying on price competition through low factor costs, including low wages. The fallacy is due to the fact that any advantage thus acquired is likely to be ephemeral and easily eroded; on the other hand, advantages based on technological superiority and quality are likely to be long-lasting and cumulative. Worries about technology, the power of TNCs over it and their accountability have recently extended to the area of consumption. Consumers throughout the world – and particularly in industrialized countries – have realized the dangers of having no countervailing power to help them direct the use of technology in less harmful and destructive ways. The worries voiced and the lack of power extend to the spheres of private consumption – mainly in relation to the health and safety of food – and public consumption – mainly in relation to environmental issues.

17.4   Labour

There are various effects of international production on labour. In the previous section some effects on the acquisition and development of skills were mentioned. The main effects are related to employment and to industrial relations.

Effects on employment

In the mid-seventies TNCs were responsible for the employment of over 45 million people worldwide (Enderwick, 1985, pp. 45–6). The UNCTC (1988) gives a more recent estimate of 65 million people directly employed by TNCs worldwide and at least double this figure for the indirect employment effects.

The standard, 'common sense', *prima facie* conclusion as regards employment effects is to say that the FDI creates extra jobs in the host country while it is likely to detract from job creation in the home country. This is in line with the 'classical assumption' highlighted in chapter 16. The job creation effects in host countries are commonly accepted as a foregone conclusion; this conclusion is reinforced by many authors by addition of the positive employment effects of the exports generated by TNCs. However, a closer look at the type of investment, the assumptions about alternative scenarios and the indirect effects of FDI may make us more cautious in drawing conclusions.

The position employment effects on the host country may disappear or look less good if we allow for the following:

1   FDI that involves acquisition of existing enterprises does not create extra jobs unless it is the basis for further investment; in some cases, following rationalization, it may reduce jobs.
2   If we assume a 'reverse classical' situation (see chapter 16) FDI is likely to crowd out domestic investment and thus to result in no net addition to jobs. There may, in fact, be a lower net addition to jobs

by the TNCs compared with job creation by domestic firms, if we allow for the fact that TNCs tend to create more capital-intensive capacity.[8]

Any conclusion on job losses in the home country must be based on clear and realistic assumptions about alternatives. If the home country economy is already working at full capacity or if it is working below capacity but the investment opportunities are taken up by other enterprises (domestic or foreign) there is no reason why the outward investment should result in job losses.

On a purely speculative level we may want to consider the 'no transnationals worldwide' alternative. Could we say anything about employment in the situation of no or little transnational development? This is, of course, a purely theoretical and indeed unrealistic alternative. My personal impression on this is that transnationalism worldwide is likely to create wider investment opportunities; this is because their ability to plan the production process worldwide may give TNCs the opportunity to develop products and processes that might not have been efficient in a 'national only' context. Looked at from this point of view we would have to conclude that – *ceteris paribus* – transnationalism worldwide adds to employment opportunities.

The employment effects go well beyond the direct effects created by FDI (whether actual or linked to potential alternative scenarios). There are many effects that are *indirect*: they come about through the effects of FDI on trade, on competition or on technology and its spread.

In section 17.1 the effects on trade were analysed. Trade effects generate indirect positive or negative employment effects; some of these effects are linked to the global planning of the production process. The balance of payments effects of FDI are likely to generate adjustments in prices and production leading to changes in employment.[9]

The technology effects considered in section 17.3 are also likely to generate employment effects. The overall volume of world employment, its geographical structure and its composition are indirectly influenced by the effects of TNCs' activities on trade and technology. The employment of unskilled, young, female labour in LDCs is connected to the type of components located in these countries and to the ability to locate the section of the production process requiring higher skills somewhere else.

Other effects on employment may come about via the effects that TNCs have on the market structure. Cowling (1982) claims that the competitive elements usually associated with imports no longer work, particularly for the UK economy, as trade is largely controlled by TNCs themselves. Cowling and Sugden (1987b) push the argument further and conclude that transnationalism increases the degree of monopoly. Such an increase leads to lower levels of effective demand and capacity utilization, and hence to a tendency towards stagnation and therefore to world unemployment.

The Cowling and Sugden arguments and their criticism have already been considered in chapter 15. The point that should be stressed here is not so much the issue about an increase in the degree of monopoly (which may or may not have happened) but the fact that indirect employment effects can come about in a variety of ways, including changes in market power.

One consequence of the globalization of production and the changing patterns of activities is that they may create extra difficulties in *assessing market power* for various reasons, in particular:

1   The usual indicators of the performance and behaviour of single subsidiaries may be misleading as assessors of structure for the following reasons: the performance of a single subsidiary may be biased and distorted by the company's overall strategy on location of production, transfer prices etc.; the actual market power of a TNC is likely to be more than the sum of power that might be attributed to units in single countries.
2   The recent tendency towards an increase in alliances and joint ventures is likely to increase the degree of monopoly.[10]

General *indirect* employment effects may, of course, also derive from the usual multiplying macro effects of investments; there are also indirect effects of horizontal and vertical linkages that TNCs may create in the economic systems.[11]

Effects on labour's strength and bargaining power

Labour and trade unions have often shown a considerable distrust of TNCs and their practices towards labour. To what extent is such distrust justified? Do TNCs' practices weaken the power of organized labour or strengthen it? Is labour utilization and exploitation in TNCs more intensive than in indigenous enterprises?

There is evidence that labour productivity is higher in TNCs than in domestic firms in many countries and particularly the UK. Enderwick (1985, pp. 75–80) gives evidence of a 32 per cent gap in the productivity of UK manufacturing in the late 1970s between foreign-owned and domestic-owned firms. This result is produced after some allowance is made for the possible differences in productivity of the different sectors in which the two groups of firms operate. Of course, the productivity gap could be explained by a variety of causes, including the size of plants, capital intensity, technology and high R&D intensity. However, we could also ascribe it, to some extent, to higher labour utilization or to superior managerial skills towards labour.

There is a considerable amount of literature on industrial relations in

TNCs and on their labour utilization practices.[12] Some of this literature is based on case studies of particular companies or on the analysis of specific industries. Most studies compare the labour relations practices of foreign firms operating in a particular country with the practices of domestic firms. Thus the emphasis has been on the effects that different managerial skills and different cultural backgrounds have on the labour relation practices of large companies. This type of analysis is, to some extent, inevitable; it is also useful in many respects. However, it makes it difficult to assess the practices of transnationals in general (whether home-based or foreign ones) against the practices of firms that are only or predominantly national. The impact of transnationalism *per se* on labour–capital relations is thus lost.

Many differences in TNCs' labour relations practices may, in fact, derive from their size and related technological advantage. However, here I shall concentrate, mainly, on specific differences deriving from transnationalism rather (or more) than size.

In their relations with labour, as in many other fields, TNCs have the advantage of being able to draw on a wide range of expertise deriving from their size and their spread of operations, which puts them in contact with a variety of industrial relations practices. The managerial skills needed for industrial relations are easily transferable although, of course, they need adaptation to local customs and cultures. There is some evidence that TNCs often tend to 'transfer' to the host country the industrial relation practices of their own home country. As newcomers in a host country TNCs can bargain (and often impose as part of the package) new practices that would be very difficult or impossible for old established domestic firms dealing with existing unions and their practices.

Different labour practices are one aspect of the conscious or unconscious attempts by many TNCs to distance themselves from domestic enterprises. Another aspect of this is their preference for unilateral bargaining and their reluctance to join employers' associations.

A related issue is that of the centralization of decisions. The feeling that decisions are taken far away from the scene of operations has always been a source of concern for labour and trade unions. This is understandable as the geographical and cultural distance, combined with the bureaucratic difficulties of dealing with many managerial layers, puts labour in a difficult position; this is bound to be the case as labour is essentially national and often 'local' in its organizational structure and culture. However, in practice, it is not clear to what extent these particular fears are justified. There is some evidence that, within multi-plant establishments, TNCs tend to operate in a more centralized fashion than domestic enterprises; however, it also seems that, within TNCs, labour relations are the most decentralized function.[13]

Connected with centralization and foreignness is the issue of careers for local managers in host countries. Many companies are known to give preference for top managerial jobs to home country nationals and, in particular, to people drawn from their own home base. This creates tensions with local white collar and managerial labour.

Many foreign TNCs are believed by the host country's labour to be foot-loose and thus to create unstable situations. Opinions differ on the degree to which TNCs are prepared to move from country to country. Moving out of a country, previously invested in, is expensive. However, there are various degrees of 'pulling-out'. The company may divest by not renewing depreciated capital and by slowly running down a particular subsidiary. The company may also fail to re-invest in the country any of the profits realized there. The threat of withdrawing future jobs by relocating planned investment can be used as a strong bargaining device towards labour.

The spread of production over many countries can be a source of flexibility for TNCs as they may take advantage of their plurality of sourcing to even out difficulties deriving from disruption of production in a particular location. This is the result of the fact that, while companies can achieve high levels of global planning, unions have, so far, been unable to organize themselves on a multi-country basis.

Enderwick (1982) takes the view that the weakening of labour as a result of TNCs' activities is an unjustifiably overemphasized issue. He considers two effects on labour: employment and industrial relations. The employment effects of FDI have been a main worry in the USA, while the industrial relations issue and the possible weakening of labour have been a main concern of British trade unions. He considers both these fears to be exaggerated. The worry over job losses stems – according to Enderwick – from the adoption of the 'wrong' model for the explanation of FDI. The US economic and political environment has been greatly influenced by the Hymer–Kindleberger and Vernon models, which have both led to pessimistic conclusions regarding outward FDI and a related loss of jobs for the USA. He concludes that Dunning's eclectic model, with its stress on ownership and location advantages and industry analysis, is likely to lead to less pessimistic results.

Of course, Enderwick's 'optimistic' conclusions could only be accepted if we were given evidence that Dunning's is the model that applies to the USA, that the effects on jobs are attenuated (as claimed by Enderwick) and that a less significant job loss is indeed compatible with Dunning's model. The conclusions could only be established by empirical tests.

Enderwick's conclusions on the effects on industrial relations are again rather optimistic for labour. He concentrates on the fact that TNCs operate a vertically integrated production process across countries. He concludes that the interdependence between subsidiaries results in 'acute sensitivity to production disruption' (p. 37). He gives as a measure of the high interdependency the large amount of intra-enterprise trade taking place across countries. He writes:

In fact, multinational status may even strengthen the relative bargaining power of organised labour. Where MNCs are created by a process of internalisation of imperfect external markets, the flow of products and information within the enterprise replaces distinct and discrete external transactions. The distinguishing feature of internal exchange is the retention of property rights. This serves to increase the interdependence between related affiliates. (Enderwick, 1982, p. 37)

His conclusion is reached by comparing a situation in which the vertical links occur across countries *but are internalized* via the operations of a single TNC, with a situation in which the vertical links are implemented across countries but by many firms, therefore there is *no internalization*. In this writer's view this comparison tells us something about the effects on labour's strength of *internalization versus externalization*, not of multinationality.

If we want to draw conclusions on the effects of *multinationality as such* on labour's strength, we should compare two situations, both characterized by *internalization* but differing in whether internalization occurs domestically or multinationally. If these two situations are compared the result is that the labour force is geographically fragmented in one case, but operates in a single country in the other; in both cases it is under the same ownership umbrella.

It has already been explained (in chapter 14) why multinational internalization is likely to weaken labour compared with the case of domestic internalization. My overall conclusion is that the geographical fragmentation of labour across many nations resulting from companies' internalization over many countries, rather than one, definitely weakens labour. Of course other trends might push in the opposite direction: vertical integration on an internal or external basis increases the risk of the spreading of damage caused by disruption at one point in the chain. However, if properly used by management, it can also be an instrument of division between labour working in different sectors or countries: workers in a given country and/or sector may be laid off (or fear they might be laid off) because of the loss of production due to stoppages caused by other workers in a vertically related sector.

Many effects of TNCs' activities on labour operate at both micro and macro levels. The micro and macro effects on labour fragmentation of the spread of production over many countries have already been considered in chapter 14.

As new labour practices, cultures and values spread from sector to sector and country to country, the effects on labour can be very long lasting and deep.

17.5   Sovereignty and the effectiveness of domestic policies

An issue often raised in the economic and political literature on TNCs is connected with sovereignty of the nation *vis-à-vis* the activities and power of TNCs. The problems are usually analysed with regard to the LDCs and their dependence on AICs and, in particular, the degree to which the inward activities of TNCs make LDCs dependent on the home countries of the TNCs. The issue has often been presented as one of dichotomy between two sets of countries: AICs and LDCs. In reality the problem is a much wider one. It largely originates from the centrality of decision-making by TNCs and from the degree to which decisions taken outside the country are likely to affect the national economy. Worries over the inward activities of TNCs may range from fears of interference in local political decisions to fears about environmental, safety and health standards, or fears of loss of cultural identity.

It would be naive, however, to think that the sovereignty issue relates to inward investment only, and the LCDs only. The central problem is, in fact, one of the multinationality and globality of decisions of certain institutions versus the 'national' character of single countries. The more a country is dominated by transnational companies (whether home-based or foreign-based) the more decisions about its production are taken on a global basis rather than on a narrow national basis.

Moreover, and this is crucial, a high level of multinational domination is likely to give a wide international orientation to a country's economic policies often at the expense of national capital and interest groups.[14] Pressures towards free trade policies may be a case in point. At the international level foreign policy may be kept in line with the interests of the home-based TNCs, which can exercise significant pressure on home governments; the size and direction of official aid to LDCs may, for example, follow the interests of outward investment. On a similar line, Stopford and Turner (1985, p. 214) mention the use of TNCs as 'transmission belts' for political messages from one country to another: an action in favour of or against a particular TNC may be interpreted as a sign of the direction of future foreign policy.

The more a country is dominated by TNCs, the more difficult it may be to ensure the effectiveness of domestic policies. This problem may affect various types of policies, such as competition, fiscal, monetary and trade policies. Domestic monetary policy can be rendered ineffective by the movements of large amounts of funds across countries by TNCs in response to changes in interest rates; high interest rates will then attract funds and increase money supply rather than decrease it. Similarly, banks can avoid overall direct control on their deposits by expanding in countries free from such controls.[15] The effectiveness of trade policy can be severely constrained by the large amounts of intra-firm trade coupled with the manipulation of transfer prices. There are many reasons for the failure of Keynesian demand management policies: increased multinational domination of national economies is likely to be one of them. The difficulties created stem partly from size and power but mainly from the transnationality of operations and globality of decisions.

A particular case in point is the issue of manipulation of transfer prices. The scope for manipulation is given by the links across nations, particularly the vertical internal links which render necessary and profitable the movements of components across countries. The reasons for pricing at levels different from arm's length prices are well known and include: minimization of tax liability worldwide; transfer of profits over and above the limits allowed by national governments; avoidance of exchange controls; penetration of new markets. The various reasons do not all necessarily work in the same direction.

There are, of course, some constraints to the manipulation of transfer pricing, including accounting ones and the need to exercise proper checks on the efficiency of individual branches. Nevertheless, the scope can be quite wide, particularly in all the cases in which comparable arm's length pricing does not exist or is difficult to establish, and, at the same time, outside control is very difficult.[16]

The main macro effects of the manipulation of transfer prices include ineffectiveness of domestic policies, loss (or gain) of extra tax revenue for governments, overall loss of tax revenue for all the countries considered together, and effects on the balance of payments and exchange rates, including the circumvention of exchange controls. There are also considerable distributional effects of transfer prices manipulation: for a start, 'surplus' is transferred from country to country and from the public sphere of tax revenue to the private sphere of companies' profits. Other distributional effects may come about indirectly via the effects on the balance of payments, on currency movements, exchange rates, trade, etc. In fact the distributional effects of TNCs' activities can go well beyond the effects of transfer prices manipulation: the geographical distribution of output, employment and incomes may be affected by their locational and sourcing policies; the functional distribution of income is affected by the technology, by the labour strategies and by the market power of TNCs.

In conclusion, transnationality and globalism in the planning and control of production create difficulties in the implementation of policies and in the control of national economic systems. As market power becomes transnational, it leads to difficulties in assessing it, but also to difficulties in implementing competition policies. As TNCs become more and more responsible for trade, the control of trade becomes more and more removed from national governments and pressure mounts for trade policies in line with the interests of TNCs. As larger amounts of trade become internal to firms the control over pricing, balance of payments and overall tax revenue becomes more difficult.

17.6   Growth and de-industrialization

As already mentioned, the effects of TNCs have often been analysed with reference to LDCs; however, concern over some negative effects of TNCs' activities on AICs has been growing. The UK has been a focus of concern, partly because of its high degree of 'maturity', partly because of the domination of its economy by TNCs and partly because of the de-industrialization process which its economic system has undergone.

TNCs are characterized by high technology, high productivity and advanced managerial and marketing techniques, and are, in general, high performers. Static welfare-type analyses would see the spread of their operations as transferring capital from abundant to scarce countries, transferring know-how and technology and generally seizing the best opportunities, thus leading to a worldwide maximization of welfare. The rosy picture of neo-classical analysis has, in the past, often been obscured by doubts about the benefits of TNCs' activities for LDCs. However, it is perhaps a sign of the growing concern over the growth and power of TNCs that there has recently been considerable literature on the possible negative effects of TNCs' activities on the performance of developed countries.

Enderwick (1987) points out the significance of TNCs' activities in the UK economy in terms of employment, profits and exports. He reports (pp. 1–2) how the top 69 UK-based MNCs plus the UK subsidiaries of foreign-owned multinationals were responsible for 59 per cent of UK manufacturing employment in 1981; they were also responsible for 72 per cent of the total UK reported profits in the same year, and for 82 per cent of exports. These figures clearly highlight how the vicissitudes of the UK economy cannot be seen separately from the operations of TNCs. TNCs in general, including UK-based TNCs, are high performers and yet the UK economy is a very poor performer; how can this be explained?

Enderwick (1987) points out how the UK-based TNCs showed atypical behaviour in the period 1977–81 in their employment pattern. The UK is unique among the developed countries in the fact that its MNEs, 'while increasing overall overseas employment', were 'responsible for a huge decline in domestic employment. This pattern was not displayed by MNEs from other nations' (p. 21). Enderwick – a follower of Dunning's eclectic approach – concludes that this shows that UK-based TNCs have ownership advantages which are best exploited overseas because of 'the declining locational attractiveness of the UK as a production base' (p.10).

Cowling (1984) argues that the international nature of British capital together with the high penetration of the UK by foreign capital has contributed to the weakening of the UK economy and accelerated the pace of de-industrialization at the same time that it has been creating problems for LDCs. He concludes his paper as follows: 'Not only is rapid de-industrialization the outcome for many of the older industrialised economies in a world of mobile industrial capital, but it is part of a negative-sum global game. Flexible capital, rather than leading to an efficient allocation of the world resources, leads in the opposite direction' (p. 20). He reaches his conclusion by focusing on the 'nomadic' nature of transnational capital and on the fact that its movements from country to country are motivated not by efficiency but 'by issues of control and distribution – the control of the work process by those who hire labour, and distribution in favour of those who control the location of production' (p. 17).

The existence of large foreign-owned capital operating in the UK has greatly contributed to the increase in import penetration. Cowling cites the situation in the motor manufacture industry and market. He writes:

> Whilst the share of the British car market captured by imports rose dramatically from 33% in 1975 to over 50% today, the Japanese share of the market rose from 9% to only 11%, whereas the share of imports from EEC rose from 20% to 38%, and a substantial fraction of this increase can be traced to the activities of the UK-based American assemblers, who have chosen to source an increasing proportion of their sales in the UK from their facilities on the continent. Ford dominates the UK car market with a share of around 30%, more than half of which has, in recent years, been sourced from plants outside the UK. It is, in fact, the biggest car importer into the UK. (p. 14)

On the connections between British capital and the British economy, Cowling thinks that the international nature and the related international opportunities of British capital have made it more mobile and weakened its operations in the UK, thus leading to a weaker economy; the long-term effect could be one of vicious cumulative causation.

We have already considered Radice's analysis (1984) of the vertical disintegration effects in the UK economy of the international vertical integration of capital: the effects are clearly negative and likely to accelerate the long-term process of decline. Similar conclusions on the negative effects of FDI on de-industrialization can be reached by concentrating on some balance of payments effects of FDI. Rowthorn and Wells (1987) give a detailed analysis of the effects of the structural changes in trade and related balance of payments components on the manufacturing sector of the UK economy. They distinguish two types of de-industrialization:

1 *Positive* de-industrialization, which is a characteristic of mature

economies, with a dynamic manufacturing sector in which high productivity growth leads to loss of jobs. Such loss is, however, compensated by the growth of the service sector, where employment grows faster than in the manufacturing sector, because of lower productivity levels and growth, and because of growing demand stimulated by the 'health and dynamism' of the manufacturing sector and hence of the economy as a whole.

2 *Negative* de-industrialization, characterized by a poor performance of the manufacturing sector where loss of jobs is accompanied by a slow-down in output and productivity. This leads to a poor growth performance of the economy and to uncompetitiveness in a cumulative vicious circle. Given the poor overall performance of the economy, the loss of manufacturing jobs cannot be compensated for by increases in the services sector.

Rowthorn and Wells see the UK economy as characterized by both elements of de-industrialization. They concentrate on the effects of changes in the structure of UK trade on de-industrialization. In their view, the UK has undergone autonomous structural changes in the non-manufacturing commercial account of the balance of payments caused by related autonomous structural changes of trade in food, raw materials, oil and non-government services. These changes have created a 'squeeze' on the manufacturing trade balance; this has led to a decline in manufacturing surplus and hence to a deterioration in the manufacturing sector of the economy, with the consequent loss of jobs, poor performance and de-industrialization. Their analysis raises many questions, including fundamental questions about methodology and policy questions about the 'inevitability' of what has been and is happening in the UK economy.[17]

One of the basic assumptions in the Rowthorn–Wells analysis is that a surplus in the non-manufacturing balance squeezes out the manufacturing contribution to the balance of payments, thus affecting negatively the manufacturing sector of the UK. Their analysis is mainly in terms of the effects of changes in the commercial sector and hence relates to the effects of a surplus in the commercial non-manufacturing trade on the manufacturing trade.

They also have a brief discussion on the contribution of foreign investment to the balance of payments. I have already mentioned (section 17.2) the possiblity that, in countries with a long tradition of outward foreign investment, such as the UK and the USA, the net inflow of interest, profits and dividends may in any one year be higher than the net outflow for new investments. This 'positive' balance of payments effect may, under special circumstances, turn out to have negative real effects; the economy can be caught in what Rowthorn and Wells call the 'wealth trap', by which they mean '*the automatic* process by which a country which is intrinsically a capital exporter may become a rentier nation' (p. 353). If the net inflow of interest, profits and dividends grows at a rate higher than the growth rate of the domestic economy (a very likely circumstance) the economy may absorb more manufacturing imports and experience a rise in its exchange rate; the overall result may be a negative effect on manufacturing trade.

Rowthorn and Wells give very limited weight to the possible negative effects of their 'wealth trap' on the manufacturing sector of the UK and thus on the de-industrialization process, partly because of their undue concentration on the effects of the so-called 'autonomous' changes in non-manufacturing trade. Indeed they hardly mention at all the role of TNCs in trade. However, a closer analysis of the 'wealth trap' issue might lead us to conclude that countries with a long tradition of outward foreign investment are likely to experience overall net 'positive' effects on the balance of payments. These may cause a rise in the exchange rate; in a situation in which the economy cannot – or is not allowed to, by monetary and fiscal policies – expand to meet the extra demand generated by the inflow of incomes, the overall long-term effect will be a weakening of the manufacturing sector with loss of jobs and 'negative' de-industrialization.

One should point out that there is nothing 'inevitable' in this process. Appropriate policies could divert the surplus generated by the net inflow of incomes from abroad into the acquisition of new equipment and the general modernization of the manufacturing sector. This would ensure the strengthening of the economy in the long run and a move towards positive, not negative, de-industrialization.

There are various lessons to be learnt from a full analysis of Rowthorn and Wells's 'wealth trap'. First, the overall balance of payments effects of FDI must be looked at in dynamic terms; if that is done we will see that what may start as an outflow, with negative effects on the balance of payments, may turn into a net inflow with positive balance of payments effects. Secondly, what may at first appear as a series of purely financial flows turns out, when properly analysed, to have serious effects on the real sector of the economy. Thirdly, it is clear that what may be to the benefit of TNCs and their shareholders (overseas investment) might turn out to cause job losses for other groups in the domestic economy: private and social benefits do not always go hand in hand. Fourthly, in this as in other issues, domestic policies towards FDI, and towards the use of incomes from abroad and of the balance of payments surplus they may generate, may be of crucial importance to the overall performance of the domestic economy.

Porter (1990), in an impressive study of competitive advantages of industries and nations, stresses the need to put firms and industries rather than macro elements at the basis of any analysis of the long-term economic performance of nations. He takes as 'the best measures of international competitive advantage either (1) the presence of substantial and sustained exports to a wide array of other nations and/or (2) significant outbound foreign investment based on skills and assets created in the home country' (p. 25). The nations that gain advantages are those that concentrate on the most productive industries. At the same time the nation can play an essential role in securing the competitive success of its firms through the provision of a congenial economic environment, institutions and policies.

Porter stresses the role of outward FDI and the multinational firm in gaining competitive advantages. He rightly considers outward FDI and exports as complementary; successful firms, industries and nations are involved in high levels of exports and outward FDI. TNCs have special relationships with the home country as the country in which they originate and first develop their products and whose working culture they absorb and adopt. Companies derive special benefits from the economic environment of the home nation and also give to it various advantages that lead to high productivity, exports and outward FDI.

Porter's interesting and comprehensive analysis seems, however, to neglect the large and increasing role of *inward* FDI in developed countries. In chapter 2 we saw evidence of large and increasing cross-country FDI and large intra-industry FDI. Is this pattern compatible with the notion that successful firms and nations are those that specialize in particular products and industries and then gain an advantage in exporting and investing abroad in those products? Does the presence of inward FDI in a developed nation signal low competitive advantage? To what extent does this apply to the UK history of large inward FDI and economic decline? These are questions that are stimulated by Porter's analysis; the answers to them may need further research work.

From the various works analysed in this section we can extract the following conclusions:

1   Enderwick sees de-industrialization as caused by locational disadvantages within the UK; the link between TNCs and de-industrialization is not one of causation.
2   Cowling sees TNCs causing de-industrialization through their footlooseness and through the pursuit of their specific objectives.
3   The activities of TNCs can contribute to the de-industrialization process through the operation of Rowthorn and Wells's 'wealth trap'.
4   From Porter's analysis we may infer a positive role for TNCs in gaining competitive advantages for themselves and for the nation from which they originate.

17.7   TNCs, uncertainty, rates of return and de-industrialization

In the previous section an attempt was made to present some links between de-industrialization and transnationalism. They all seem rather tenuous and it would be difficult, on any of them or even on all of them cumulatively, to take transnationalism as 'the' (or even 'a') cause of de-industrialization and low capital accumulation. Possible stronger links may be seen if we consider the generation of investment alternatives and the role of uncertainty. In order to illustrate these two points we shall take a little detour via some recent interpretations of Keynes.

The post-Second World War interpretations of Keynes have had, among others, the following effects. They have led to a 'Keynesian analysis' in which risk, uncertainty and expectations have disappeared; they have also led to policy prescriptions that have concentrated on short-term counter-cyclical measures, on fiscal policy, on demand management implemented largely via the direct or indirect manipulation of public and private consumption. More recent interpretations are now moving away from this 'Keynesian' approach in an attempt to render justice to Keynes's thought. One of the cornerstones of the new wave of interpretations is based on the attempt to put uncertainty at the centre of the analysis, in line with Keynes's original theory. The post-Keynesian school is largely responsible for this new wave of re-interpretations.[18]

A recent re-interpretation has been put forward by Meltzer (1988). According to Meltzer, Keynes saw the effects of risk and uncertainty as leading to high interest rates; this is for various reasons, in particular because the divorce of lenders from borrowers means that the risk for both sets of people must be taken into account in the interest rate. The end result is that the rate of interest is usually too high to secure a level of investment leading to a socially 'optimal capital stock'.

Meltzer thus argues, convincingly, that 'Keynes's principal concern was to reduce the divergence between private and social returns to investment and increase the scale of output by reducing uncertainty' (p. 309). The policy prescriptions, on this interpretation, are along three main lines: (a) public investment in order to supplement the insufficient private level; (b) any measure leading to a reduction in the degree of uncertainty, as this would lower the rate of interest and thus generate higher levels of private investment – this would include the work of national and international institutions directed towards higher stability and lower uncertainty; (c) the establishment of set 'rules' and 'norms' on fiscal and monetary policies, thus creating a more stable, less uncertain macro environment.

According to Meltzer, concentration on fine-tuning and short-run aggregate demand management has prevented economists and politicians from seeing Keynes's principal message; more importantly, it has increased the degree of instability and uncertainty in the economy, thus leading to effects opposite to the ones Keynes wished to see come about. In theory, fine-tuning could have led to higher stability via increasing confidence in the government's ability and willingness to regulate the trade cycle. In practice, it has led to increased instability and uncertainty for a variety of reasons including the following: incompetence; objective difficulties in assessing the desirable scale, type and time of intervention; lack of fixed, set 'norms' which entrepreneurs could take as a guide for medium- and long-term planning; intervention geared to the political more than the economic cycle.

Given the above points on the interpretation of Keynes's thought and on the shortcomings of the Keynesian analysis and policies, I now move on to consider their relationship to TNCs' activities. I shall, at the same time, try to analyse the effects on the macro economy.

The conclusion reached by this author is that TNCs' activities have contributed to a lower rate of capital formation and thus have contributed to de-industrialization in the UK in the following ways.

1   Given their opportunity for global scanning and planning, TNCs are able to gain higher rates of return by investing abroad and/or by a combination of domestic and foreign investment. This has tended to increase the domestic marginal rate of return and thus the rate at which firms are prepared to invest in the UK. A country that is very highly dominated by the activities of transnational companies, and where this domination process starts first, finds itself in a disadvantaged position relative to other countries; this negative relative position will contribute to the well-known process of cumulative causation in de-industrialization. As we shall see in more detail in chapter 18, Britain has been the leader, not only in the starting of transnational activities, but also in the scale of overall multinational domination of its economy.

2   Global scanning combined with electronic technology in communications and ease of movement of funds across frontiers by TNCs may have contributed to raising the rate of return on purely financial investment. This will have raised the marginal rate of return required on real capital formation. Similarly, high rates of return on the services sector (particularly the financial services) may have raised the marginal rate of return on the manufacturing sector investments.

3   TNCs may have contributed to the increase in the level of uncertainty in the domestic economy for the following reasons:

(a)   because, given the TNCs' global planning and their locational alternatives for production, any given country can be less certain of attracting investment within its confines;
(b)   because the activities of TNCs reduce the effectiveness of domestic economic policies and thus the stability of a given country, as argued in section 17.5.

Both outward activities of domestic TNCs and inward activities of foreign TNCs contribute cumulatively to the increase in the level of uncertainty.

In conclusion, TNCs' activities may have contributed to the process of de-industrialization in the UK via:

1   The generation of alternatives for investment, which raised the required marginal rate of return on domestic real investment. These alternatives were in terms of worldwide location of investment and in terms of services versus manufacturing sectors, and financial versus real investments.
2   The increase in the overall level of uncertainty in the economy.

However, it is not claimed here that TNCs' activities are the only or main cause of de-industrialization in the UK; they are likely to have been a strong contributing factor.

De-industrialization is, in fact, unlikely to have a single cause, and indeed it must be seen as a dynamic process in which causes cumulate through time. We cannot, however, ignore the fact that the UK is the economy where the de-industrialization process is most advanced and the one that is most highly dominated by TNCs.

18

Multinational Domination of National Economies

Facts by themselves are silent.
                                                A. Marshall, *The Present Position of Economics*

18.1 Introduction

The impact of TNCs' activities on national economies varies a great deal from country to country. The differences are related not just to the level of development; there are, undoubtedly, considerable differences among countries at different stages of development, as would be expected, but there are also considerable variations between developed market economies. There is, for example, widespread feeling that the role played by TNCs in the British economy is greater than the role played by TNCs in other comparable developed Western economies.[1]

This chapter presents some indicators designed to capture the extent to which an economic system is dominated by TNCs; estimates are given for Britain and for some of the major developed countries. Assessment of the relevance and impact of TNCs' activities on national economies helps towards an assessment of direct and indirect effects of such activities.

As highlighted in chapters 1 and 2, the activities of TNCs take different forms; besides, TNCs' control over production spans much wider than control over their direct production. However, as the aim of this chapter is to present some indicators of multinational domination of national economies, we have to confine ourselves to developing indicators from existing statistics; this means that the data and indicators will refer to FDI as a *proxy* for international production. In interpreting the results, the reader must bear in mind the following points. First, the official data on

This chapter is a modified and updated version of a paper originally published in the *International Review of Applied Economics* in 1989.

FDI do not distinguish between acquisitions of controlling interests in existing firms and investment in greenfield plants;[2] this means that although FDI incorporates productive capacity and assets that are additional for the investing company (and the home country), the assets and capacity are not always additional for the host country and for the world economy. Secondly, TNCs' effective control over production spans much wider than is shown by the data and indicators presented here. This is because the FDI data cannot take account of the wider control over production exercised through non-equity involvement by TNCs (see chapter 2).

The next section of this chapter is devoted to a general comparative overview of the relative positions of major developed market economies as regards FDI. Section 18.3 introduces a multinational domination ratio and gives estimates for major developed Western countries; estimates for the UK are in section 18.4. Section 18.5 presents a first attempt at using a global approach in estimating elasticities of trade with respect to FDI for the UK. Section 18.6 draws some conclusions.

18.2   Relative position on FDI: an international overview

Any attempt to assess the impact of FDI on domestic economies must necessarily take into account their relative size. Tables 18.1 and 18.2 give international comparisons of foreign direct investment and international production in relation to various indicators of the size of domestic economies.

Table 18.1 gives trends in the ratios of outward and inward direct investment as a percentage of gross domestic fixed capital formation (GDFCF) for major developed countries. Two countries show very significant results: the Netherlands and the UK. In both cases there is large and increasing FDI in relation to the size of GDFCF for both inward and outward flows; the outward ratio, in particular, shows a tremendous jump in the 1980s. The USA shows increasing ratios for inward flows in relation to GDFCF but decreasing relative outward flows. Japan's trends are in the opposite directions to the USA's: increasing outward trends and decreasing inward ones.

Table 18.2 gives the average value of international production as a percentage of exports and GDP for selected years (1968–88) and ten industrialized Western economies.[3] The ratio of international production to exports gives us an idea of trends and comparisons of internationalization and integration as a whole. Does internationalization take more the form of exports or the form of international production for any particular country and time? Looking at the data for each country through time, we see that some countries show a trend towards an increase in inter-

Table 18.1 Flow of direct investment from and into developed market economies as percentage of gross domestic fixed capital formation, 1960–1987

Country	Outward			Inward		
	1960–9	*1970–9*	*1980–7*	*1960–9*	*1970–9*	*1980–7*
Canada	1.2	2.3	5.8	4.7	2.4	1.1
USA	3.4	4.4	2.2	0.4	1.2	3.9
Belgium–Luxembourg	0.7	2.6	2.5	4.3	6.2	6.6
France	1.2	1.4	3.1	1.1	1.8	2.2
Federal Republic of Germany	1.2	2.1	3.2	2.2	1.8	0.6
Italy	1.4	0.8	2.1	2.5	1.7	1.4
Netherlands	4.7	6.8	16.8	3.6	4.4	6.2
Sweden	1.7	3.0	5.2	1.5	0.7	1.0
UK	4.8	7.7	14.1	3.3	3.9	6.7
Japan	0.4	0.9	1.7	0.2	0.2	0.1
Australia	0.6	1.1	2.2	8.4	6.1	4.8
Averages	1.9	3.0	5.4	2.9	2.8	3.2

Values are averages for the period.

Source: IMF *Balance of Payments Yearbook*, 1988; OECD, 1987, for 1980–7; UNCTC, 1983a, pp. 41 and 44, for 1960–79.

nationalization via international production rather than via exports. Comparisons of ratios of international production to exports across countries are, of course, highly affected by the degree of openness of the economies considered and the relative importance of exports. A more meaningful ratio for international comparisons may be the ratio of international production to GDP presented in table 18.2. The average ratios show a clear ranking in the relevance of international production in relation to the size of the country (measured by its GDP): the Netherlands and the UK come top with Japan, Italy and Australia bottom. In terms of trends in individual countries, the tendency has been for an increase in all the countries except the USA. The data used for table 18.2 give estimates for *total* exports, international production and GDP; a sector or industry analysis might show different patterns.

From trends shown in tables 2.1, 2.2, 2.6, 18.1 and 18.2, Britain's position in the international context can be summarized in the following points:

1   It is still responsible for a high share of outward investment; its share

Table 18.2 International production as percentage of exports and GDP in ten selected industrialized countries, 1968–1988

	UK	Netherlands	USA	Canada	FRG	France	Italy	Japan	Australia	Belgium and Luxembourg
International production as a percentage of Exports										
Average 1968–79	107.0	104.6	191.6	44.2	25.6	41.6	18.2	33.0	n.a.	n.a.
Average 1980–8	128.7	99.8	155.8	63.7	31.1	n.a.	20.6	32.5	24.3	13.5
International production as a percentage of GDP										
Average 1968–79	27.2	46.8	13.8	11.0	6.4	7.1	3.7	4.0	n.a.	n.a.
Average 1980–8	36.2	58.2	12.5	17.7	9.4	n.a.	5.4	4.6	4.4	9.3

n.a.: not available.
For some countries a year may be missing from the period over which the averages are calculated.

Sources: OECD, 1987; IMF, 1988 and 1989

of outward FDI among the developed market economies was 18.5 per cent in 1960, decreased in the late sixties and seventies, reaching 11.1 per cent in 1978, and increased again to over 15 per cent in the eighties (Table 2.1). It ranks second to the USA in terms of the overall outward share, though the outward flow in relation to the size of its domestic capital formation (table 18.1) places it in first position, together with the Netherlands.

2 In relation to other countries it has a very high rate of involvement through international production compared with exports (table 18.2).

3 The ratio of international production to GDP places the UK in a very high position in the international league, second only to the Netherlands (table 18.2); similar results are shown by the ratio of outward FDI to GDFCF (table 18.1).

4 Together with the Netherlands it shows the highest, and increasing, ratios of inward *and* outward FDI in relation to GDFCF (table 18.1).

5 It is home to over 10 per cent of the largest TNCs in the world; this puts the UK in third position worldwide after the USA, with almost 46 per cent, and Japan, with almost 16 per cent (table 2.6).

18.3 Multinational domination of national economies: international comparisons

The data from tables 18.1 and 18.2, analysed in the previous section, give some idea of the impact of FDI on national economies. None the less, the full extent of the overall impact of FDI and of the possible domination of national economies by TNCs is not captured by analysing inward and outward activities separately.

In chapter 16 arguments were given in favour of taking a *global* approach in assessing the effects of international production; by a global approach is meant one that considers *both* inward and outward activities rather than concentrating on the direction of the flow of investment. Following this approach, the aim is now to arrive at an indicator that can help assess the comparative relevance across countries and industries of those effects of international operations that are connected with the overall volume and spread of FDI. I am aware that the impact and effects of TNC activities have many aspects and dimensions; indeed, the activities themselves are varied and their full relevance and spread can be only partially caught by data on foreign direct investment. However, as the aim is to arrive at a single and simple indicator, using official statistics, the analysis will be confined to FDI only.

In order to capture the full effects of the two-way flow both inward and outward FDI are incorporated. GDFCF was chosen as the normalizer since it is the domestic indicator nearest to foreign direct investment.[4]

The indicator presented in equation (18.1) was eventually arrived at. It has been called the *multinational domination ratio* (MNDR), because it attempts to measure the overall impact of domestic and foreign TNCs (as measured by their FDI activities) on domestic economies.[5]

$$\text{MNDR} = \frac{\text{FDI}\,(\text{I} + \text{O})}{\text{GDFCF}} \times 100 \qquad\qquad (18.1)$$

Where: FDI is foreign direct investment; I + O is inward and outward; GDFCF is gross domestic fixed capital formation.

Table 18.3 contains estimates of this ratio for some major industrialized countries. On a year-to-year basis the data are likely to be affected by cyclical fluctuations in GDFCF. This is why averages have been calculated so that the comparisons can be made on the basis of long-term trends. The ratios show considerable differences among countries; the ranking puts the UK and the Netherlands in the top positions and Japan and Italy in the bottom positions.

Looking at countries' positions through time we notice that most countries have seen an increase in their multinational domination ratio; the increase is very considerable for the UK and the Netherlands. These two countries have, through time, become more and more dominated by TNCs' activities. It is interesting to note that the UK and the Netherlands also show increasing ratios of international production to GDP (table 18.2) through time. The results of tables 18.2 and 18.3 reinforce each other. The Federal Republic of Germany and Japan show low values of MNDR, particularly Japan. However, the ratios are increasing in both countries and this is accompanied by a tendency towards higher outward involvement in relation to volume of exports and to GDP (see table 18.2).

The ratios in table 18.3 refer to total FDI and total GDFCF. It was felt that it would be interesting to have a more detailed analysis for manufacturing. I have, therefore, tried to construct a similar indicator for various manufacturing industries and different countries. However, this proved rather difficult for the following reasons.

The only comparable data on FDI that it was possible to obtain were stock data.[6] An appropriate normalizer for these data would have been the net stock of capital for those industries and countries. Data on domestic capital stock are, however, on the whole, less reliable – for reasons related to both economic theory and statistics – than the corresponding flow data on GDFCF. Besides, and this was obviously crucial, it is virtually impossible to get comparable data on capital stock across countries and industries. I therefore had to rely on a variable constructed from GDFCF as a 'normalizer'. Appropriate regrouping of GDFCF data was necessary to arrive at data comparable with the classification used for foreign assets. The following indicator was, eventually, arrived at:

Table 18.3 Multinational domination ratios: ratio of foreign direct investment (outward and inward) as percentage of GDFCF, 1960–1987, for 11 industrialized Western countries

	USA	Japan	FRG	France	Canada	Italy	UK	Nether-lands	Sweden	Belgium and Lux.	Australia	Average all countries
Average 1960–69	3.7	0.6	2.5	2.0	5.7	4.2	8.1	6.5	n.a.	n.a.	n.a.	4.1
Average 1970–79	5.4	1.0	3.7	3.6	5.3	3.0	12.1	11.2	n.a.	n.a.	n.a.	5.7
Average 1980–87	6.1	1.8	3.8	5.3	6.6	3.5	20.8	22.9	7.2	9.1	7.0	9.5

n.a.: not available.

Sources: OECD, *National Accounts* (various issues); IMF, *Balance of Payments Yearbook* (various issues); IMF, 1989, *International Financial Statistics*

$$MNDR_t = \frac{FDA\ (I + O)_t}{\sum\limits_{n=0}^{4} GDFCF_{t-n}} \times 100 \qquad\qquad (18.2)$$

For t = 1965, 1970, 1975 and where:

$MNDR_t$ = Multinational domination Ratio at end of year t;

$FDA\ (I + O)_t$ = Inward + Outward Foreign Direct Assets at end of year t

GDFCF = Gross Domestic Fixed Capital Formation.

This is essentially a ratio related to stocks rather than flows (as in MNDR of table 18.3); the underlying assumption is that the sum of GDFCF over the previous five years gives a reasonable estimate of the domestic capital stock. Table 18.4 gives results for the ratios for various countries and for nine manufacturing industries as well as for total manufacturing. There are various problems attached to this indicator and the related estimates which means that the results must be considered with much more caution than those from table 18.3.[7]

The data in table 18.4 show ratios that are considerably higher than those in table 18.3. This partly reflects the fact that FDI involvement in manufacturing is higher than for the economy as a whole, to which the data in table 18.3 refer.[8] From table 18.4 the picture we get is one in which the ranking still sees the UK at the top in terms of multinational domination of its manufacturing sector, while Japan is at the bottom. The ranking is similar to that of table 18.3. Both the UK and Japan show increases through time in their ratios for total manufacturing. Looking at the nine industries, we see the following. Taking the average for the five countries it is noticeable that the ratio has increased between 1970 and 1975 in all the industries considered. The industries which share the highest domination ratios across countries are those involving engineering.

The overall picture we get from all the sets of data in tables 18.3 and 18.4 is one of substantial unevenness in the spread of multinational domination across countries and industries. If we accept that considerable effects, particularly on trade, labour and the effectiveness of domestic policies, derive from the activities of TNCs, then we must expect the weight of these effects to be unevenly spread among countries and sectors.

18.4 Multinational domination ratios: the UK situation

An attempt was made to get a more detailed picture of the UK situation in terms of its various industries and the relative relevance of various countries with which the UK has FDI links. Table 18.5 gives average

Table 18.4 Multinational domination ratios in five industrialized countries, manufacturing industries, 1965, 1970 and 1975; percentages

Industries	USA			UK		Japan			Federal Republic of Germany		Sweden		Average of five countries	
	1965[a]	1970	1975	1970	1975	1965	1970	1975	1970	1975	1970	1975[b]	1970	1975
FDT	36.45	38.30	44.65	113.44	130.05	1.07	0.86	1.64	27.31	36.31	11.79	19.34	38.34	46.40
CAP	52.99	40.58	52.59	66.10	91.66	2.91	2.28	4.47	37.93	48.92	53.25	40.19	40.02	47.56
PFM	23.25	22.68	36.64	42.06	28.43	1.88	1.39	2.36	26.60	49.93	25.67	23.75	23.68	28.22
MIE	104.15	59.14	82.70	98.50	129.87	4.38	3.53	4.27	37.17	55.61	137.90	97.70	67.25	74.03
EE	60.63	42.08	70.14	174.14	163.39	2.06	2.66	6.25	44.40	68.87	84.88	87.97	69.63	79.32
TE	65.78	56.57	65.04	50.81	52.81	1.55	1.08	2.61	38.58	36.34	6.97	11.59	30.80	33.68
TLCF	14.83	12.62	15.96	39.78	55.74	2.63	3.68	12.64	26.14	37.92	12.38	17.59	18.92	27.97
PPP	26.13	21.47	26.80	59.28	98.95	3.11	3.51	4.39	9.19	15.94	11.59	14.32	21.01	32.08
OMI	12.57	20.08	23.54	48.23	59.44	0.61	0.75	1.78	7.68	9.71	6.32	9.54	16.61	20.80
Total manu-facturing	39.42	34.98	46.82	73.20	85.55	2.11	1.93	4.87	29.97	40.28	30.43	29.42	34.10	41.39

FDT: food, drink, tobacco. CAP: chemical and allied products. PFM: primary and fabricated metals. MIE: mechanical and instrument engineering. EE: electrical engineering. TE: transport equipment. TLCF: textiles, leather, clothing and footwear. PPP: paper, printing and publishing. OMI: other manufacturing industries.
[a] Outward FDI refers to 1966.
[b] Outward FDI refers to 1974.

Sources: Dr J. Clegg for data on FDI assets; *UN Yearbook of Industrial Statistics*, 1976 and previous issues, for GDFCF; *IMF Balance of Payments Yearbook*, various issues, for exchange rates

multinational domination ratios for various manufacturing industries. The results show considerable variations from industry to industry and different dynamics through time; for total manufacturing the ratio has increased from 41.1 per cent in the 1970s to 58.9 per cent in the 1980s.

The data in table 18.3 and 18.5 refer to flows: FDI and GDFCF. However, the global effects deriving from inward and outward TNCs' activities are likely to be related not just to the year-to-year new activities, but also to the accumulation of linkages and thus to the cumulative FDI over the years: hence more to the stock than the flow of FDI. The higher the level of TNCs' productive capacity, its spread throughout the world and its level of activity, the higher is, for example, the scope for movements of components and funds across the world. Therefore, the higher is the scope for international trade, intra-firm trade and transfer prices manipulation.

In order to take account of the effects of accumulation, calculations were made to arrrive at multinational domination ratios using stock data rather than flows. The following equation has been used:

$$\text{MNDRK}_t = \frac{\text{K FDI (I + O)}_t}{\text{DFK}_t} \times 100 \qquad (18.3)$$

Where: MNDRK_t is the multinational domination ratio at the end of year t (stock data); K FDI $(I + O)_t$ is the book value of stock of FDI (inward plus outward) at the end of year t; DFK_t is the value of domestic capital stock (net fixed assets) at the end of year t.

The ratios in table 18.6 are the results of equation (18.3). They are more stable than those in table 18.5 as the latter show a more erratic behaviour because of year-to-year variations in foreign and/or domestic investment. The indicators based on stock data (table 18.6) are more reliable. They show a tendency towards considerable increase in the indicators for most industries and particularly for total manufactures and all industries. The MNDRK for manufacturing industry moves from around 24–25 per cent in the 1970s to over 30 per cent in the mid and late 1980s. The ratio for total industry moves from around 6 per cent in the 1970s to over 12 per cent in the mid and late 1980s.

I also wanted to capture the overall FDI (inward and outward) involvement of the UK with various countries or areas. It would have been meaningless to construct multinational domination ratios similar to the ones just discussed, since it does not make sense to allocate the UK GDFCF by country. I have instead calculated percentage distribution of stock of FDI (inward and outward) for each country or area. The data (table 18.7) show that the biggest overall FDI (inward and outward) involvement for the UK is with the USA and Western Europe, and that in both of these areas it has increased. The overall involvement with the

Table 18.5 UK multinational domination ratios, flow data, manufacturing and total industries, averages 1972–1979, 1980–1987; percentages

	Food, drink, tobacco	Chemicals	Metal	Mechanical and electrical engineering	Motor	Textile	Paper, printing, publishing	Rubber	Other manufacturing[a]	Total manufacturing	Total all industries
1972–9	63.2	63.5	11.6	58.4	41.5	20.8	42.2	19.0	38.2	41.1	n.a.
1980–7	78.0	94.5	34.6	55.7	13.3	49.0	25.6	−23.7	144.0	58.9	18.4

n.a.: not available.
[a] Includes shipbuilding.

Sources: CSO *Business Monitor* (MA4), 1987 and previous years; CSO *UK National Accounts*, 1987 and previous years

Table 18.6 UK multinational domination ratios, book value and capital stock data, main manufacturing industries and total for all industries, end of year 1971–1987; percentages

Year	Food, drink, tobacco	Chemicals	Metal	Mechanical engineering	Electrical engineering	Motor	Textiles	Paper, printing, publishing	Rubber	Other manufacturing	Total manufacturing	Total all industries
1971	44.5	25.1	13.1	38.8	46.5	14.6	15.8	18.6	28.0	17.4	25.6	7.4
1978	39.5	30.8	8.9	32.4	36.2	12.3	12.1	21.6	19.3	17.5	23.8	5.8
1981	38.5	35.7	7.5	28.9	36.1	14.1	10.9	18.5	20.4	14.5	23.8	5.7
1984	36.8	49.1	14.1	35.6	46.4	15.1	15.4	17.8	15.6	32.3	30.8	12.4
1987	42.2	52.6	14.0	30.5	48.3	19.5	13.3	30.5	9.4	37.8	34.0	12.5

Sources: CSO Business Monitor (MA4), 1987 and previous editions; CSO UK National Accounts, Blue Book, 1987 and previous editions; Capital stock data supplied directly by the Department of Trade and Industry

Table 18.7 UK book value of foreign direct investment (inward plus outward), selected countries and main areas, 1962–1987; percentage distribution

	1962	1971	1981	1987
Western Europe	15.6	22.4	24.5	33.2
Belgium–Luxembourg	1.5	1.8	1.9	1.8
France	2.4	3.1	3.6	3.7
Federal Republic of Germany	1.5	3.5	4.7	3.5
Irish Republic	1.4	1.8	1.8	0.9
Italy	1.0	1.6	1.0	1.1
Netherlands	2.1	3.9	4.0	13.9
Sweden	0.7	1.1	1.4	0.9
Switzerland	2.9	3.2	3.3	3.9
North America	38.7	39.9	44.7	45.1
Canada	13.5	8.5	6.2	5.7
USA	25.2	30.9	38.5	39.4
Other developed countries	19.8	20.4	15.3	9.9
Australia	10.9	11.1	8.5	5.6
Japan	0.0	0.3	1.1	2.0
South Africa	6.6	7.3	5.0	1.5
Rest of the world	25.9	17.2	15.5	11.8
World	100.00	100.00	100.00	100.00

Source: CSO *Business Monitor* (MO4), various years

rest of the world (mainly LDCs) has declined very considerably. A decline is also shown in figures related to some 'Commonwealth' countries, such as Australia, Canada and South Africa.

In summary, the overall picture that emerges for the UK is clear: an economy which is very highly dominated by TNCs compared with other industrialized countries, and for which the domination ratios (for the economy as a whole and for manufacturing) are increasing.

18.5 Trade and FDI: a preliminary attempt to use a 'global' approach

The theoretical points made in chapter 16 have led to the estimates presented in the two previous sections of this chapter. Both theoretical and empirical results point to the desirability of considering the overall global, two-way flow of activities in assessing the effects of TNCs. By looking together at both inward and outward FDI, we get a more realistic assessment of the impact of TNCs' activities on domestic economies. Among the effects that are likely to be better understood and assessed by a global approach, are those on labour, the effectiveness of economic policies and trade. Detailed estimates of the various effects are outside the scope of this work. However, as a preliminary example, an attempt has been made to consider how a global approach can contribute to the assessment of trade effects.

In chapters 16 and 17 it was argued that there is a need to consider the cumulative effects on trade of both inward and outward investment; this was done on the assumption that a foreign link – whether generated by outward or by inward activity – is likely to lead to movements of components, services etc., and thus to trade. Any increase in trade thus generated is likely to be related to the overall spread of international production rather than to the direction of FDI. This leads to the need to consider both outward and inward FDI in the assessment of FDI effects on trade. The issue of the functional relationship between trade and foreign direct investment would, of course, have to be considered in the context of a fully specified trade model involving other relevant variables. This is outside the scope of this work.

I have, however, attempted some preliminary estimates of elasticities of trade with respect to overall foreign direct investment. The elasticities (tables 18.8 and 18.9) have been calculated as ratios of growth rates of trade over growth rates of book value of FDI (inward and outward). There are strong *a priori* reasons to believe that there is complementarity between trade and foreign direct investment (see chapter 17). The results obtained for elasticities seem to corroborate the complementarity hypothesis.

Table 18.8 gives elasticities for the 1970s and 1980s[9] of total trade, imports and exports with respect to book value of FDI. All elasticities are positive, with the exception of the rubber industry for the 1980s. The negative values for this industry result from the large decline in outward stock between 1978 and 1987. The elasticities of exports were all greater than 1 in the 1970s; so were the elasticities of imports, with the exception of food-drink-tobacco and paper-printing-publishing. Total trade – imports and exports – followed a similar pattern to imports elasticities in the 1970s.

In the 1980s *all* exports elasticities declined compared with their 1970s values. Many imports elasticities declined but some increased (metal, mechanical engineering and textiles); this pattern is largely reflected in total trade. The decline in elasticities in the 1980s is likely to be due to the deepening of the recession and its effects on trade. The large increase in FDI in the 1980s would also have had an immediate depressive effect on elasticities; however, if our arguments are correct, this increase in overseas involvement is likely to generate extra trade (both imports and

Table 18.8 UK elasticity of imports, exports and total trade (imports plus exports) with respect to total book value of foreign direct investment, main manufacturing industries, averages for the 1970s and 1980s

Elasticity	Years[a]	Food, drink, tobacco	Chemicals	Metal	Mechanical engineering	Electrical engineering	Motor	Textiles	Paper, printing, publishing	Rubber	Other manufacturing	Total manufacturing	Total all industries
%M / %KFDI(I + O)	1970s	0.87	1.15	1.22	1.63	1.72	2.94	2.10	0.95	3.30	1.42	1.31	n.a.
	1980s	0.82	0.93	1.26	1.96	1.52	0.93	2.88	0.95	-7.64	0.60	1.04	0.58
%X / %KFDI(I + O)	1970s	1.22	1.06	1.23	1.27	1.47	1.40	1.50	1.06	2.36	1.27	1.16	n.a.
	1980s	1.07	0.84	0.96	1.06	1.26	0.84	1.42	0.85	-4.96	0.34	0.85	0.42
%(M + X) / %KFDI(I + O)	1970s	0.96	1.10	1.23	1.37	1.57	1.91	1.81	0.97	2.71	1.33	1.23	n.a.
	1980s	0.90	0.87	1.10	1.42	1.39	0.87	2.10	0.91	-6.27	0.49	0.94	0.51

na: not available. M: imports; X: exports. KFDI (I + O): stock of FDI (inward + outward). %: percentage change.
[a] See note 9 to chapter 18.

Sources: CSO Business Monitor MO4 and MQ10 (various years)

exports) in the future. Essentially there may be lags in the relationship between the growth of FDI stock and the growth of trade that are not fully captured by the very simple elasticities presented here.

Elasticities of imports are higher than exports elasticities for total industries, total manufacturing and for most manufacturing industries. If the causal relationship between FDI and trade were corroborated, these results would suggest that, in the UK, the impact of FDI on trade, while strong for trade as a whole, is higher for imports.

Calculations have also been made of similar elasticities for total manufacturing and the main countries with which the UK has strong trade or international production links (table 18.9). The elasticities of total trade with respect to total (inward and outward) foreign direct investment are again all greater than 1, with the exception of the Netherlands, Japan and South Africa; for the latter two countries it is clear that integration has increasingly taken the direct investment route rather than the trade route. The elasticity of imports is higher than the elasticity of exports for all countries except the Irish Republic. This confirms the results obtained in the industrial breakdown analysis (table 18.8).

It should be pointed out that I am aware of not having established functional relationships and that a properly specified functional relationship is likely to involve various variables in the explanation of trade. None the less, the main trends in the results seem relevant: positive elasticities for almost all the data in tables 18.8 and 18.9; elasticities greater than 1 in most cases; and elasticities of imports greater than elasticities of exports in most cases.

This last result can have significant repercussions: if it is corroborated that as a result of FDI imports increase faster than exports, we have to look carefully at the employment effects of such results. It could be that any positive employment effects of inward FDI are counterbalanced by the negative employment effects of more than proportional increases in imports. And, in fact, in the 1970s most elasticities of imports, with respect to inward FDI only, are well above unity, denoting growth rates of imports well above the growth rates of the stock of inward FDI. The only industries for which this is not the case are food-drink-tobacco and paper-printing-publishing (see table 18.10). In the 1980s most elasticities show a decline compared with the 1970s values with the exception of mechanical engineering, textiles, paper-printing-publishing and rubber.

On the whole, it seems that these preliminary results warrant further research to try to test functional relationships and estimate elasticities in the context of a fully specified model in which *overall FDI appears as one of the variables affecting trade* and appropriate lags can also be used.

Table 18.9 UK elasticities of imports, exports and total trade with respect to book value of total foreign direct investment in selected countries and areas, total manufacturing, averages 1962–1984

Countries and areas	%M % KFDI (I + O)	%X % KFDI (I + O)	% (M + X) % KFDI (I + O)
Belgium and Luxembourg	1.25	1.05	1.14
France	1.14	1.07	1.10
FRG	1.11	0.99	1.06
Italy	1.64	1.47	1.55
Netherlands	1.06	0.90	0.98
Irish Republic	1.09	1.15	1.12
USA	1.21	1.17	1.18
Japan	0.64	0.40	0.58
South Africa	0.81	0.69	0.63
Total developed countries	1.26	1.04	1.16
Total developing countries	1.47	1.15	1.24
World	1.30	1.03	1.17

M: imports. X: exports. KFDI (I + O): stock of foreign direct investment (inward + outward). %: percentage change.

The growth rates used refer to 1975–84 for trade, and to 1962–81 for foreign direct investment (except for Japan, for which they refer to 1968–81).

Sources: Trade data supplied directly by Department of Trade and Industry; foreign direct investment data, CSO *Business Monitor*, MO4.

18.6   Conclusions

The overall world picture is one of increasing involvement in international production by the major capitalist economies. The UK share of outward FDI among the DMEs decreased in the 1970s and increased in the 1980s. Its outward involvement, however, is very, very high and increasing in relation to the size of the domestic economy.

Our attempts to measure the degree to which domestic economies are dominated by TNCs through their foreign direct investment, show great disparities across major capitalist developed countries. The UK economy shows very high and increasing ratios. The 1980s, the decade of Thatcherism, saw an increasing degree of internationalization of the British economy. Both inward and outward investment have become more relevant in relation to the size of the economy and in relation to the domestic capital formation. The British economy as a whole and most of its manufacturing

Table 18.10 UK elasticities of imports with respect to book value of inward foreign direct investment in main manufacturing industries, total manufacturing and total all industries, averages for the 1970s and 1980s

Elasticity	Years[a]	Food, drink, tobacco	Chemicals	Metals	Mechanical engineering	Electrical engineering	Motor	Textiles	Paper, printing, publishing	Rubber	Other manufacturing	Total manufacturing	Total all industries
% M	1970s	0.89	1.48	2.83	1.65	1.69	2.97	1.45	0.79	4.01	1.46	1.48	n.a.
% KFDI(I)	1980s	0.56	0.84	0.73	2.54	1.50	1.04	1.97	0.90	5.42	1.10	1.05	0.56

n.a.: = not available. M: imports. KFDI (I): stock of inward foreign direct investment. %: percentage change.
[a] See note 10 to chapter 18.

Sources: CSO *Business Monitor, MO4, MQ10,* 1989 and previous years

industries have become more 'dominated' by TNCs. The removal of exchange controls and general deregulation seem to be reflected in the results on multinational domination of the British economy.

There is evidence that both UK foreign direct investment (inward and outward) and UK trade have been increasing in the past 25 years. However, the growth of trade (both imports and exports) has been higher than the growth of foreign direct investment for total manufacturing and for most of the manufacturing industries. The related values for elasticities seem to suggest a relationship of complementarity between FDI and trade, particularly with imports.

Although more research needs to be done to establish proper functional relationships and give detailed estimates of the effects, some broad conclusions can be drawn from the results presented. First, if countries are unevenly affected by transnational activities and unevenly dominated by them in terms of their foreign direct investment, we would also expect uneven effects on their domestic economies. Such uneven effects are likely to manifest, in particular, in the areas of labour strength, trade, the effectiveness of domestic economic policies and growth.

These considerations very much apply to the UK, which more or less tops the league in terms of multinational domination of its domestic economy, and whose share of imports and exports in GDP is large. Future domestic policies ought to take account of this situation and try to counteract any negative effects. In particular, the full effects on trade of the overall (inward and outward) foreign investment ought to be given particular attention, especially the possible strong effects on imports.

With regard to labour there are two issues: the employment effects and the effects on labour strength. Any assessment of the employment effects of FDI should take due account of the indirect effects derived via the FDI effects on trade, bearing in mind that, while the direct effects of inward and outward FDI can be considered to move in opposite directions, the indirect trade effects are more likely to be cumulative. With regard to the effects on labour strength, it appears that the process of geographical dispersion brought about by multinational activities leads to geographical fragmentation and general segmentation of the labour force. This has profound implications for a labour movement that wants to counteract such effects: the strategies may have to allow for the growing internationalization process by fostering links across the ownership–management divide and across frontiers for employees of the same transnational company.

The results also suggest a considerable degree of unevenness across major capitalist economies in the effectiveness of economic policies. This may warrant tighter domestic policies, and attempts on the part of governments to regain control of the economy for those countries (particularly Britain) that are very highly dominated by TNCs.

Conclusions on Part III

The effects of the activities of TNCs on the economy and society are very wide-ranging and significant. The internationalization of economic systems throughout the world is increasing and extending to new areas, including Eastern Europe. Economic systems are becoming more dominated by multinational activities.

It is interesting to try to disentangle political rhetoric from economic reality in Britain. During the 1980s the dominant British political leaders spoke a rhetoric of nationalism and sovereignty, encouragement of small business and market supremacy. However, the reality is: (a) a growing internationalization of the economic system; (b) a considerable increase in multinational domination of the economic system; (c) an increase in transactions that bypass the market – such bypassing has particularly strong effects and distortions when the internal transactions take place across countries; (d) an increase in non-market (and non-governmental) control as more and more TNCs become involved in joint ventures, sub-contracting and licensing.

I am aware that chapters 17 and 18 have often concentrated on the negative rather than the positive effects of transnational activities; this has, partly, been the result of a deliberate decision to highlight problems in order to stimulate the search for solutions. It should, however, be stressed that I do not advocate a retreat away from current trends in internationalization and a nostalgia for 'national' companies; I consider this not only impossible, but indeed undesirable. TNCs have been and are a force for progress. The advantages they bring are in terms of technology, the transmission of cultural trends, raising aspirations and the consciousness of what can be achieved, bringing peoples closer together. They are evidence of what can be achieved by the coordination of production on a large scale and across countries, by getting people from many countries and backgrounds working towards common goals.

Transnationalism, coordination and control, which TNCs represent, can be strong elements for progress but they can also create serious problems, as has been highlighted in the previous pages. The problems created by TNCs are different from, more wide-ranging and more serious than the problems created by national firms. There are, however, some points common to most problems created by TNCs:

1   The problems are generated by the fact that some institutions plan and operate transnationally while other institutions are, by their own nature or for historical reasons, unable to operate transnationally in the same way and to the same extent; for example, governments, labour organizations, consumers' organizations. In the case of consumers the problems are compounded by the lack of organization, even at the national level.
2   Transnationality in itself has, therefore, generated extra power in one group without countervailing power in others.
3   The problems are economic and social in nature but they have strong political overtones deriving from the general power of TNCs.
4   Many problems – whether strictly economic, or social, cultural or environmental – generate the need for public intervention. However:
5   Given the transnationalism of activities, public intervention becomes more difficult; indeed national economic policies (whether demand or supply management or longer-term industrial policy) are becoming less and less effective.

Following point 5, it is an irony that some Western countries have moved towards less economic management, less intervention, lower levels of planning at the macro level, at a time when more planning goes on at the micro level and this micro planning becomes more powerful with the use of information technology. It may be also considered an irony that some political forces should resist more integration within the EC on the grounds that it would lead to loss of sovereignty. In reality the major loss of sovereignty has already occurred in the economic sphere through the power of TNCs (enhanced by the policies often advocated by the same political forces!). One cannot help wondering whether what is being feared in a full European integration is the loss of sovereignty or the strengthening of countervailing power to the TNCs.

A full understanding of the effects of TNCs' activities requires full incorporation of internationalization issues with the body of economic theory. So far economists have either neglected TNCs' activities or dealt with them separately from the main body of analysis and theory, even in as close an area as international trade. Thus both analysis and the effects of TNCs' activities have been seen as 'addenda', almost 'footnotes', to the existing framework of analysis. What we may need is a full analysis of the extent to which the advantages and power given by transnationalism to some economic agents in modern economic systems invalidate the framework of analysis of our economic theory; and thus the extent to which economic relationships and models ought to be reconsidered. This would also lead to a reconsideration of the overall framework for policies.

This book has, deliberately, not dealt with policies. However, some general principles do emerge from the analysis of trends and effects presented. If the arguments previously presented are accepted, it follows that if we want to retain some positive feature of TNCs' activities and reduce problems, we should consider:

1 Some public control over the operations of TNCs; the degree of control should vary according to the sectors in which they operate and the nature and extent of the problems generated.
2 Improvements in the flow of information between national agencies regarding TNCs' activities.
3 More openness and parliamentary scrutiny on issues related to the process leading to economic policies. The aim of such scrutiny would be to detect the existence of pressures towards particular policies that might be in the interest of TNCs but not of the nation as a whole or of large groups within it (workers, consumers). This is particularly relevant to issues of trade policy or safety issues, including those related to the food industry and the environment.
4 Encouragement of international integration and harmonization of policies with the aim of reducing or eliminating some of the problems (for example, the manipulation of transfer prices).
5 Implementation of policies designed to reduce the level of uncertainty in the economy in order to encourage long-term investment. Measures designed to deal with points 1 to 4 would help to reduce uncertainty; the establishment of medium- and long-term fiscal and monetary norms may be necessary to achieve a less uncertain macroeconomic environment.
6 In terms of the strategy of intervention, preventative measures should be preferred to *ex post* controls, which often tend to be less effective and to be resented as they are considered punitive.
7 Facilitating the establishment of 'transnational countervailing power' and transnational links among institutions that do not currently possess a strong international infrastructure, particularly trade unions, consumers and, to some extent, governments.

The notion of 'countervailing power' was developed by Galbraith (1952). The power he was concerned with was monopoly power deriving from increased concentration of production; he believed that the increased monopoly power in production was gradually being counteracted by the power of workers (through their unions), of consumers (through the power of organized retailers) and of farmers. The end result seems to be some kind of equilibrium in which countervailing power balances the power of large oligopolists and is therefore to be welcomed. Galbraith was dealing entirely with the power of national firms exercised in the national context of the USA.

The power considered in this book derives specifically from transnationalism rather than from concentration of production, though the two aspects may be related and, often, self-reinforcing. I do not think that the advantages and power of transnationalism are, at present, evenly spread between social groups and agents or between countries. Thus we are far from a self-equilibrating balancing situation.

Galbraith saw the role of the government as helping other agents (workers, consumers, farmers) to achieve or strengthen their countervailing power. In the analysis here presented governments themselves are in need of countervailing power to counteract their loss of power deriving from the transnationalism of production. None the less, governments must be seen as the primary motor in the pursuit of strategies and policies directed towards the creation of countervailing power for themselves and for other economic agents.

19

Summing Up

There are some themes considered throughout this book which might be worth summarizing.

1 The relevance of *control* in understanding the development of TNCs, their activities and their power; a theme taken from Hymer (1960) and Cowling and Sugden (1987a).
2 A *strategic* approach considered to be relevant to: (a) the analysis of the development in internal organization of firms, following Chandler (1962) and Hymer (1971); (b) the analysis of TNCs' behaviour and its relation to theories of international production – strategies towards markets and rivals and strategies towards labour have been considered; (c) the assessment of effects of international production.
3 Emphasis has been put throughout the book on issues of *production* and its planning and control, more than, or as much as, on issues of markets, demand and exchange. This point has been considered relevant in terms of firms' organization, and explanations of international production and its effects.
4 *Transnationality per se* has been given a prominent role in terms of the general advantages and power it confers and in particular in terms of the planning of production and production processes.
5 It follows from point 4 that if transnationality gives extra power and advantages and if it creates extra problems one policy direction to follow is to build *poles of countervailing power* for institutions that do not possess such power. This is a theme touched on at various points.
6 In the assessment of effects, the stress has been on transnationality and *globality* rather than the direction of the flow of investment. This

is reflected in the analysis of methodological issues, in the assessment of effects on specific areas (such as trade) and in the assessment of the overall macro impact on national economies.

7   Many *theories* have been presented; none constitutes 'the answer' to determinants of international production. Nevertheless, they are witness to a substantial body of knowledge in this area of economics. The need to test theories against empirical evidence, as well as for their internal coherence, has been an underlying theme.

Notes

1 The Internationalization Process: Agents and Conditions

1 On the history of TNCs, see Hertner and Jones (1986).
2 For an analysis of theoretical and historical points on the U- and M-forms, see Auerbach (1988). A critical analysis is also in Aglietta (1976, 4.III).
3 The controversy goes back to the study of modern corporations by Berle and Means (1932).
4 This issue is further developed in chapters 5 and 17.

2 Trends in Internationalization

1 The data in tables 2.1 and 2.2 are expressed in nominal, not real value and hence do not allow for inflation. As comparisons between countries and over time are based on percentages, the bias due to working with nominal values should not be too great. Besides, any attempt at presenting real value statistics raises the question of the appropriateness of the deflator used and possible bias introduced by the deflator itself. For these reasons it was decided not to attempt to deflate the data and to present them more or less as in the UNCTC publications from which they derive.
2 A detailed analysis of the determinants of intra-industry FDI is in Dunning and Norman (1986); Cantwell (1989) explores the relationship between intra-industry FDI and technological advantages of various countries.
3 Of course, these statistics tell us the story only from the point of view of equity participation and FDI. As highlighted in section 2.1, point 9, there has been an increase in non-equity forms of international involvement in production with a large share directed towards LDCs. However, it is doubtful

whether, in relative terms, such involvement can compensate for the relative shift of the FDI share away from LDCs; this is because FDI is still, by far, the main form of overall international involvement in production.

4   Magdoff (1966, p. 110, note 14), writing about the expansion of US bank branches abroad, wonders:

Is there perhaps an affinity between United States branch banking abroad and social revolution? In 1917, the largest concentration of United States branch banks in any one foreign country was in Russia. Prior to the Chinese revolution the largest concentration of United States branch banks in the Far East was in China. And Cuba was also a long-time favorite for United States banking: prior to the Cuban revolution, Cuba was host to the largest number of United States bank branches.

Whether we take foreign banking as a serious predictor of social revolution or not, the fact is that the changing structure and technology of international banking has made 'foreign branches of banks' an obsolete indicator of international banking activity, thus undermining Magdoff's simple rule of thumb!

5   Licensing agreements are agreements between two companies (one of which could be a TNC and the other a domestic company) according to which the licensor grants the use of industrial property rights (e.g. trade mark and knowledge over production processes and products) in return for royalties and fees. A 'turnkey operation' is 'an agreement between a company in one country – usually an advanced industrialized country – and a company in another country under which the former designs, constructs, and commissions a plant and is paid partly with the future output generated by the new plant' (Grimwade, 1989, p. 450).

6   'Customs items 807.00 and 806.30 permit an importer, under certain restrictive conditions, to pay the normal duty for the product imported only on the value added abroad: no duty is paid on the value of the US parts or materials incorporated. Evidently not all products which involve international subcontracting will necessarily qualify under these customs items' (Sharpston, 1975, p. 95). Some of the work on goods imported under these items may take place in export processing zones. However, some of the imports under the above categories may, of course, originate with affiliates of the importer TNC; the 'proxy' used by Sharpston may not be a very good one.

7   For details of the advantages and problems of this type of arrangement, see UNCTC (1988, pp. 166–9).

8   Hladik (1985) contains a detailed analysis of joint ventures and their effects, based on a sample of 420 US–foreign JVs formed between 1974 and 1982. The determinants of JVs are explored in Contractor and Lorange (1988) and Buckley and Casson (1988). Walmsey (1982) looks at some managerial aspects of JVs. A good analysis of JVs is in United Nations (1989).

9   Willmore (1979) clarifies the distinction between the measurement of intra-industry trade and the concept of intra-industry specialization. In the same volume, Agmon (1979) relates intra-industry trade to the oligopolistic structure of production.

10 A comprehensive analysis of US intra-firm trade and its determinants is in Helleiner (1981).

11 Victoria Chick (1979, p. 143) remarks that: 'The phenomenon of transfer

pricing has obscured still further the already fuzzy distinction between trade and capital flows. It has long been known that leads and lags in payments for trade are a form of short-term capital flow, often used by traders to move out of currencies expected to depreciate. The same use can be made of under – and over – invoicing.'

12 The managerial difficulties created by transfer prices are highlighted by Harvey-Jones (1988), former ICI Chairman, when he writes: 'I have never known a large or a small organization which doesn't have endless problems about the prices at which an intermediate that is manufactured in one part of the company is transferred to another. It is a source of almost endless belly-aching and can produce a fantastic head of managerial and emotional steam' (p. 141). Similarly, Lorenz (1989), in an article related to the managerial problems of the Zanussi–Electrolux merger, highlights the enormous amount of time that high-level managers have to spend to iron out conflicts over transfer prices between divisions in various countries. Of course, similar problems can arise in large non-private institutions, particularly as more and more of them are moving towards strict performance indicators for single units within the overall organizations.

3 Classical Writers on Imperialism

1 Lenin takes the term 'combination' from Hilferding.
2 In particular he criticizes K. Kautsky for his stress on industrial capital from the point of view of both the colonizing and the annexed country. Other strong criticisms of Kautsky relate to the fact that Kautsky does not see imperialism as an inevitable phase of capitalism and its inner workings, and that he thus divorces politics from economics.
3 This methodological point will be reconsidered in chapter 12.
4 A clear detailed treatment of the issue of improvement to agricultural produce related to improvements in manufactures, with particular reference to the UK, is in Rowthorn and Wells (1987, chapter 6).
5 Lee (1971) contains some interesting comments on this and other points of Luxemburg's work.
6 On this point see Sweezy (1942, chapters X and XI).

4 The Realization Problem Back in Fashion

1 Hobson's and Luxemburg's books are not, however, cited in the Baran and Sweezy works considered here.
2 Sweezy (1939) had, in fact, previously presented a theory of prices under oligopolistic conditions which gave theoretical backing to the empirical observation of price stability. His approach and other similar ones were further developed by Stigler (1947). Both Sweezy's and Stigler's articles have been reprinted in American Economic Association Series, *Readings in Price Theory* (1953), London: George Allen and Unwin, pp. 404–39.
3 For a discussion on the falling tendency of the rate of profit, see Sweezy (1942, chapter VI).

5   Some Recent Marxist Approaches

1   This point is also stressed by Aglietta (1976), particularly in relation to control over labour.
2   Some of the points made here on Fröbel et al.'s work derive from a review of their book (Ietto-Gillies, 1982).
3   An introduction to Babbage's work and intellectual contributions is in his biography by Hyman (1982).
4   'Free productive zones' are, in the terminology of Fröbel et al., more or less equivalent to what are here called 'export processing zones'.
5   I have already highlighted the effects of such developments on the internal organization of large firms (see chapter 1).

6   Foreign Investment within the Neo-classical Paradigm

1   Acocella mentions that his presentation is adapted from the work by Bertin (1972). In the analysis, rates of return and interest rates coincide, given the neo-classical assumptions.
2   For example, Jasay (1960), Pearce and Rowan (1966), Johnson (1970) and Beenstock (1977).
3   See, in particular, Samuelson (1948, 1949), Stolper and Samuelson (1941) and Rybczynski (1955).
4   On the control of trade by TNCs and on the empirical and theoretical consequences of this, there is more in chapter 17.
5   See, for example, the clearly argued paper by the philosopher of science Musgrave (1981), as well as those by the economists Samuelson (1963), Coddington (1972), Katouzian (1980) and Pheby (1988).
6   Recently Cowling and Sugden (1987a, b) have emphasized the contradiction between the perfect competition assumption and the profit maximization assumption. This point is reconsidered in chapter 15, where I discuss Cowling and Sugden's theory.

7   Foreign Direct Investment and Market Imperfections: the Hymer and Kindleberger Approach

1   The issue of Hymer's awareness of Coase's work, and of the relevance of transaction costs economies for the theory of MNCs, has recently been the topic of much controversy. This is highlighted by the paper by Horaguchi and Toyne (1990). Although Hymer's thesis contains no reference to Coase, Hymer's (1968) article does; this paper also shows that he took the role of transaction costs in internationalization very seriously.

8 The Product Life Cycle and Foreign Direct Investment

1 I shall not deal in detail with the technological gap or other theories of international trade, as they are outside the scope of this book. I shall, however, touch on some aspects of the theories that have a bearing on the product life cycle theory of international production.

2 The 'Leontief paradox' raises interesting methodological issues for economists and philosophers of science. Leontief's findings appear to falsify the factor proportions theory of trade. Instead of rejecting the theory, economists have been extremely busy looking for modifications to some of the assumptions in order to accommodate the paradox. This is one instance that shows the difficulty of applying the Popperian falsifiability criteria in science and particularly in economics. The difficulties are highlighted by the so-called 'Duhem–Quine thesis'. This thesis points out how testing is never related to a single hypothesis, but to a cluster of hypotheses and assumptions; thus, scientists can never be sure which hypothesis has been falsified. This leaves the door open for endless modifications to auxiliary assumptions in order to salvage the basic theory. Some of these modifications are *ad hoc* procedures devised to allow scientists to go on using discredited theories. In economics, where ideological elements are very relevant, the tendency to use *ad hoc* procedures may be stronger than in other disciplines. Discussions on these points are in Katouzian (1980), Keat and Urry (1975), Lakatos (1978) and Pheby (1988). The original theories are in Duhem (1905), Quine (1951) and Popper (1959).

3 By the time Vernon wrote his 1977 book, his research student F. T. Knicker-bocker (1973) had completed and published his theory showing that FDI from various firms tends to accumulate in particular geographical areas (see chapter 13). Vernon discusses the follow-the-leader hypothesis with regard to various product markets.

9 Currency Areas and Foreign Direct Investment

1 Aliber illustrates the various cases with two graphs (figures 1 and 2 on pp. 25 and 26 respectively).

2 One complication arises from the fact that official statistics on FDI are collected on the basis of financial flows and that the distinction between short-, medium- and long-term flows is not always easy to draw.

10 Horizontal and Vertical Integration, Diversification and the MNE: Caves's Approach

1 In a 'strategy' approach the main determinant of decision and action is the desire, on the part of the economic agent(s), to acquire advantages over other economic agents. The strategies can be directed towards rival producers, governments or labour and be related to products, processes, location, inputs,

markets or a combination of these and other elements. An 'efficiency' approach is one that stresses the efficient use of resources as the main determinant of decision and action. Both approaches are profit-driven, though the emphasis may be long-run for the 'strategy' and short-run for the 'efficiency' approach. A strategy may lead to an inefficient use of resources in the short run (e.g. low penetration prices for a new market), although it may turn out to be very profitable and efficient in the long run.

11   Internalization as an Explanation for International Production

1   Markusen (1984) uses the concepts of 'public goods' and 'jointness' with respect to the firm to analyse multi-plant economies deriving from firm-specific activities such as R&D, advertising, marketing, distribution and management services. He develops an efficiency model of international production based on multi-plant economies.

2   The authors write on this point: 'For example, in the absence of discrimination a monopoly of a factor input may be exploited only by charging a uniformly high price which encourages substitution against the input. A discriminatory tariff based on the derived demand curve for the factor would more or less maintain the *average* price of the factor while removing entirely the incentive to substitute against it. It would therefore increase the monopolist's profit without reducing that of his customers. It follows that when discriminatory pricing in an external market is impracticable, internalization of the market through merger of the firms concerned will potentially increase their combined profits by facilitating discriminatory pricing' (Buckley and Casson, 1976, pp. 37–8).

3   The issue of buyer uncertainty over quality as an incentive for backward integration is further explained in Casson (1982, pp. 34–5). On the risks for the sellers of the debasement of quality for a branded good or service by the distributor see also Williamson (1981, pp. 1549–50).

4   Many of the authors who have either originated or embraced the internalization theory seem aware of the dangers of slipping into tautology. For example, Casson (1982) writes: 'Internalization is in fact a general theory of why firms exist, and without additional assumptions it is almost tautological' (p. 24). Buckley (1983) expresses similar doubts when he writes: 'At its most general, the concept of internalisation is tautological; firms internalise imperfect markets until the cost of further internalisation outweighs the benefits' (p. 42). Teccc (1983) thinks that 'the tautological nature of transaction costs or "internalisation" reasoning can be avoided' (p. 51) by distinguishing between those transactions that can be dealt with at lowest cost by the market and those that can be dealt with at lowest cost by the MNE.

5   The relationship between efficiency of internalization and endogenous or exogenous market imperfections is explained in more detail by Yamin and Nixson (1988). It should be noted that Buckley (1983) accepts that 'It is a valid criticism of the internalization rubric that market imperfections are taken as exogenous to the (internalizing) firm' (p. 45).

12   Dunning's Eclectic Approach

1   The 'why' and 'where' analysis is clearly spelt out in Dunning (1980).
2   A discussion of methodological issues in a special case of theories that have a large number of adjustable parameters is in Gillies (1989); the case discussed has many similarities with the eclectic theory.

Introduction to Section IV

1   An attempt to demarcate between efficiency and strategic approaches is in note 1 of chapter 10.
2   For example, Acocella (1975) links FDI to stages of economic development and suggests that in modern oligopolistic structures FDI has the strategic role of breaking 'barriers to expansion'.

13   Oligopolistic Reactions as an Explanation for Foreign Direct Investment

1   The data used by Knickerbocker refer to phase I of the project, covering the history of international expansion between 1900 and 1967 for 187 large US firms; phase II refers to a similar study of 200 non-US based firms. Details of data sources and methodology are in Knickerbocker (1973, chapter 2).
2   This point has similarities with Vernon's (1974) idea of innovation-based oligopoly, as illustrated in chapter 8.
3   The difficulty of making forecasts in a world of industries dominated by a few giants is mentioned by Knickerbocker himself (1973, pp. 201–2).
4   Knickerbocker's doctoral dissertation and Caves's first article (1971) seem to have been produced contemporaneously; neither of the two authors refers to the other.

14   Transnational Corporations and Strategies towards Labour

1   See in particular Fröbel et al. (1980), discussed in chapter 5.
2   Malcolmson (1984, p. 120) highlights how 'in the case of labour, the market transaction is not the only transaction that is relevant'. For example, he points out elements that are very relevant for costs, such as the fact that: '*Ceteris paribus*, employees . . . retain an interest in working less hard or ensuring that the job takes long enough that they have to be paid at overtime rates.'
3   Most of the material in this chapter derives from Ietto-Gillies (1988).
4   See on this point chapter 8 in Leadbeater and Lloyd (1987).
5   As mentioned in chapter 1, Cowling and Sugden (1987a) deal with sub-contracting in relation to large corporations and in particular TNCs. However, their concern is different from the one dealt with here. They consider the issue of control, and thus power – in particular, market power – that large corporations have over sub-contractors.

6 For a clear presentation of the 'flexibility offensive' and related issues, see Atkinson and Gregory (1986). Graziani (1989) discusses the role of decentralization and the growing precariousness of labour as part of the restructuring of the Italian economy in the late 1960s and early 1970s.

7 On these points, see Friedman (1977) and Michalet (1980).

8 A comprehensive critical analysis of the problems facing the theory of the segmented labour market, and its relation to the core–periphery view of the macroeconomy and industrial structure, is in Fine (1987); this work also contains an extensive bibliography on the subject.

9 On some of the difficulties emerging from sub-contracting arrangements, in particular in relation to quality controls, see Casson (1984).

10 Enderwick (1985, p. 148) writes on this issue: 'To date, transnational union action has been limited in both its form and effectiveness. . . . There has been a tendency for unions to concentrate on the first two stages of co-operation, the exchange of information and consultation.' This point is also confirmed by one of the results of a survey of foreign-owned companies and trade unions in the USA by Greer and Shearer (1981). With reference to the responses by companies, they write: 'the vast majority (81.5 per cent) reported that the unions representing their U.S. employees have not cooperated with unions in other countries to strengthen their U.S. positions. Furthermore, the majority (77.8 per cent) did not expect their unions to increase multinational cooperative efforts' (p. 46).

15   Transnational Monopoly Capitalism

1 The full effects of both inward and outward FDI and other activities are not, however, analysed by Cowling and Sugden. These are considered in chapter 16. Chapter 18 presents a concept and estimates of a multinational domination ratio which, as an indicator of the power and dominance of TNCs over a national economy, gives the sort of evidence that Cowling and Sugden (1987b) seemed to be searching for in their chapter 3.

2 The work leading to chapters 14 and 18 of this book was being developed more or less at the same time as Cowling and Sugden's work; none of us was aware of the others' work and thus proceeded independently. This has led to results often showing interesting analogies, common points and differences; in some cases the focus on different aspects leads to stronger conclusions, in others it leads to a different analysis and conclusions.

3 They fruitfully move away from the idea of 'monopolistic advantage' and this allows them to explain the activities of both new transnationals and already established ones; this point is highlighted by Cowling and Sugden themselves (1987b, p. 25, note 20).

4 This is an area to which Cowling (1982) had already made a considerable contribution. For further comments on this part of Cowling's work see Ietto-Gillies (1983).

5 For example, Fine and Harris (1985, pp. 93–4) point out how, despite the rise of large MNCs, the largest firms' concentration ratios have tended to remain fairly constant; they link this to the increase in the geographical spread of activities. See also Auerbach's (1989) review of Cowling and Sugden

(1987b) for a critique of the link between transnational corporations and the increase in the degree of monopoly. Auerbach (1988, chapter 9) develops the thesis of increased competitiveness in the twentieth century resulting from, among other things, improved technology of transport and communication.

16   Methodological Issues

1 See among others Stopford and Turner (1985), UNCTC (1983b), Stopford (1979) and Hood and Young (1979).
2 Dunning (1981, chapter 13) is one author who specifically addresses methodological issues both in terms of analysis and in terms of the assessment of policy prescriptions.
3 The term 'methodological issues' is here used in a wide sense; it includes issues about the breadth and type of effects to be considered, as well as issues related to how to conduct the analysis.

17   Effects

1 Helleiner (1981) provides good evidence on this point.
2 The United Nations Conference on Trade and Development (1978, p. 20) quotes a particular type of intra-firm trade involving exactly the same commodity. 'Frequently the only change involved is a transfer of the "materials" into different-sized containers for sale in the final market as "finished products". A good example is provided by two Paris laboratories which buy their vitamin B-12 from a producer in the Paris region, but have the substance sent to Antwerp, Geneva, Hamburg and Monaco before it is returned to Paris. Prices triple or quadruple during the 1,000-mile circuit.' However, cases like this, in which the simple manipulation of transfer prices can lead to large profits, are likely to be exceptional; the usual transactions are more likely to be in parts, components and semi-manufactured products belonging to the same industrial group.
3 Dunning (1982, p. 430, note 6) reports a good example: 'IBM's trade in computer parts is intra-firm and intra-industry; Phillips' trade of TV sets and steam irons is intra-firm but inter-industry.'
4 For a clear presentation of the literature on intra-industry trade and its determinants, see Grimwade (1989, chapter 3).
5 From this section it should be clear that the relationship bewteen IIT and IFT is not an obvious one. It is not therefore surprising that Helleiner (1981, p. 7) finds 'no overall correlation between available measures of intra-firm and intra-industry trade.' This is reinforced by the fact that he correlates intra-firm trade related to imports only, with intra-industry trade indicators that, by definition, relate to both imports and exports.
6 An analysis of the effects of TNCs' activities on LDCs is in Jenkins (1987).
7 Best's critique of the M-form of internal organization was considered in chapter 1.
8 The case here is far from clear-cut since the higher capital intensity of TNCs' subsidiaries usually derives from their concentration in capital-intensive sectors.

9 This point is developed by Russell (1978), as mentioned in chapter 16.
10 Concern over the growth of 'international cartels' through strategic alliances was expressed at a conference on anti-trust in Berlin in June 1990, as reported by Marsh (1990). See also section 2.1, point 10.
11 On these points, see UNCTC (1988, chapter XIII).
12 See in particular the good critical survey by Enderwick (1985, chapters 4 and 5).
13 On these various issues see Enderwick (1985).
14 For an analysis of problems and conflicts between nation states and international capital see Murray (1971). Rowthorn (1971) considers, among other things, the effects of British international capital on British capitalism. The tensions and conflicts deriving from TNCs' activities in relation to national governments and rival companies are examined by Vernon (1977). This work by Vernon deals specifically with the effects of activities of TNCs.
15 On these and other policy elements, particularly in relation to harmonization within the EC, see Panić (1991).
16 As Casson (1986, p. 10) writes: '. . . intra-firm trade is more difficult to subject to outside scrutiny than arm's length trade. Centralized management of intra-firm trade gives a foreign parent company direct control over both the imports and exports of its overseas subsidiary. If the subsidiary company dominates one of the key industries in the host economy, the policies of the foreign management may have a crucial effect on the balance of payments and the stability of the exchange rate in the host economy.'
17 An exposition and critique of Rowthorn and Wells's thesis is in Ietto-Gillies (1990); see also the reviews by Auerbach (1989), Thirlwall (1988) and Prowse (1987).
18 The link between Keynes's long-term expectations and the probability of social groups is explored by Gillies and Ietto-Gillies (1991).

18   Multinational Domination of National Economies

1 For example, Fine and Harris (1985, p. 120) write: 'Multinational corporations have had much greater significance for the British economy than for West Germany, Japan and comparable countries.'
2 See the IMF definition of foreign direct investment given in the appendix to chapter 1.
3 The value of international production has been calculated from the data for stock of outward foreign direct investment. A factor of 2.0 has been applied to these 'capital stock' data to derive the related 'output' data. This is the method used by the United Nations Department of Economic and Social Affairs (1973, p. 159, table 19).
4 The reader must, however, remember that, given the IMF definition of FDI, the data on FDI and GDFCF are not fully comparable (see section 18.1 on this point). However, this does not affect the comparability of our ratios across countries and through time.
5 The indicator is not, of course, designed to capture the impact of domestic activities by domestic TNCs, e.g. the domestic activities of UK transnational companies. Besides, the 'multinational domination ratio' here presented is

essentially a macro indicator designed to capture some macroeconomic effects. It differs from other indicators of multinational activity. In particular, Stopford et al. (1980) give estimates for the degree of internationalization of a company by using the ratio of 'sales of overseas subsidiaries and direct export from home' over 'total worldwide sales' for particular companies (p. xxiv). Buckley et al. (1978) use the concept of 'degree of multinationality', defined as the ratio of 'sales of overseas affiliates and associates' divided by 'total worldwide sales' for given MNCs. These very useful ratios are essentially different from our indicator in that they are more micro-orientated and they concentrate on outward operations only. Their aim is different from the one that led to our 'multinational domination ratio'.

6 There were indeed very serious data problems because there are no official comparable statistics on foreign direct investment by country and industry. Dr J. Clegg of Bath University has, however, constructed some data for five countries (the USA, the UK, Japan, West Germany and Sweden) and ten industries using a variety of sources (Clegg, 1987). He kindly made the data available to me, before publication of his book, for which I am very grateful. The data have been constructed only for three years (1965, 1970 and 1975). They are expressed in dollars. They are estimates of net assets, and hence of stock data rather than flow data as in table 18.3.

7 Among the problems are the following: (a) the numerator expresses net values and the denominator gross values; (b) the denominator is not exactly a capital stock estimate but only an approximation of it; (c) there are doubts about the reliability of the data (see note 6) on foreign assets and their comparability across countries, industries and time; (d) the outward and inward data do not always refer to the same year (see the notes to table 18.4).

8 However, the UK ratios in table 18.4 are considerably higher than the detailed ratios calculated for the UK industries (table 18.6). This throws some further doubts on the data used for table 18.4. In particular, the following two problems may be responsible for the high ratios: (a) the sum of GDFCF over five years may be an underestimate of the value of domestic capital stock, and this affects the denominator of indicator (2), thus giving higher ratios; (b) it was impossible to counteract cyclical effects in the data in table 18.4 since only two years were available. These problems should not, however, affect too badly the comparability across industries and countries within table 18.4, as the data across countries and industries are equally affected.

9 The 1970s data relate to average growth rate of book value of FDI between 1971 and 1978 and average growth rate of trade between 1970 and 1979; the 1980s estimates are arrived at by using average growth rates of book value of FDI between 1978 and 1987 and average growth rates of trade between 1980 and 1987.

Bibliography

Acocella, N. (1975) *Imprese Multinazionali e Investimenti Diretti: le Cause dello Sviluppo*. Milan: Giuffré.

Ádám, G. (1975) Multinational Corporations and Worldwide Sourcing. In Radice, H. (ed.), *International Firms and Modern Imperialism*. Harmondsworth: Penguin, 89–103.

Aglietta, M. (1976) *A Theory of Capitalist Regulation. The US Experience*. 1987 Edition. London: Verso.

Agmon, T. (1979) Direct investment and intra-industry trade: substitutes or complements? In Giersch, H. (ed.), *On the Economics of Intra-Industry Trade*. Tübingen: J. C. B. Mohr (Paul Siebeck), 49–67.

Agnelli, U. (1990) Thinking big as frontiers tumble. *Times Higher Education Supplement*, 26 June.

Aharoni, Y. (1971) On the definition of a multinational corporation. *Quarterly Review of Economics and Business*, 11 (3), 27–37.

Aliber, R. Z. (1970) A theory of direct foreign investment. In Kindleberger, C. P. (ed.), *The International Corporation*. Cambridge, MA: MIT Press, 17–34.

Aliber, R. Z. (1971) The multinational enterprise in a multiple currency world. In Dunning, J. H. (ed.), *The Multinational Enterprise*. London: Allen and Unwin, 49–60.

Amin, S. (1974) *Accumulation on a World Scale. A Critique of the Theory of Under-Development*. New York: Monthly Review Press.

Aquino, A. (1978) Intra-industry trade and inter-industry specialisation as concurrent sources of international trade in manufactures. *Weltwirtschaftliches Archiv*, 114 (2), 275–96.

Atkinson, J. and Gregory, D. (1986) A flexible future. *Marxism Today*, April, 12–17.

Auerbach, P. (1988) *Competition: the Economics of Industrial Change*. Oxford: Blackwell.

Auerbach, P. (1989a) Review of 'De-Industrialization and Foreign Trade' by Rowthorn, R. E. and Wells, J. R. (1987). *International Review of Applied Economics*, 3 (1), 107–12.

Auerbach, P. (1989b) Review of 'Transnational Monopoly Capitalism' by Cowling, K. and Sugden, R. (1987). *International Review of Applied Economics*, 3 (1), 115–21.

Babbage, C. (1832) *On the Economy of Machinery and Manufactures*. London: Charles Knight.

Baran, P. A. and Sweezy, P. M. (1966a) Notes on the theory of imperialism. *Monthly Review*, March, 15–31.

Baran, P. A. and Sweezy, P. M. (1966b) *Monopoly Capital. An Essay on the American Economic and Social Order*. 1968 edition. Harmondsworth: Penguin.

Beenstock, M. (1977) Policies towards international direct investment: a neo-classical reappraisal. *Economic Journal*, 87, 533–42.

Belassa, B. (1974) Trade creation and trade-diversion in the European Common Market. *Manchester School*, XL11(2), 93–135.

Bergstrand, J. H. (1983) Measurement and determinants of intra-industry international trade. In Tharakan, P. K. M. (ed.), *Intra-Industry Trade*. Amsterdam: North Holland, 201–41.

Berle, A. A. and Means, G. C. (1932) *The Modern Corporation and Private Property*. New York: Commerce Clearing House.

Bertin, G. Y. (1972) *L'investissement international*. Paris: Presses Universitaires de France.

Best, M. (1986) Strategic planning, the new competition and industrial policy. In Nolan, P. and Paine, S. (eds), *Rethinking Socialist Economics*. Cambridge: Polity Press, 182–97.

Bhagwati, J. N. (1973) The theory of immiserizing growth: further applications. In Connolly, M. B. and Swoboda, A. K. (eds), *International Trade and Money*. Toronto: University of Toronto Press, 45–54.

Brecher, R. A. and Diaz Alejandro, C.F. (1977) Tariffs, foreign capital and immiserizing growth. *Journal of International Economics*, 7, 317–22. Reprinted in Bhagwati, J. N. (ed.) (1981) *International Trade: Selected Readings*. Cambridge, MA: MIT Press.

Buckley, P. J. (1983) New theories of international business: some unresolved issues. In Casson, M. C. (ed.), *The Growth of International Business*. Boston: Allen and Unwin, 34–50.

Buckley, P. J. and Casson, M. C. (1976) A long-run theory of the multinational enterprise. In Buckley, P. J. and Casson, M. C. (eds), *The Future of the Multinational Enterprise*. London: Macmillan, 32–65.

Buckley, P. J. and Casson, M. (1988) A theory of cooperation in international business. In Contractor, F. J. and Lorange, P. (eds), *Cooperative Strategies in International Business: Joint Ventures and Technology Partnership Between Firms*. Lexington, MA: Lexington Books.

Buckley, P. J., Dunning, J. H. and Pearce, R. D. (1978) The influence of firm size, industry, nationality and degree of multinationality on the growth and profitability of the world's largest firms, 1962–1972. *Weltwirtschaftliches Archiv*, 114 (2), 243–57.

Bukharin, N. (1917) *Imperialism and World Economy*. 1987 edition. London: Merlin Press.

Cantwell, J. (1989) *Technological Innovation and Multinational Corporations*. Oxford: Blackwell.

Casson, M. C. (1982) Transaction costs and the theory of the multinational enterprise. In Rugman, A. M. (ed.), *New Theories of the Multinational Enterprise*. London: Croom Helm, 24–43.

Casson, M. C. (1984) *A Theory of the International Division of Labour*. University of Reading Discussion Paper in Economics, Series A, No. 151.

Casson, M. C. and associates (1986) *Multinationals and World Trade*. London: Allen and Unwin.

Caves, R. E. (1971) International corporations: the industrial economics of foreign investment. *Economica*, 38, 1–27. Reprinted in Dunning, J. H. (ed.) (1972) *International Investment*. Harmondsworth: Penguin, 265–301.

Caves, R. E. (1982) *Multinational Enterprise and Economic Analysis*. Cambridge: Cambridge University Press.

Central Statistical Office (1988 and previous years) *Business Monitor MA4 Supplement. Census of Overseas Assets*. London: HMSO.

Central Statistical Office (1989 and previous years) *Business Monitor MA4, Overseas Transactions*. London: HMSO.

Central Statistical Office (1989 and previous years) *Business Monitor MO4. Census of Overseas Assets*. London: HMSO.

Central Statistical Office (1989 and previous years) *United Kingdom National Accounts*. London: HMSO.

Central Statistical Office (1989 and previous years) *Business Monitor MQ10. Overseas Trade Analysed in Terms of Industries*. London: HMSO.

Chandler, A. D. (1962) *Strategy and Structure: Chapters in the History of the Industrial Enterprise*. Cambridge, MA: MIT Press.

Channon, D. F. (1973) *The Strategy and Structure of British Enterprise*. Cambridge, MA: Harvard University Press.

Chick, V. (1979) Transnational corporations and the evolution of the international monetary system. In Crough, G. J. (ed.), *Transnational Banking and the World Economy*. Transnational Corporations Research Project, University of Sydney, 129–77.

Clegg, J. (1987) *Multinational Enterprise and World Competition: a Comparative Study of the USA, Japan, the UK, Sweden and West Germany*. London: Macmillan.

Coase, R. H. (1937) The nature of the firm. *Economica*, IV, 386–405. Reprinted in Stigler, G. J. and Boulding, K. E. (eds), (1953) *Readings in Price Theory*. London: Allen and Unwin, 331–51.

Coddington, A. (1972) Positive economics. *Canadian Journal of Economics*, February.

Contractor, F. J. and Lorange, P. (1988) Why should firms cooperate? The strategy and economic basis for cooperative ventures. In Contractor F. J. and Lorange, P. (eds), *Cooperative Strategies in International Business: Joint Ventures and Technology Partnership Between Firms*. Lexington, MA: Lexington Books, 3–28.

Cowling, K. (1982) *Monopoly Capitalism*. London: Macmillan.

Cowling, K. (1984) *The Internationalization of Production and Deindustrialization*. Mimeo.

Cowling, K. and Sugden, R. (1987a) Market exchange and the concept of a transnational corporation: analysing the nature of the firm. *British Review of Economic Issues*, 9 (20), 57–68.

Cowling, K. and Sugden, R. (1987b) *Transnational Monopoly Capitalism*. Brighton: Wheatsheaf.

Currie, J. (1985) *Export Processing Zones in the 1980s. Customs Free Manufacturing*. London: EIU Special Report No. 190.

Dicken, P. (1986) *Global Shift. Industrial Change in a Turbulent World*. London: Paul Chapman.

Duhem, P. (1905) *The Aim and Structure of Physical Theory*. English edition 1962. New York: Atheneum.

Dunning, J. H. (1971) Comment on the chapter by Professor Alibert. In Dunning, J. H. (ed.), *The Multinational Enterprise*. London: Allen and Unwin, 57–60.

Dunning, J. H. (1977) Trade, location of economic activity and the MNE: a search for an eclectic approach. In Ohlin, B., Hesselborn, P. O. and Wijkman, P. M. (eds), *The International Allocation of Economic Activity*. London: Macmillan, 395–431.

Dunning, J. H. (1979) The UK's international direct investment position in the mid-1970s. *Lloyds Bank Review*, April, 1–21.

Dunning, J. H. (1980) Explaining changing patterns of international production: in defense of the eclectic theory. *Oxford Bulletin of Economics and Statistics*, 41 (4), 269–95.

Dunning, J. H. (1981) *International Production and the Multinational Enterprise*. London: Allen and Unwin.

Dunning, J. H. (1982) A note on intra-industry foreign direct investment. *Banca Nazionale del Lavoro Quarterly Review*, 139, 427–37.

Dunning, J. H. (1983) Changes in the level and structure of international production: the last one hundred years. In Casson, M. (ed.), *The Growth of International Business*. London: Allen and Unwin, 84–139.

Dunning, J. H. and Norman, G. (1986) Intra-industry investment. In Gray, H. P. (ed.), *Uncle Sam as Host*, Greenwich, CT: JAI Press, 73–94.

Dunning, J. H. and Pearce, R. D. (1981) *The World's Largest Enterprises*. Farnborough: Gower.

Dunning, J. H. and Rugman, A. (1985) The influence of Hymer's dissertation on the theory of foreign direct investment. *American Economic Review*, 75 (1), 228–32.

Emmanuel, A. (1969) *Unequal Exchange: a study of the Imperialism of Trade*. 1972 edition. London: New Left Review.

Enderwick, P. (1982) Labour and theory of the multinational corporation. *Industrial Relations Journal*, 2, 32–43.

Enderwick, P. (1984) The labour utilisation practices of multinationals and obstacles to multinational collective bargaining. *Journal of the Industrial Relations*, 26, 345–64.

Enderwick, P. (1985) *Multinational Business and Labour*. Beckenham: Croom Helm.

Enderwick, P. (1987) *Multinational Restructuring and U.K. De-industrialisation*. Mimeo.

Fine, B. (1987) *Segmented Labour Market Theory: a Critical Assessment*. Birkbeck College Discussions Papers in Economics, 87/12.

Fine, B. and Harris, L. (1985) *The Peculiarities of the British Economy*. London: Lawrence and Wishart.

Frank, A. G. (1980) *Crisis in the World Economy*. London: Heinemann Educational.

Frank, A. G. (1981) *Crisis in the Third World*. London: Heinemann Educational.

Frankel, M. (1965) Home versus foreign investment: a case against capital exports. *Kyklos*, 18, 411–33.

Friedman, A. L. (1977) *Industry and Labour. Class Struggle at Work and Monopoly Capitalism*. London: Macmillan.

Friedman, M. (1953) *Essays in Positive Economics*. Chicago: University of Chicago Press.

Fröbel, F., Heinricks, J. and Kreye, O. (1980) *The New International Division of Labour*. Cambridge and Paris: Cambridge University Press and Editions de la Maison des Sciences de l'Homme.

Galbraith, J. K. (1952) *American Capitalism. The Concept of Countervailing Power*. 1968 edition. Harmondsworth: Penguin.

GATT (1986) *International Trade 1985/86*. Geneva: GATT.

Gillies, D. A. (1989) Non-Bayesian confirmation theory, and the principle of explanatory surplus. In Fine, A. and Leplin, J. (eds), *Proceedings of the 1988 Biennial Meeting of the Philosophy of Science Association*, 2 (12), 373–80.

Gillies, D. A. and Ietto-Gillies, G. (1991) Intersubjective probability and economics. *Review of Political Economy*, 3 (4), November.

Gray, H. P. (1975) Two-way international trade in manufactures: a theoretical underpinning. *Weltwirtschaftliches Archiv*, 109, 19–39.

Graziani, A. (1989) *L'economia Italiana dal 1945 a oggi*. Milan: Il Mulino.

Greer, C. R. and Shearer, J. C. (1981) Do foreign-owned U.S. firms practice unconventional labor relations? *Monthly Labour Review*, 104, 44–8.

Grimwade, N. (1989) *International Trade: New Patterns of Trade, Production and Investment*. London: Routledge.

Grubel, H.G. and Lloyd, P. J. (1975) *Intra-Industry Trade*. London: Macmillan.

Gruber, W., Mehta, D. and Vernon, R. (1967) The R & D factor in international trade and international investment of United States industries. *Journal of Political Economy*, 75 (1), 20–37.

Harvey-Jones, J. (1988) *Making it Happen. Reflections on Leadership*. London: Collins.

Heckscher, E. (1919) The effect of foreign trade on the distribution of income. In Ellis, H. and Metzler, L. A. (eds) (1950), *Readings in the Theory of International Trade*. London: Allen and Unwin, 272–300.

Helleiner, G. K. (1981) *Intra-Firm Trade and the Developing Countries*. London: Macmillan.

Hergert, M. and Morris, D. (1988) Trends in international collaborative agreements. In Contractor, F. J. and Lorange, P. (eds), *Cooperative Strategies in International Business*. Lexington, MA: Lexington Books, 99–109.

Hertner, P. and Jones, G. (1986) *Multinationals. Theory and History*. Aldershot: Gower.

Hilferding, R. (1912) *Das FinanzKapital*. Vienna: Wiener Volksbuchhandlung.

Hirsch, S. (1965) The United States electronics industry in international trade. *National Institute Economic Review*, 24, 92–7.

Hirsch, S. (1967) *Location of Industry and International Competitiveness*. Oxford: Clarendon Press.

Hladik, K. J. (1985) *International Joint Ventures. An Economic Analysis of US Foreign Business Partnerships*. Cambridge, MA: Lexington Books.

Hobson, J. A. (1902) *Imperialism: a Study*. 1988 edition. London: Unwin-Hyman.

Hood, N. and Young, S. (1979) *The Economics of Multinational Enterprise*. London: Longman.

Horaguchi, H. and Toyne, B. (1990) Setting the record straight: Hymer, internalization theory and transaction cost economics. *Journal of International Business Studies*, 21 (3), 487–94.

Hufbauer, G. C. (1966) *Synthetic Materials and the Theory of International Trade*. London: Duckworth.

Hufbauer, G. C. and Adler, M. (1968) *Overseas Manufacturing Investment and the Balance of Payments*. Washington: US Treasury Department.

Hyman, A. (1982) *Charles Babbage: Pioneer of the Computer*. Oxford: Oxford University Press.

Hymer, S. H. (1960) *The International Operations of National Firms: a Study of Direct Foreign Investment*. Cambridge, MA: MIT Press (published 1976).

Hymer, S. H. (1968) La grande 'corporation' multinationale: analyse de certaines raisons qui poussent à l'intégration internationale des affaires. *Revue Economique*, 14 (6), 949–73.

Hymer, S. H. (1970) The efficiency (contradictions) of multinational corporations. *American Economic Review*, 60 (2), 441–8. Reprinted in Cohen, R. B., Felton, N., Van Liere, J. and Nkosi, M. (eds) (1979), *The Multinational Corporation: a Radical Approach*, Papers by S. H. Hymer. Cambridge: Cambridge University Press, 41–53.

Hymer, S. H. (1971) The multinational corporation and the law of uneven development. In Bhagwati, J. W. (ed.), *Economics and World Order*. London: Macmillan, 113–40. Reproduced in Radice, H. (ed.) (1975), *International Firms and Modern Imperialism*. Harmondsworth: Penguin, 113–35.

Ietto-Gillies, G. (1982) Review of *The New International Division of Labour* by Fröbel, F., Heinrichs, J. and Kreye, O. (1980). *Marxism Today*, 44–5.

Ietto-Gillies, G. (1983) Monopoly capitalism and the UK economy: a review article. *Studi Economici*, 21, 57–75.

Ietto-Gillies, G. (1988) Internationalization of production: an analysis based on labour. *British Review of Economic Issues*, 10 (23), 19–48.

Ietto-Gillies, G. (1989) Some indicators of multinational domination of national economies: analysis for the UK and other developed countries. *International Review of Applied Economics*. 3 (1), 25–45.

Ietto-Gillies, G. (1990) Was deindustrialization in the UK inevitable? Some comments on the Rowthorn–Wells analysis. *International Review of Applied Economics*, 4 (2), 209–23.

IMF (1977) *Balance of Payments Manual*, 4th edn. Washington, DC: IMF.

IMF (1989 and previous years) *Balance of Payments Yearbook*. Washington, DC: IMF.

IMF (1989 and previous years) *International Financial Statistics Yearbook*. Washington, DC: IMF.

Iversen, C. (1935) *International Capital Movements*. 1967 edition. London: Frank Cass.

Jasay, A. E. (1960) The social choice between home and overseas investment. *Economic Journal*, 70, 105–13.

Jenkins, R. (1987) *Transnational Corporations and Uneven Development. The*

Internationalization of Capital and the Third World. London: Methuen.

Johnson, H. G. (1970) The efficiency and welfare implications of the international corporation. In Kindleberger, C. P. (ed.), *The International Corporation*. Cambridge, MA: MIT Press, 35–56.

Kalecki, M. (1939) *Essays in the Theory of Economic Fluctuations*. London: Allen and Unwin.

Kalecki, M. (1954) *Theory of Economic Dynamics*. London: Allen and Unwin.

Katouzian, H. (1980) *Ideology and Method in Economics*. London: Macmillan.

Keat, R. and Urry, J. (1975) *Social Theory as Science*. London: Routledge and Kegan Paul.

Kindleberger, C. P. (1969) *American Business Abroad*. New Haven, CT: Yale University Press.

Knickerbocker, F. T. (1973) *Oligopolistic Reaction and Multinational Enterprise*. Cambridge, MA: Division of Research, Graduate School of Business Administration, Harvard University.

Kojima, K. (1978) *Direct Foreign Investment*. London: Croom Helm.

Kutznets, S. (1953) *Economic Change*. New York: W. W. Norton.

Lakatos, I. (1978) *The Methodology of Scientific Research Programmes*. Cambridge: Cambridge University Press.

Lall, S. (1978) The pattern of intra-firm exports by US multinationals. *Oxford Bulletin of Economics and Statistics*, 40, 209–22.

Leadbeater, C. (1990) Marriage of convenience. *Financial Times*, 29 May, 24.

Leadbeater, C. and Lloyd, J. (1987) *In Search of Work*. Harmondsworth: Penguin.

Lee, G. (1971) Rosa Luxemburg and the impact of imperialism. *Economic Journal*, 81 (324), 847–62.

Lenin, V. I. (1917) *Imperialism, the Highest Stage of Capitalism*. 1970 edition. Moscow: Progress Publishers.

Leontief, W. (1953) Domestic production and foreign trade: the American capital position re-examined. *Proceeding of the American Philosophical Society*, 97, 332–49.

Leontief, W. (1956) Factor proportions and the structure of American trade: further theoretical and empirical analysis. *Review of Economics and Statistics*, 38, 386–407.

Lorenz, C. (1989) The Italian connection: a stark contrast in corporate manners. *Financial Times*, 23 June, 20.

Luxemburg, R. (1913) *The Accumulation of Capital*. 1971 edition. London: Routledge and Kegan Paul.

MacDougall, G. D. A. (1960) The benefits and costs of private investment from abroad: a theoretical approach. *Economic Record*, 36, 13–55.

Magdoff, H. (1966) *The Age of Imperialism*. 1969 edition. New York: Monthly Review Press.

Malcolmson, J. M. (1984) Efficient labour organization: incentives, power and the transactions cost approach. In Stephens, F. H. (ed.), *Firms, Organizations and Labour: Approaches to the Economics of Work Organization*. London: Macmillan, 87–118.

Marginson, P. (1985) The multidivisional firm and control over the work process. *International Journal of Industrial Organization*, 3, 37–56.

Markusen, J. R. (1984) Multinationals, multiplant economies and the gains from trade. *Journal of International Economics* 16 (3/4), 205–24. Reprinted in

Bhagwati, J. N. (ed.) (1981), *International Trade: Selected Readings.* Cambridge, MA: MIT Press, 457–95.

Marsh, D. (1990) Multinationals' links criticised. *Financial Times*, 19 June, 2.

Meltzer, A. H. (1988) *Keynes's Monetary Theory. A Different Interpretation.* Cambridge: Cambridge University Press.

Michalet, C. A. (1980) International sub-contracting, a state-of-the-art. In Germidis, D. (ed.), *International Sub-Contracting. A New Form of Investment.* Paris: OECD, 38–70.

Miller, N. C. (1968) A general equilibrium theory of international capital flows. *Economic Journal*, June, 78, 312–20.

Mundell, R. A. (1957) International trade and factor mobility. *American Economic Review*, 47, 321–35. Reprinted in Bhagwati, J. N. (ed.) (1981), *International Trade: Selected Readings*. Cambridge, MA: MIT Press, 21–36.

Murray, R. (1971) The internationalisation of capital and the nation state. *New Left Review*, 67, 84–109.

Murray, R. (1972) Underdevelopment, the international firm and the international division of labour. In Society for International Development, *Towards a New World Economy*. Rotterdam: Rotterdam University Press, 160–239.

Murray, R. (1985) Benetton Britain. The new economic order. *Marxism Today*, November, 28–32.

Musgrave, A. (1981) Unreal assumptions in economic theory: the F twist untwisted. *Kyklos*, 34 (3), 377–87.

Norman, G. and Dunning, J. H. (1984) Intra-industry foreign direct investment: its rationale and trade effects. Presented at the International Economics Study Group Ninth Annual Conference, Sussex University, September.

Nurkse, R. (1933) Causes and effects of capital movements. In Dunning, J. H. (ed.) (1972), *International Investment*, Harmondsworth: Penguin, 97–116.

OECD (1970) *Gaps in Technology. Comparisons Between Member Countries in Education, Research & Development, Technological Innovation, International Economic Exchanges.* Paris: OECD.

OECD (1971) *The Conditions for Success in Technological Innovation.* Paris: OECD.

OECD (1987 and previous years) *National Accounts.* Paris: OECD.

Ohlin, B. (1933) *Interregional and International Trade.* 1967 edition. Cambridge, MA: Harvard University Press.

Panić, M. (1991) The impact of multinationals on national economic policies. In Burgenmeier, B. and Mucchielli, J. L. (eds), *Multinationals and Europe 1992. Strategies for the Future.* London: Routledge, 204–22.

Panić, M. and Joyce, P. L. (1980) UK manufacturing industry: international integration and trade performance. *Bank of England Quarterly Bulletin*, 20, 42–55.

Pearce, I. F. and Rowan, D. C. (1966) A framework for research into the real effects of international capital movements. In Dunning, J. H. (ed.) (1972), *International Investment*. Harmondsworth: Penguin, 163–97.

Pearce, R. D. (1982) *Overseas Production and Exporting Performance: an Empirical Note.* University of Reading Discussion Papers in International Investment and Business Studies, No. 64.

Pearson, C. and Ellyne, M. (1985) Surges of imports: perceptions versus evidence. *World Economy*, 8 (3), 299–315. September.

Pheby, J. (1988) *Methodology and Economics: a Critical Introduction.* London: Macmillan.

Popper, K. R. (1959) *The Logic of Scientific Discovery*. London: Hutchinson.

Popper, K. R. (1963) *Conjectures and Refutations*. London: Routledge and Kegan Paul.

Popper, K. R. (1972) *Objective Knowledge. An Evolutionary Approach*. Oxford: Oxford University Press.

Porter, M. E. (1990) *The Competitive Advantage of Nations*. London: Macmillan.

Posner, M. V. (1961) International trade and technical change. *Oxford Economic Papers*, 13, 323–41.

Prowse, M. (1987) The need to bolster confidence. *Financial Times*, 30 November, 22.

Quine, W. V. O. (1951) Two dogmas of empiricism. Reprinted in *From a Logical Point of View* (1963). New York: Harper Torchbooks.

Radice, H. K. (1984) Multinational companies and the disintegration of the UK industrial economy. University of Leeds, School of Economic Studies Discussion Paper, No. 138.

Reddaway, W. B., in collaboration with Perkins, J. O. N., Potter, S. J. and Taylor, C. T. (1967) *Effects of UK Direct Investment Overseas. An Interim Report*. Cambridge: Cambridge University Press.

Reddaway, W. B., in collaboration with Potter, S. J. and Taylor, C. T. (1968) *Effects of UK Direct Investment Overseas Final Report*. Cambridge: Cambridge University Press.

Rosenberg, N. (1982) *Inside the Black Box: Technology and Economics*. Cambridge: Cambridge University Press.

Rowthorn, B. (1971) Imperialism in the seventies: unity or rivalries? *New Left Review*, 69, 31–51.

Rowthorn, R.E. and Wells, J.R. (1987) *De-Industrialization and Foreign Trade*. Cambridge: Cambridge University Press.

Rugman, A. M. (ed.) (1982) *New Theories of the Multinational Enterprise*. London: Croom Helm.

Russell, E. A. (1978) Foreign investment policy. What role for the economist? *Australian Economic Papers*, 17 (31), 193–206.

Rybczynski, T. M. (1955) Factor endowment and relative commodity prices. *Economica*, 23, 352–9.

Samuelson, P. A. (1948) International trade and the equalization of factor prices. *Economic Journal*, 58, 163–84.

Samuelson, P. A. (1949) International factor-price equalization once again. *Economic Journal*, 59, 181–97.

Samuelson, P. A. (1963) Comment on Ernest Nagel's 'Assumptions in Economic Theory', *American Economic Review*, May. Reprinted in Stiglitz, J. E. (ed.) (1966), *The Collected Scientific Papers of Paul A. Samuelson*. Cambridge, MA: MIT Press, volume 2, no. 129, 1772–8.

Sharpston, M. (1975) International subcontracting. *Oxford Economic Papers*, March, 27, 94–135.

Solinas, G. (1982) Labour market segmentation and workers' careers: the case of the Italian knitwear industry. *Cambridge Journal of Economics*, 6, 331–52.

Stigler, G. J. (1947) The kinky oligopoly demand curve and rigid prices. *Journal of Political Economy*, 55, 432–49.

Stolper, W.F. and Samuelson, P. A. (1941) Protection and real wages. *Review of Economic Studies*, 9, 58–73.

Stopford, J. M. (1979) *Employment Effect of Multinational Enterprises in the UK*, Working Paper No. 5. Geneva, ILO.

Stopford, J. M., Dunning, J. H. and Haberick, K. O. (1980) *The World Directory of Multinational Enterprises*. London: Macmillan.

Stopford, J. M. and Dunning, J. H. (1983) *Multinationals: Company Performance and Global Trends*. London: Macmillan.

Stopford, J. M. and Turner, L. (1985) *Britain and the Multinationals*. Chichester: John Wiley and Sons.

Sweezy, P. M. (1939) Demand under conditions of oligopoly. *Journal of Political Economy*, 47, 568–73.

Sweezy, P. M. (1942) *The Theory of Capitalist Development*. London: Dennis Dobson.

Teece, D. J. (1983) Technological and organisation factors in the theory of the multinational enterprise. In Casson, M. C. (ed.), *The Growth of International Business*. London: Allen and Unwin, 51–62.

Thirlwall, A. (1988) Review of *De-Industrialization and Foreign Trade* by Rowthorn, R. E. and Wells, J.R. (1987). *Economic Journal*, 98, 893–5.

United Nations (1976) *Yearbook of Industrial Statistics*. New York: United Nations.

United Nations (1978) *Statistical Yearbook*. New York: United Nations.

United Nations (1989) *Joint Ventures as a Form of International Economic Cooperation*. New York: Taylor and Francis.

United Nations Centre on Transnational Corporations (1983a) *Salient Features and Trends in Foreign Direct Investment*, ST/CTC/14. New York: United Nations.

United Nations Centre on Transnational Corporations (1983b) *Transnational Corporations in World Development*, Third Survey, ST/CTC/46. New York: United Nations.

United Nations Centre on Transnational Corporations (1985) *Transnational Corporations and International Trade: Selected Issues*, ST/CTC/54. New York: United Nations.

United Nations Centre on Transnational Corporations (1988) *Transnational Corporations in World Development. Trends and Prospects*. New York: United Nations.

United Nations Conference on Trade and Development (1978) *Dominant Position of Market Power of Transnational Corporations. Use of Transfer Pricing Mechanism*, TD/B/C.2/167. New York: United Nations.

United Nations Department of Economic and Social Affairs (1973) *Multinational Corporations in World Development*. New York: United Nations.

United Nations Economic Commission for Europe (1987) *The Telecommunication Industry. Growth and Structural Change*. New York: United Nations.

Vernon, R. (1966) International investment and international trade in the product cycle. *Quarterly Journal of Economics*, 80, 190–207.

Vernon, R. (1970) Future of the multinational enterprise. In Kindleberger, C. P. (ed.), *The International Corporation: a Symposium*. Cambridge, MA: MIT Press.

Vernon, R. (1974) The location of economic activity. In Dunning, J. H. (ed.), *Economic Analysis and the Multinational Enterprise*. London: Allen and Unwin, 89–113.

Vernon, R. (1977) *Storm over the Multinationals: the Real Issues*. Cambridge, MA: Harvard University Press.

Vernon, R. (1979) The product cycle hypothesis in a new international environment. *Oxford Bulletin of Economics and Statistics*, 41, 255–67.

Walmsley, J. (1982) *Handbook of International Joint Ventures*. London: Graham and Trotman.

Warren, B. (1980) *Imperialism Pioneer of Capitalism*. London: Verso.

Williamson, O. E. (1981) The modern corporation: origins, evolution, attributes. *Journal of Economic Literature*, 19, 1537–68.

Williamson, O. E. (1984) Efficient labour organization. In Stephens, F. H. (ed.), *Firms, Organization and Labour: Approaches to the Economics of Work Organization*. London: Macmillan, 87–118.

Willmore, L. (1979) The industrial economics of intra-industry trade and specialization. In Giersch, H. (ed.), *On the Economics of Intra-Industry Trade*. Tübingen: J. C. B. Mohr (Paul Siebeck), 185–209.

Yamin, M. and Nixson, F. I. (1988) Transnational corporations and the control of restrictive business practices: theoretical issues and empirical evidence. *International Review of Applied Economics*, 2 (1), 1–22.

Index